The Kookaburra

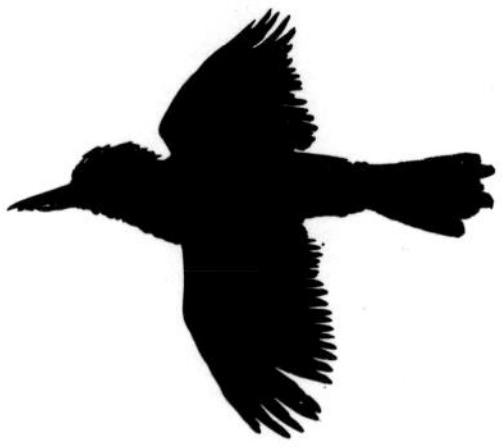

The Kookaburra

A pictorial celebration of Australia's best-loved bird

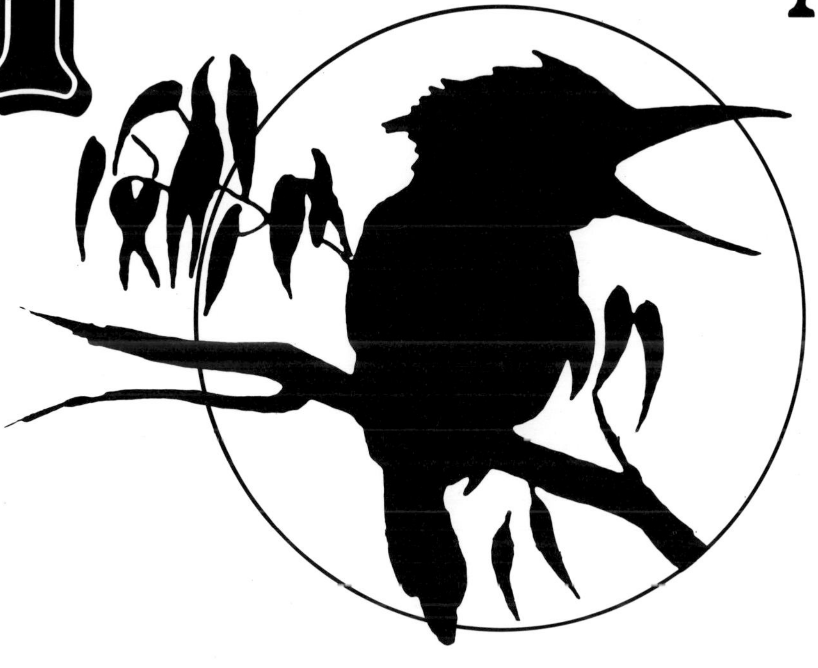

TOBY & JULIANA HOOPER

VIKING O'NEIL

THE AUTHORS

Toby and Juliana Hooper are the proprietors of Hoopers Antiques in Prahran, Victoria. *The Kookaburra* (first published as *The Laughing Australian*) is their fourth book; their others are *A Guide to Buying Antiques in Australia*, *A Guide to Collecting Australiana*, *A Pocket Guide to Buying Antiques*, and *Australian Country Furniture*. Some years ago they started collecting decorative kookaburras, and a passion for them led to this book.

Penguin Books Australia Ltd
487 Maroondah Highway, PO Box 257
Ringwood, Victoria 3134, Australia
Penguin Books Ltd
Harmondsworth, Middlesex, England
Viking Penguin, A Division of Penguin Books USA Inc.
375 Hudson Street, New York, New York, 10014, USA
Penguin Books Canada Limited
10 Alcorn Avenue, Toronto, Ontario, Canada M4V 1E4
Penguin Books (N.Z.) Ltd
182–190 Wairau Road, Auckland 10, New Zealand

First published by Thomas Nelson Australia Ltd 1982 as
The Laughing Australian
This revised edition published by Penguin Books Australia Ltd 1991

10 9 8 7 6 5 4 3 2 1

Produced by Viking O'Neil
56 Claremont Street, South Yarra, Victoria 3141, Australia
A Division of Penguin Books Australia Ltd

Designed by Tom Kurema and David Constable
Cover design by David Constable
Typeset in Garamond by Solo Typesetting, Adelaide
Printed and bound in Hong Kong through Bookbuilders Limited

National Library of Australia
Cataloguing in Publication data.

Hooper, Toby.
The kookaburra.

Bibliography.
ISBN 0 670 90215 2.

1. Kookaburra—Folklore. 2. Kookaburra in art. I. Hooper, Juliana. II. Title. III. Title: The laughing Australian

398.2458892

The logo used for the cover and the endpapers is reproduced with the kind permission of A. G. Thompson Pty Ltd

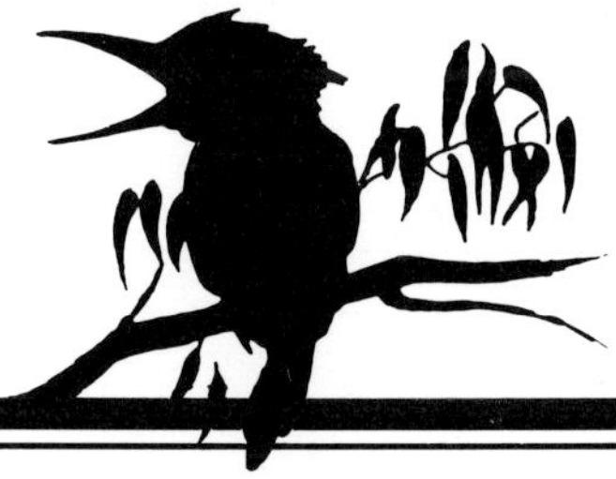

Contents

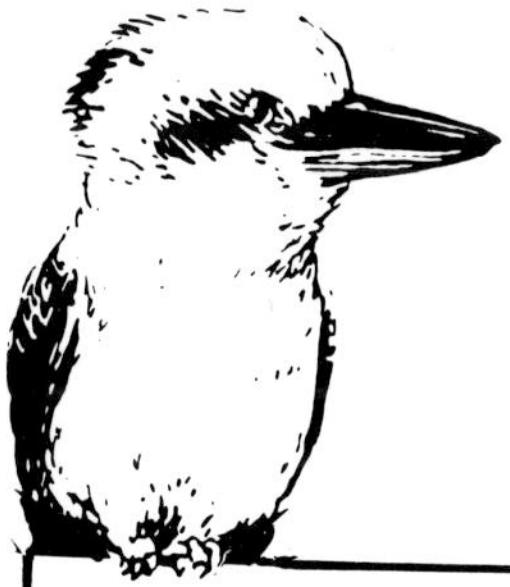

For Chloë, Justin and Nicholas

Kookaburra sits in the old gum tree,
Merry, merry, king of the bush is he,
Laugh kookaburra, laugh kookaburra,
Gay your life must be.

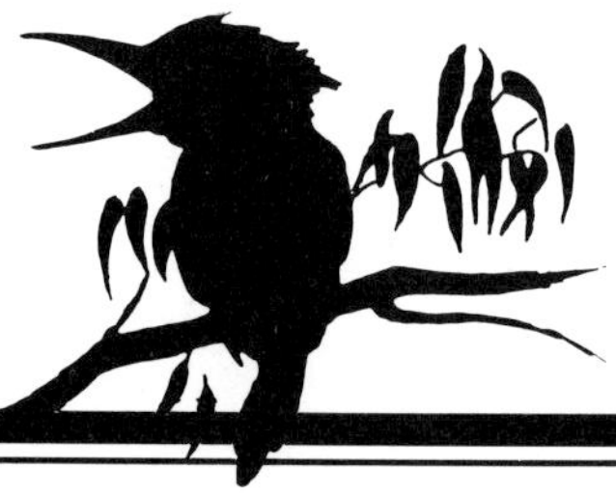

-1-
AN AUSTRALIAN SYMBOL

The kookaburra's laughter in the soft early light of dawn has woken many an Australian bushman to the expectations of a new day.

In the mellow contrast of dusk, the kookaburra's merriment has enriched the solitude of the bush and gladdened the heart of the weary traveller.

Many Australians, not only the Aborigines and early white settlers, have identified strongly with the kookaburra. Somehow this bird reflects aspects of the Australian character. There is something congenial and attractive about his cheeky stance, his fearless laugh, and even the absurd bravery of a mere kingfisher, apparently ill-equipped, taking on enormous snakes.

The kookaburra eventually emerged as a most familiar and popular symbol, although he did not achieve this position instantly.

The startlingly different kangaroo and emu emerged as Australia's first symbols. Explorers, colonists and early illustrators were intrigued by the unique Australian fauna, so different from the birds and animals in Europe and other explored territories. The kookaburra's appearance was not so unusual. He looked like a large kingfisher and his colouring blended into the bush. There was no spectacular plumage to attract a mate or catch the human eye. It was the raucous laugh that demanded attention, but some early settlers did not readily come to terms with the mirth of the kookaburra. A few

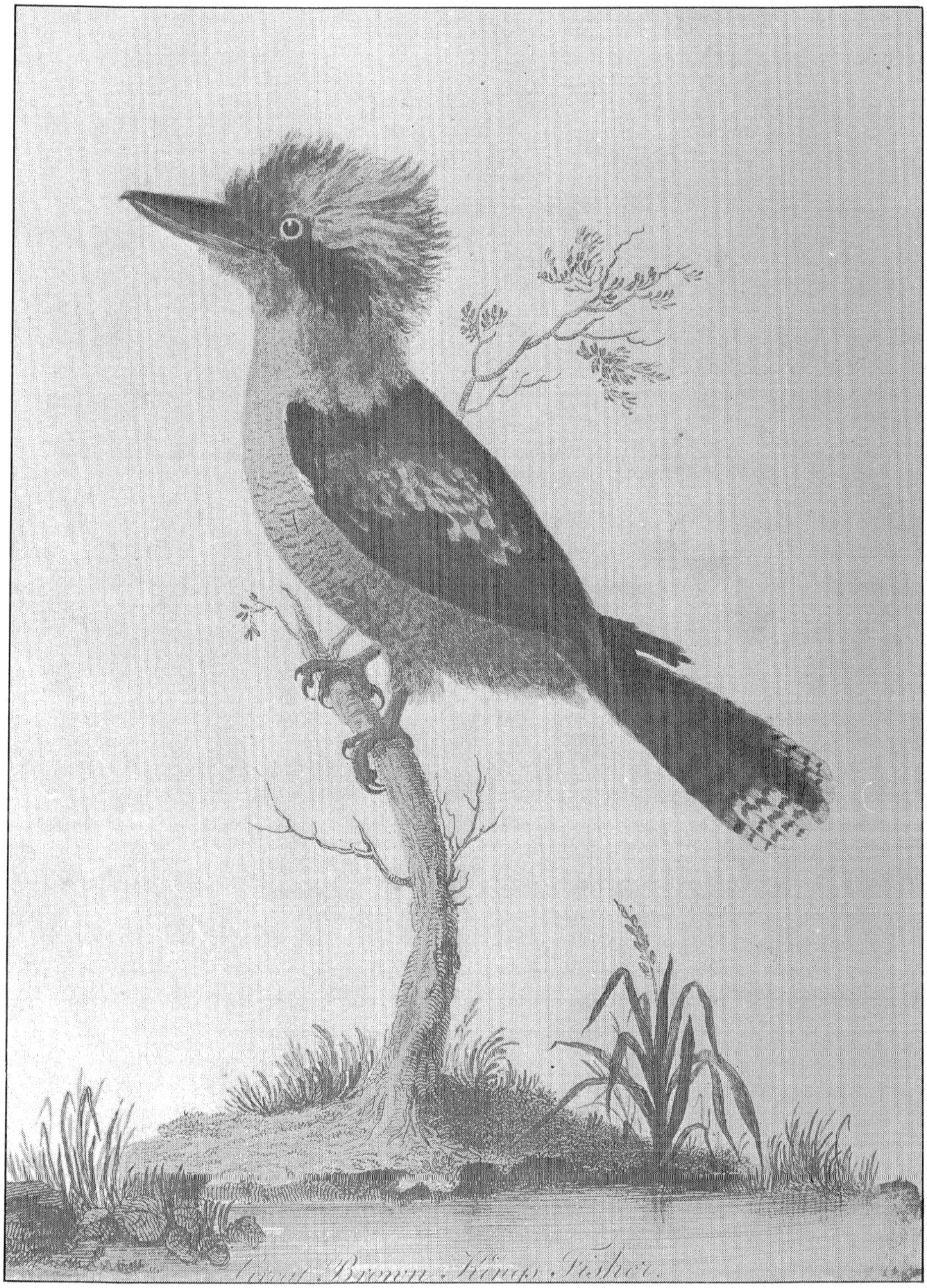

unhappy early travellers regarded the laughter as alien, or fiendish and mocking. Happily the majority of Australians found the laughter reassuring, a symbol of the mateship of the bush, and wanted to laugh along too. And so, in time, the kookaburra developed into Australia's best-loved bird.

This early engraving of the 'Great Brown Kings Fisher', published in 1790, is from *Journal of a Voyage to New South Wales* by John White, Surgeon-General to the First Fleet

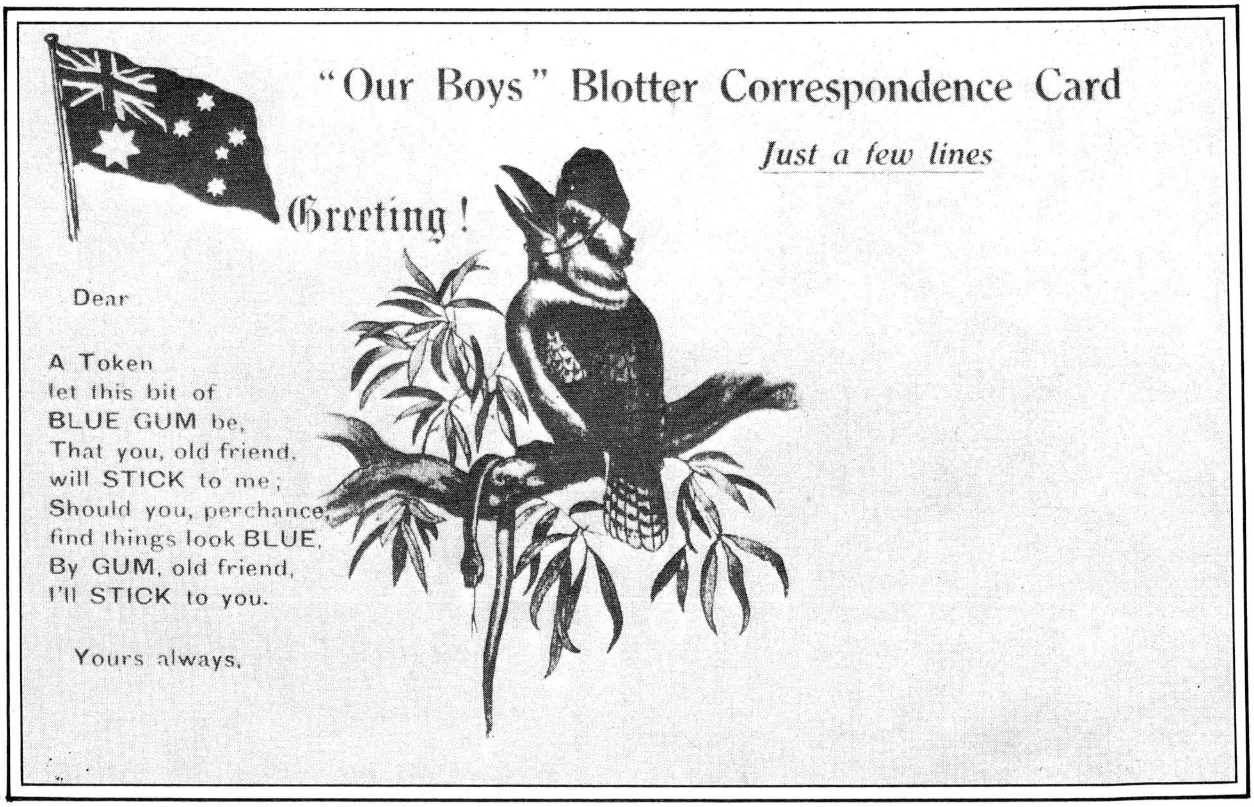

It was during the first forty years of this century, especially the period between the two wars, that the kookaburra motif had its heyday as a national symbol. In those years a host of illustrators, storytellers, craftspeople, artisans and promoters wove their pictures, tales and products around the kookaburra.

The first popular portrayal early this century was by a small number of watercolourists who repeatedly used kookaburras as subjects. Soon advertisers and promoters were registering kookaburra trademarks to capitalise on the image. The kookaburra began to appear on greeting cards and postcards, many of which were designed to be sent to friends and relatives abroad. During World War I, the kookaburra and the sprig of wattle became the two most popular 'pick-me-ups' sent to the boys in the trenches in postcard form. The kookaburra or 'Diggaburra' was pictured dressed in the

World War I postcards often featured the kookaburra, sometimes with a sprig of wattle as well. Here, the snake catcher has gum leaves

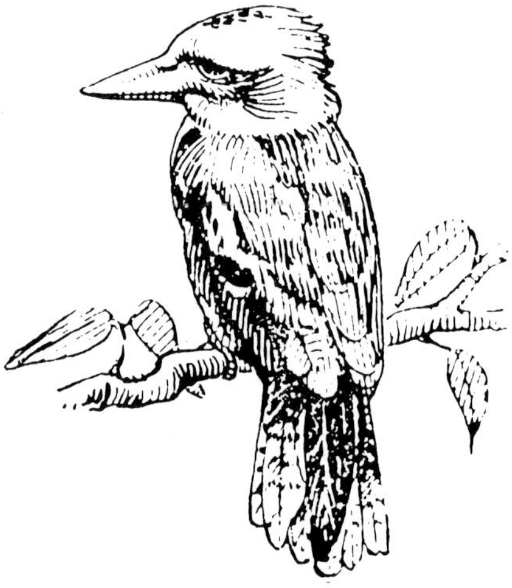

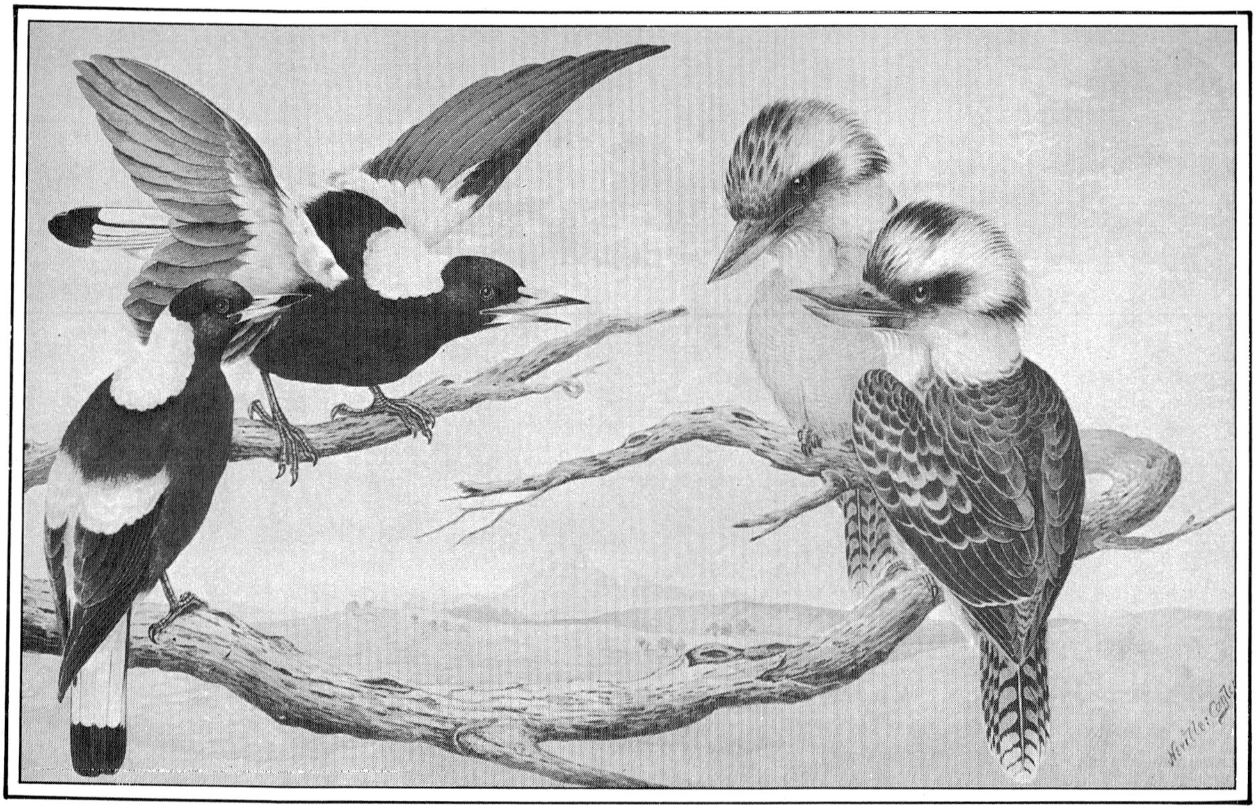

military attire of all the Australian defence forces. By this time he was firmly established in Australian hearts as part of a developing culture.

After the war, the kookaburra appeared regularly in Australian literature, particularly in children's books.

Many new kookaburra trademarks were registered in the 1920s as advertisers and promoters used the bird's popularity to help sell their products. The period between the two wars saw a further flowering of national feeling and the decorative arts flourished in the hands of hobbyists and amateurs as well as skilled artists and craftspeople.

English and European ceramic firms used Australian motifs to capitalise on this nationalism and many foreign-made kookaburras were shipped across to us on domestic crockery and decorative wares. When our own art and pottery

A territorial confrontation with some magpies: a painting by Neville Cayley senior (1853–1903), one of the most celebrated painters of kookaburras

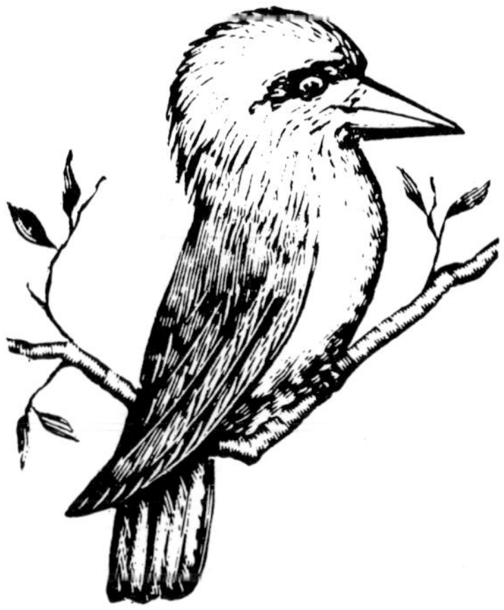

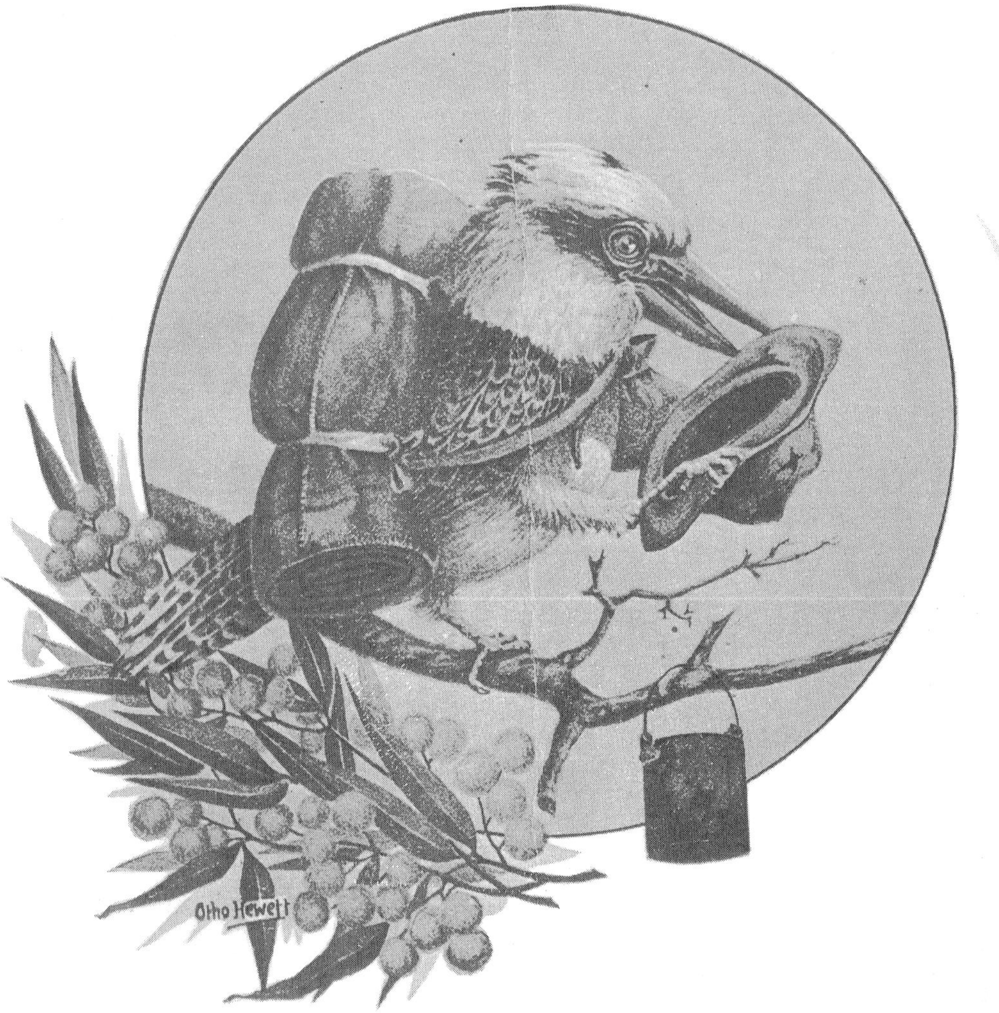

JACK SUNDOWNER

Did Jack Sundowner always use Diggaburra Tea?
This illustration by Ortho Hewett comes from *A Day in the Life of Jack Sundowner* by F. J. Mills

flourished here in the late 1920s and the 1930s, Australian potters used the kookaburra prominently in their work.

Patriotic woodcarvers, ranging from artists like the great Robert Prenzel to amateur woodworkers, incorporated kookaburras in their pieces. Flocks of pokerwork kookaburras were produced first by hobbyists and then commercially. The array of embroidered kookaburras, leatherwork kookaburras, kookaburra jewellery, metal kookaburras, and stained-glass or leadlight kookaburras produced in this period is truly amazing.

Zany characters like Jacko the performing kookaburra captured the public imagination, Little Miss Kookaburra did her kookaburra impersonations on 3LO, and every week at the 'flicks', the newsreel was sung in and out by a boisterous kookaburra chorus.

Throughout the 1930s, the kookaburra image was more familiar to ordinary people than any symbol before or since. Our gift shops and souvenir shops were crammed with all sorts of kookaburra products. There were ashtrays, cigarette dispensers, shoe horns, bookends, paperknives and all sizes of plaster kookaburras.

The surge of popularity that had attracted fine artists and woodcarvers in the early years resulted in mass-market gift shop items of generally low-quality kitsch in the late 1930s. During World War II, the kookaburra was used as the emblem of the No. 1 Bomber Squadron and the No. 453 Squadron; however, the kookaburra boom as a national symbol was over. A cuddly usurper called the koala had claimed his throne.

For a time, the kookaburra symbol was rather neglected. During the 1980s, however, people have begun to listen to the wild laughter again – those who are lucky enough to be within earshot – and artists, illustrators and advertisers are once again tapping the enormous reservoirs of goodwill that many dinky-di Aussies feel for the merry, merry king of the bush.

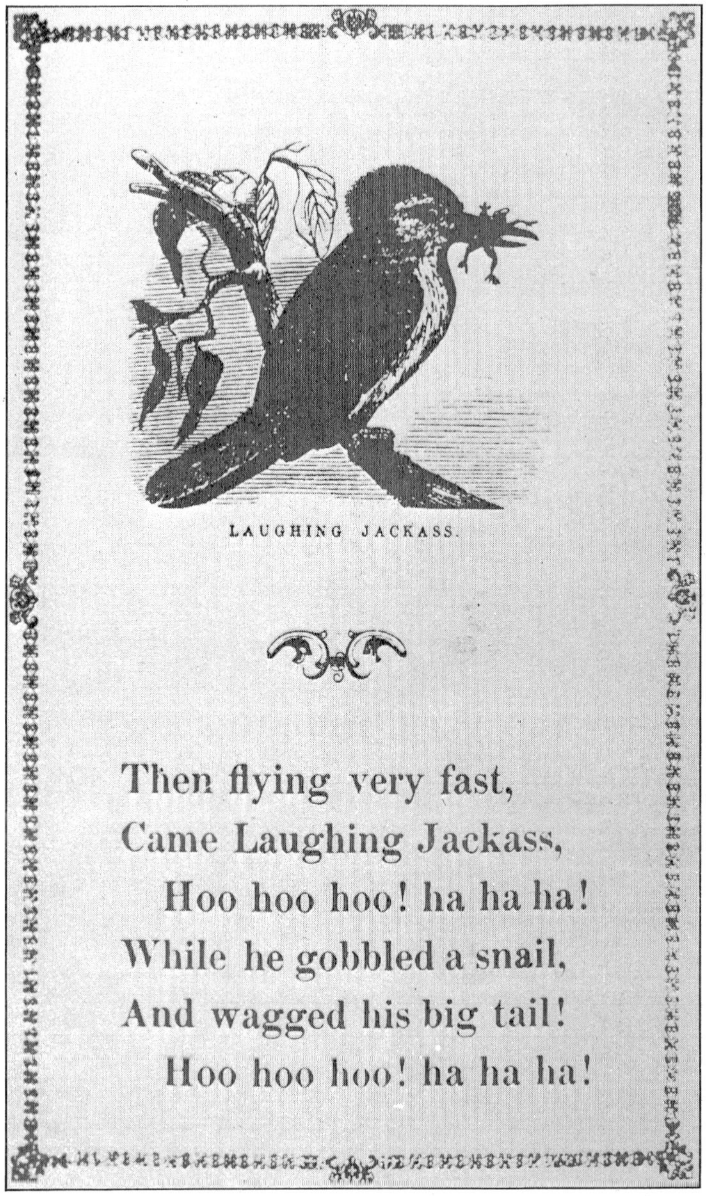
LAUGHING JACKASS.

Then flying very fast,
Came Laughing Jackass,
Hoo hoo hoo! ha ha ha!
While he gobbled a snail,
And wagged his big tail!
Hoo hoo hoo! ha ha ha!

A page from *Who Killed Cockatoo?*, a children's book published in Adelaide in 1870

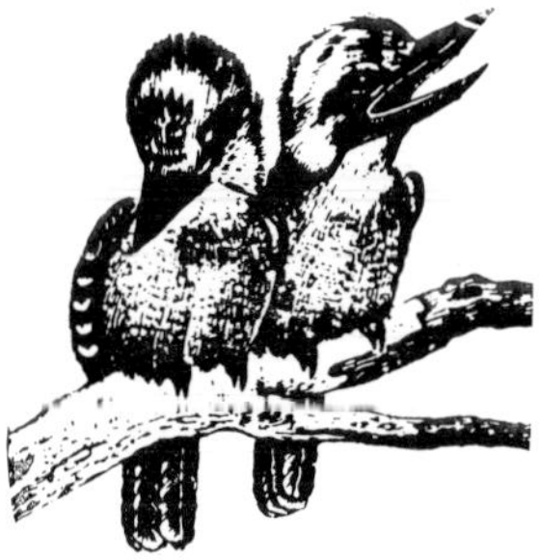

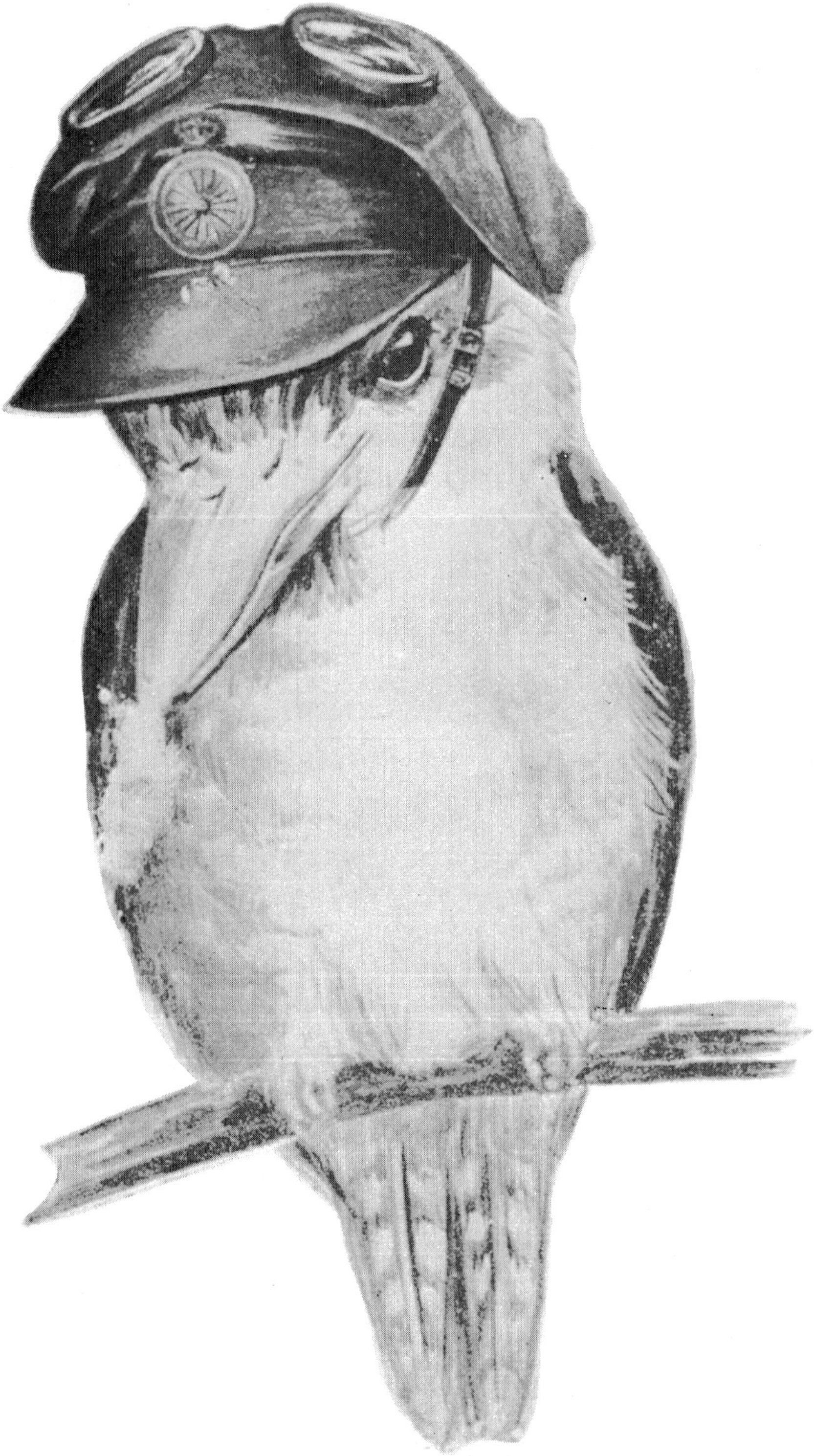

World War I postcard shows 'Diggaburra' in his Air Force regalia (opposite page)

This decorative good luck symbol has a golden Jack in a wishbone brooch (right)

Handsome pottery kookaburras by Grace Seacombe (inscribed G.S.), *c.* 1930 (below)

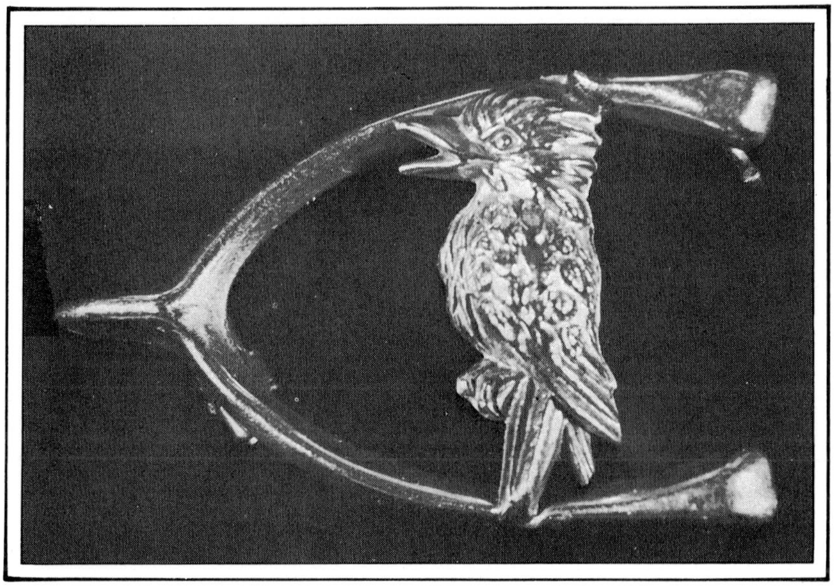

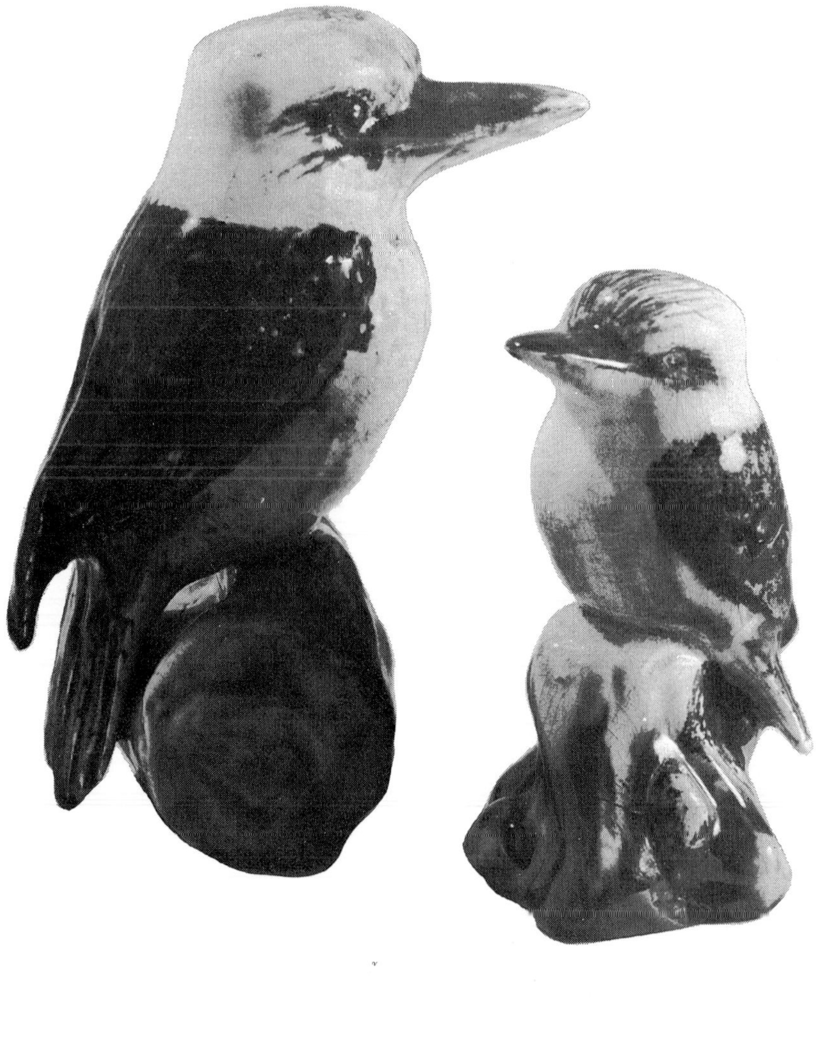

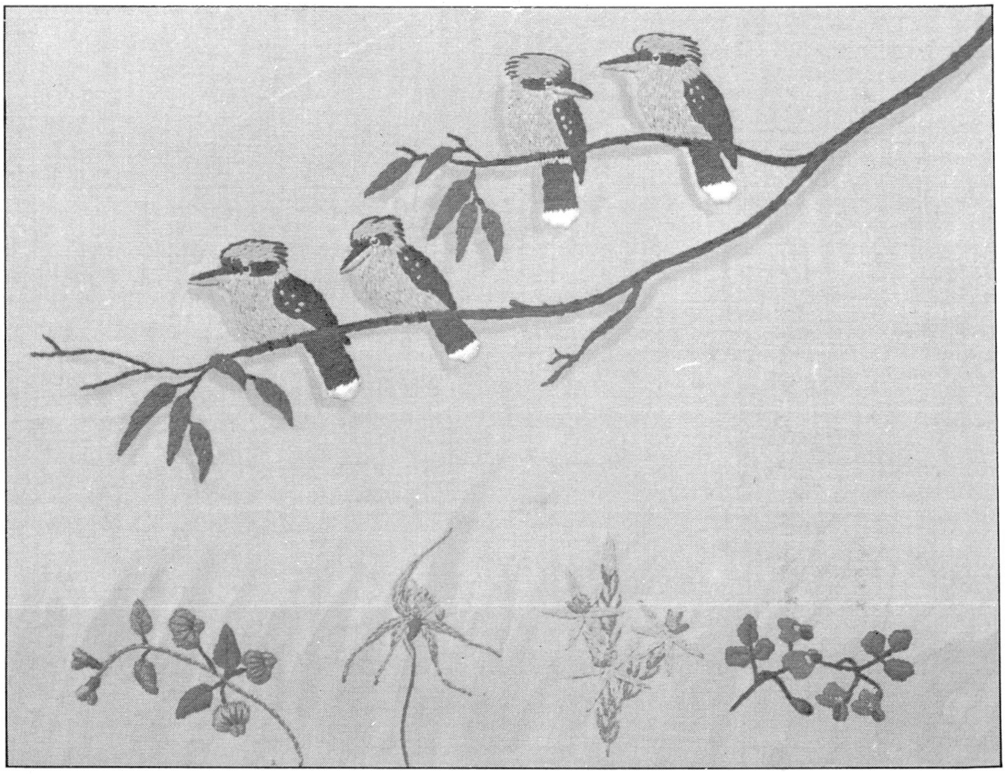

The embroidered picture (above) was decorated with watercolours after a design by Geoff Riley of Melbourne, *c.* 1930

Cast brass bookends (right)

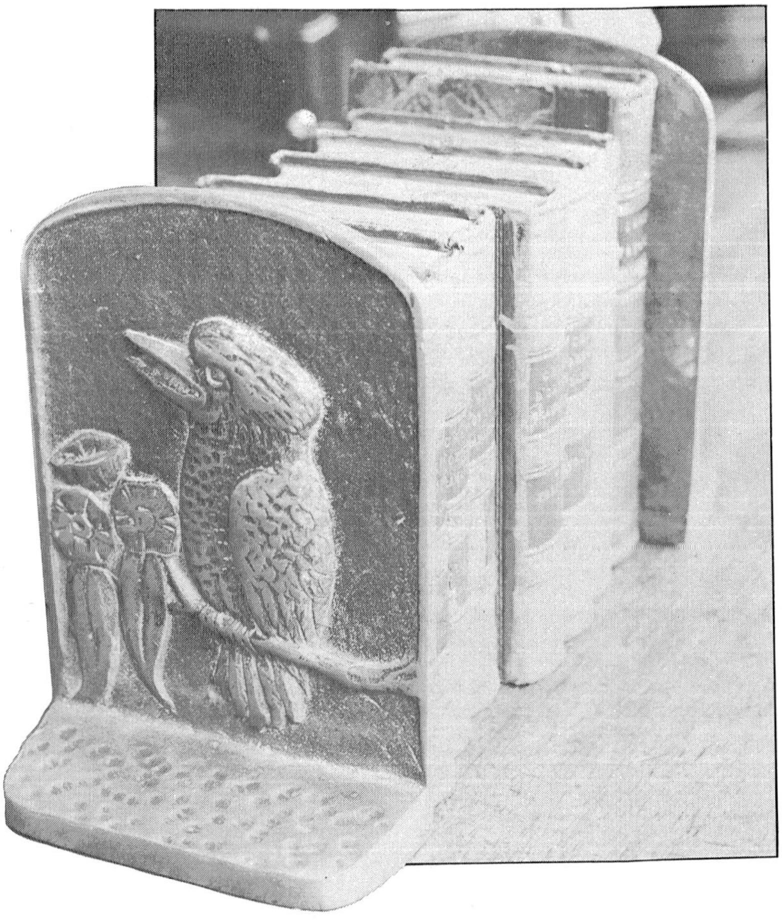

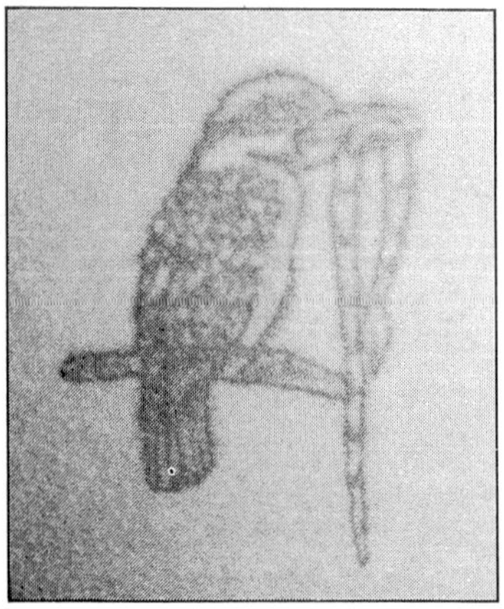

A tattoo – an unusual place for the snake catcher to be

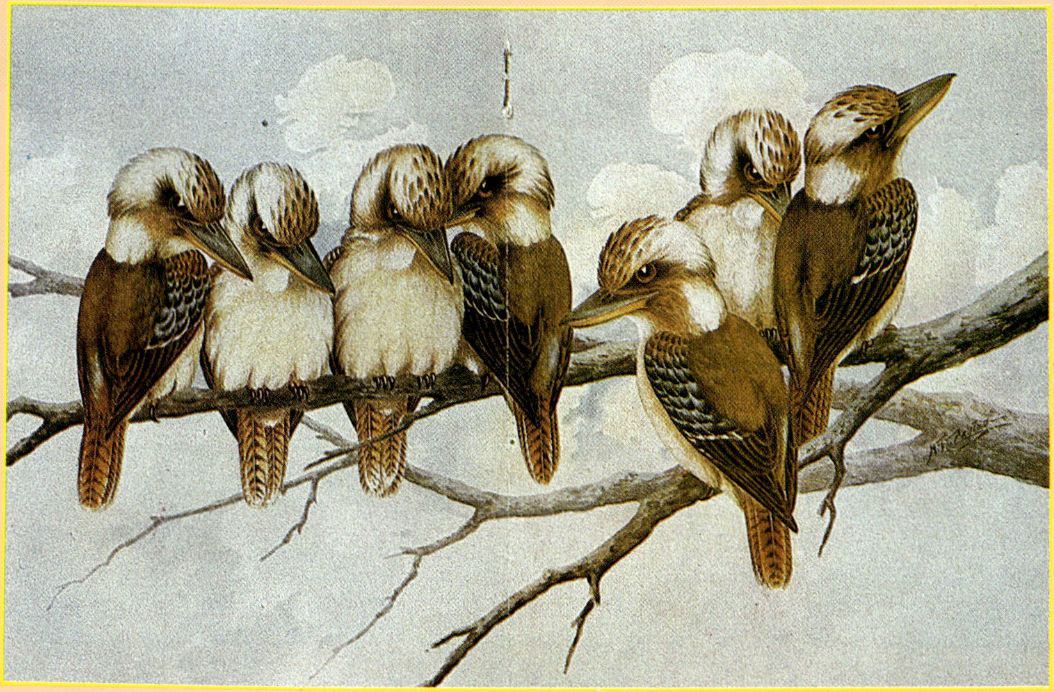

Seven Little Australians: a painting by Neville Cayley senior

Hand-coloured lithograph from John Gould's *Birds of Australia*, 1848 (below left)

Chromolithograph from G. J. Broinowski's *Birds of Australia*, *c.* 1890 (below right)

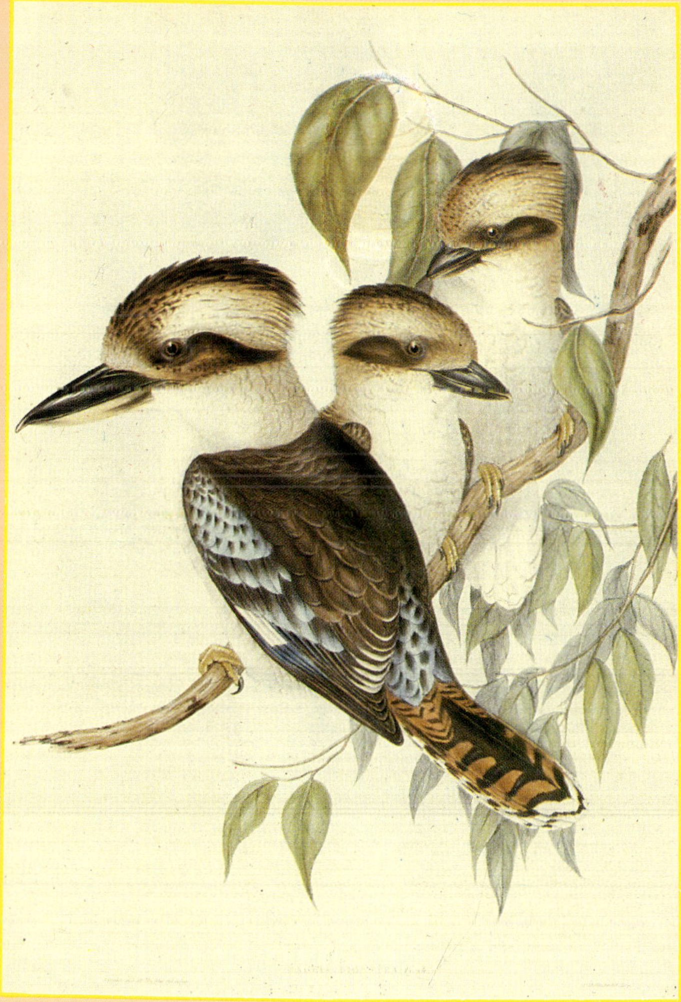

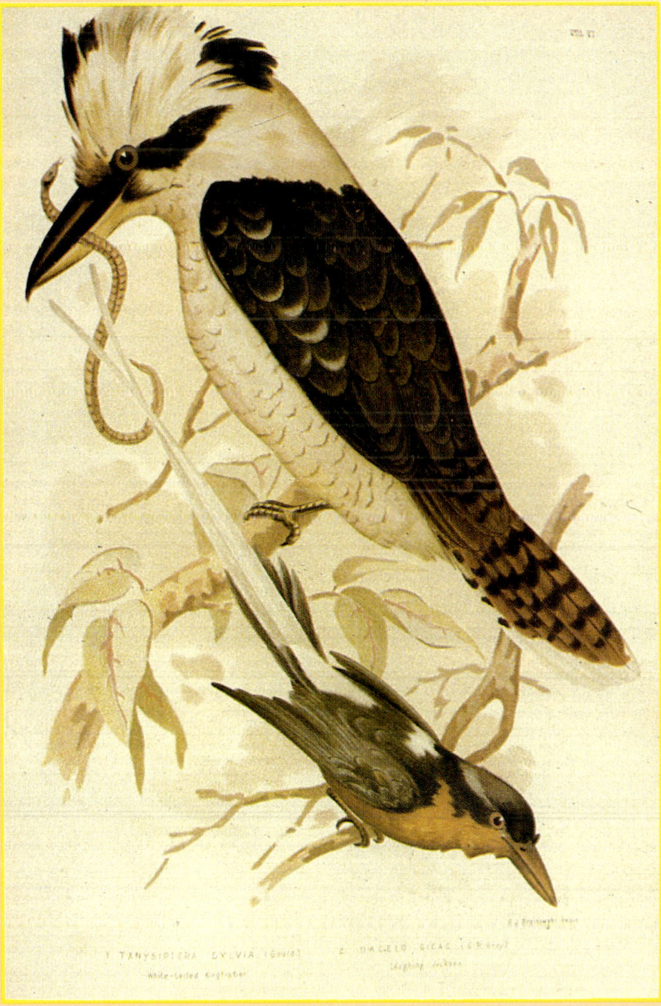

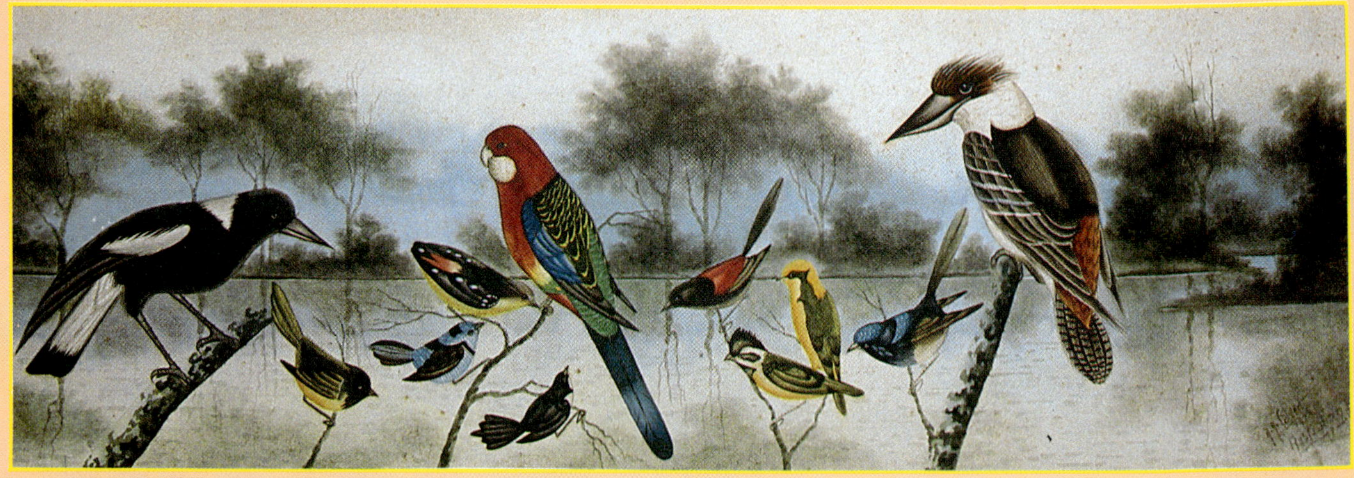

An Australian Eleven by H. H. Calvert

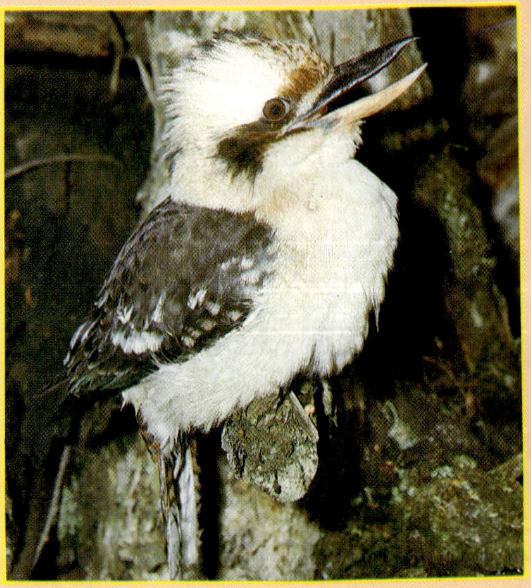

Fledgling kookaburra: photograph by Ken Stepnell (below)

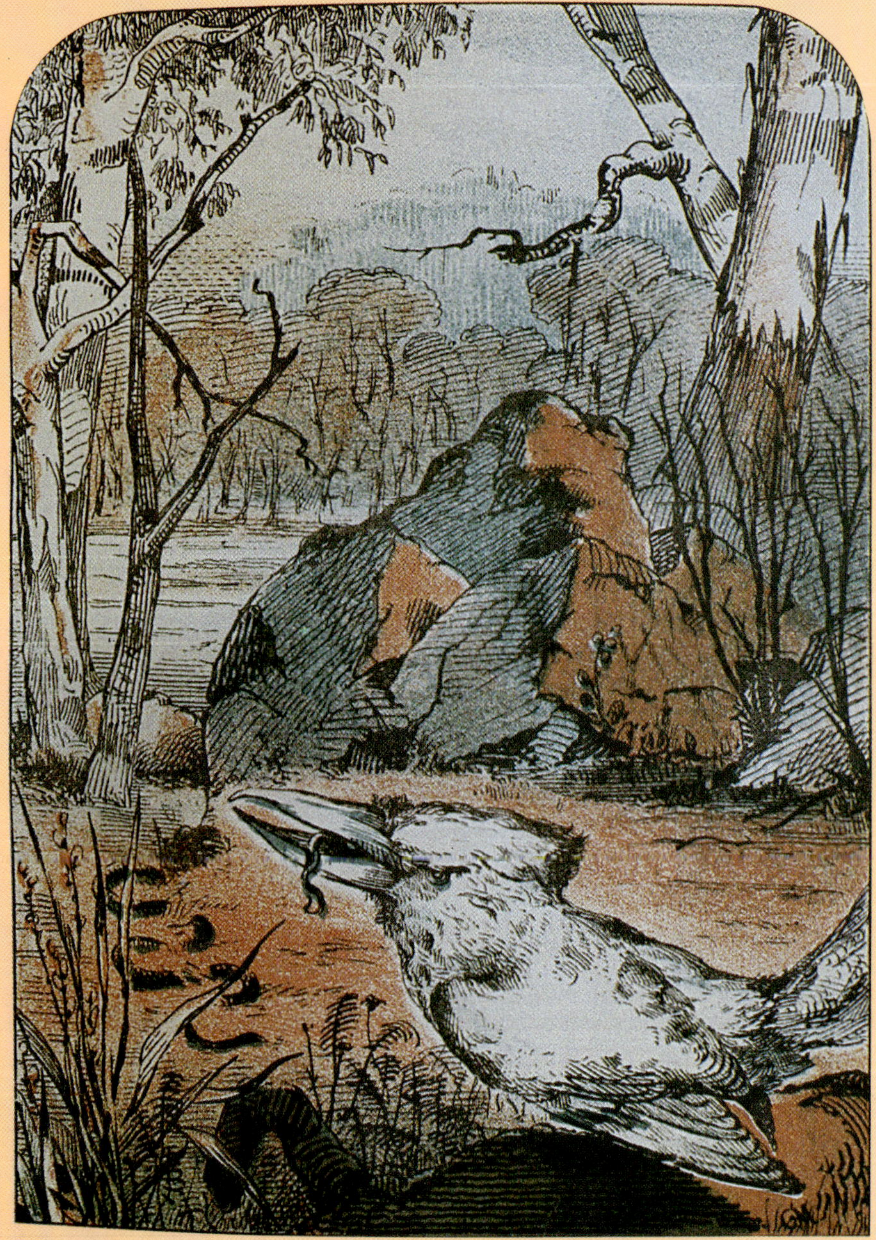

Illustration from Cyrus Mason's *The Conceited Snake*, published by George Robertson in Melbourne, 1871 (left)

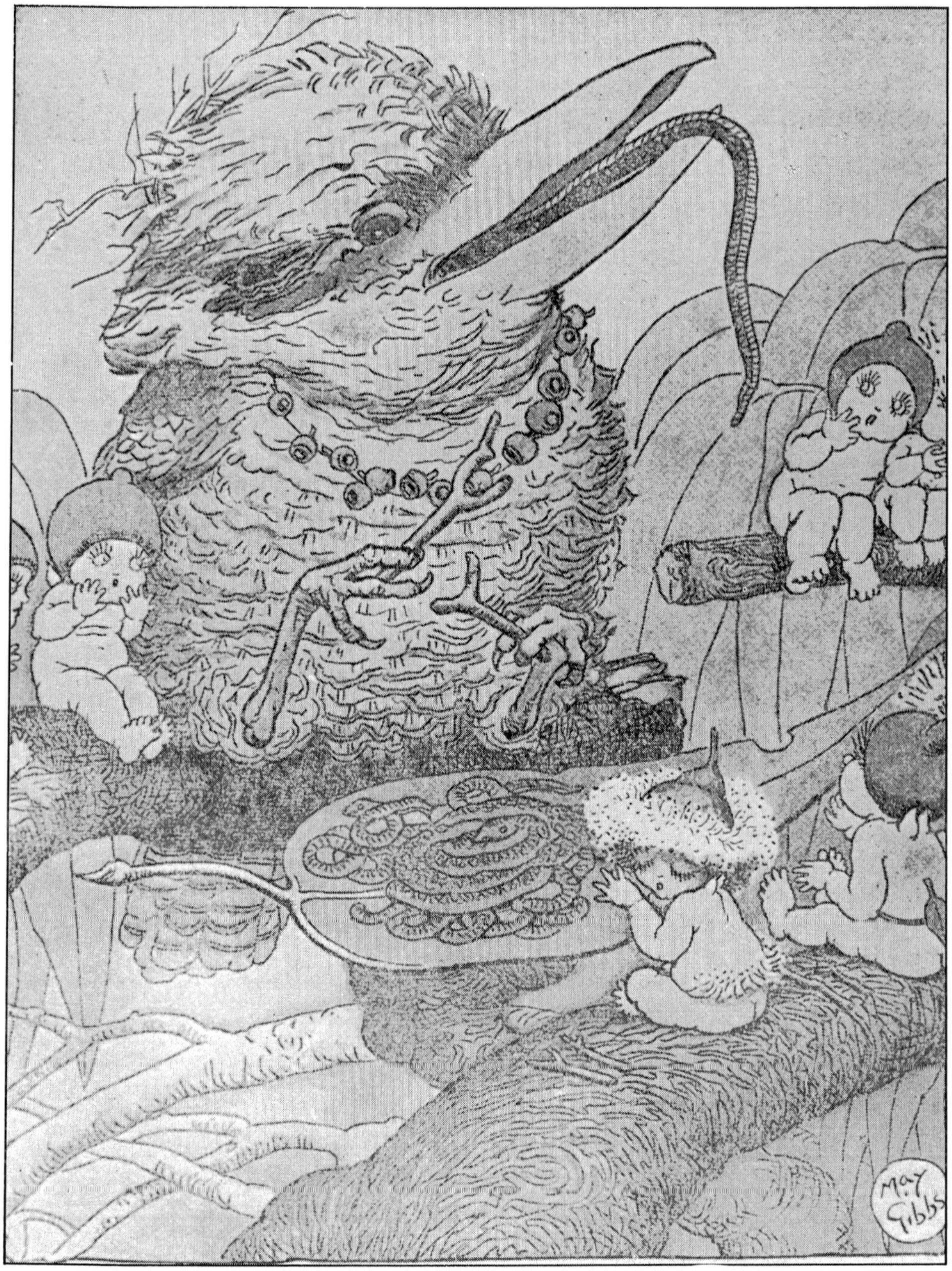

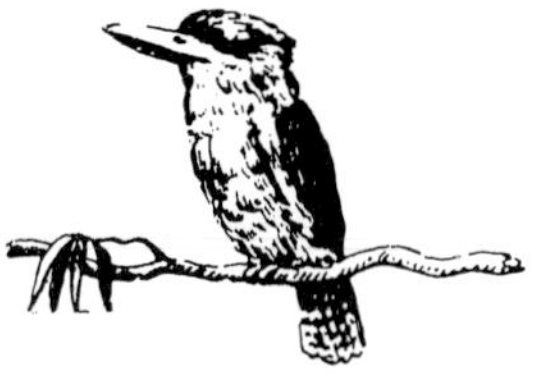

Mrs Kookaburra's Dinner Party, an illustration by May Gibbs, has charmed thousands of children

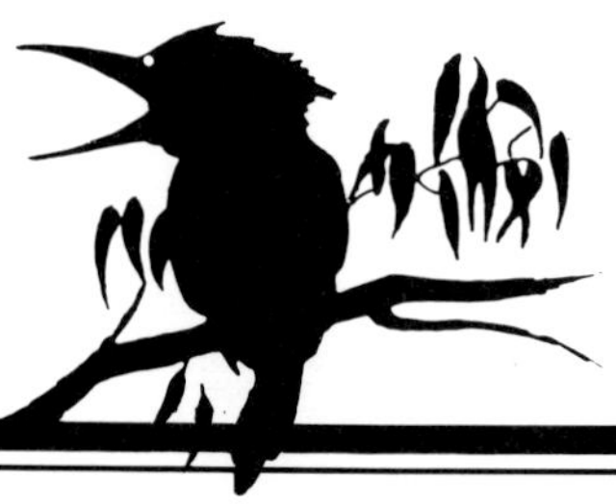

-2-
A Much-named Bird

Audibly the most noticeable Australian bush creature, the kookaburra has attracted a multitude of names and nicknames over the years.

Different tribes of Aborigines had their own names for the bird, all using strong guttural sounds. To the Aborigines, the kookaburra was the herald of the dawn and he was treated and protected as a sacred bird.

THE HERALD OF THE DAWN

The kookaburra had a noisy role in the legends of the south-eastern Australian Aborigines, with an important job to do each morning for Punjel or Agoodenout, the keeper of the sun's fire. The legend has it that before the sun's fire was lit for the first time, the world was a dark, cold, miserable place. Punjel had gathered an enormous woodpile for the Great Spirit to set alight. The Great Spirit agreed to light Punjel's fire and illuminate the world each morning, but only if all the earth's creatures could be relied upon to wake up to appreciate the morning's glory.

Punjel had to find a reliable herald to awaken everybody each morning. So on the first morning Punjel searched to find a creature who was awake to witness the lighting of the great fire. Only the kookaburra was awake, and he was perched on a branch, laughing loudly at the sight of all the bush folk fast asleep: 'Ha ha ho ho ha ha ho ho!' In no time at all, the shrieks of wild laughter woke the sleeping world – more cause for laughter. Punjel and the Great Spirit were delighted with their new herald.

In Europe the cock was the herald of the dawn. The Great Spirit provided Australia with a much more cheerful signaller!

The Aborigines bestowed upon the kookaburra a wonderful variety of names. A. H. Chisholm, writing in *Bird Wonders of Australia*, first published in 1934, sets out the following forty-five names for the bird and states that this is by no means a full list: kookaburra, kowburra, kangroburra, kakaburri, akkaburra, kakaburra, arkooburra, kouburra, kocaburra, kakooburra, karkoburra, karconbur, kookooburry, kokoparra, googooburra, cowur burra, kowkargar, gugaga, gingarga, kamminmalli, toones, doowal, kaggoo, greggoom, karkun goon, koaka, gragon, kakorim, gookergaka, koori, kooree, kulkyne, konga, koorungal, knongkrong, kooar tang, tarakook, kron, koonet, korung-korung, kangoo, wokook, burndigan, wook-wook and coarg.

After the richness of this assortment, the European descriptions seem very uninspired.

HALCYON DAYS

The kookaburra of the Australian bush seems eons away from the gods of Ancient Greece, yet there is a link. The kookaburra is a member of the kingfisher family and the Greeks had a wonderful legend about the kingfisher, or Halcyon as they named it. The legend concerns Halcyone, the daughter of Aeolus, the god of the winds, and her great love for her husband, King Ceyx.

One day, in spite of Halcyone's pleas, Ceyx sailed off on the hazardous journey to consult the Oracle at Delphi. Sadly, even his father-in-law Aeolus could not save the ship and crew from perishing in a great storm.

Halcyone, meanwhile, was praying to all the gods and to the queen of heaven to bring Ceyx back safely to her. Hera knew that Ceyx was dead and arranged for Halcyone to be sent the tragic news in a dream.

The heartbroken Halcyone went to the seashore to the spot from which Ceyx had embarked, and presently she saw the body of a man, whom she finally recognised as her husband, floating towards her. She leapt from a breakwater into the sea towards him. The gods took pity on them and changed them both into kingfishers.

Every year Aeolus calms the winds and the waves for fourteen days in the middle of winter so that his beloved Halcyone and her husband can build their nest and raise their young far out to sea.

Halcyon days indeed!

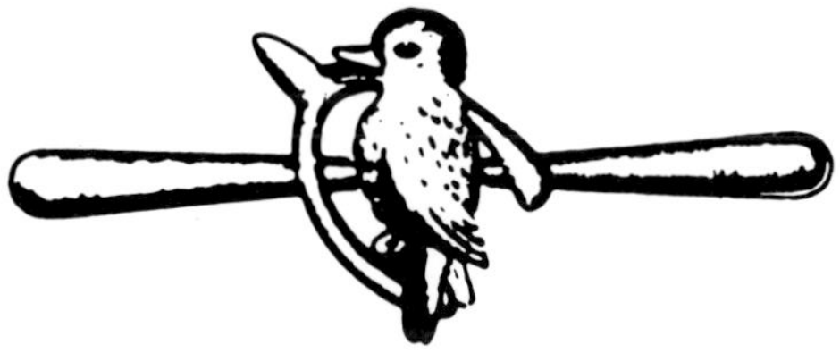

HOW THE KOOKABURRA WAS WRONGLY NAMED

Although the kookaburra has been called many names, from 1846 it was named *Dacelo gigas* by the naturalist G. R. Grey. This name continued in the official *Checklist of the Birds of Australia* until 1975. (*Dacelo* is derived from the Greek name Halcyon or Alcyone. *Gigas* means big.) Some recent publications still use the name *Dacelo gigas*.

Since 1975, Australia's favourite bird (which occurs no nearer to New Guinea than Cape York) has been officially called *Dacelo novaeguineae*. The New Guinea Dacelo! The reasons for this misleading name originate in the eighteenth century. There is still confusion over the first European sighting and the official naming of the Laughing Kookaburra, for no one is quite sure which European first saw the bird. Sir Joseph Banks brought back two specimens from Captain Cook's first voyage, 1769–1771, when the east coast of Australia was explored. However, as nothing was written about the bird or its laugh, one must assume that they shot first and looked second.

The first European to write about the kookaburra was a Frenchman, Pierre Sonnerat, whose *Voyage à la Nouvelle Guinée* was published in 1776. Sonnerat describes the

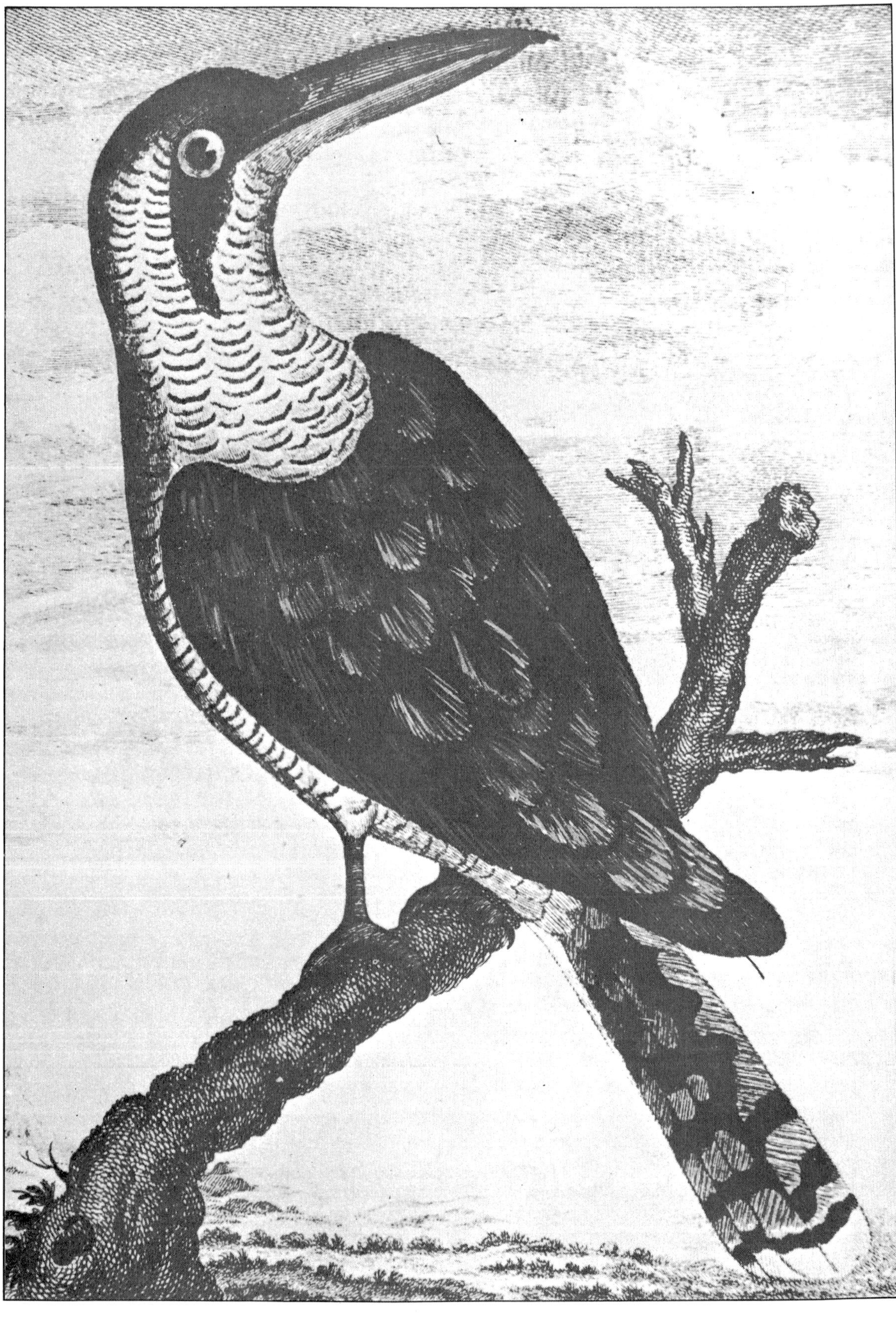

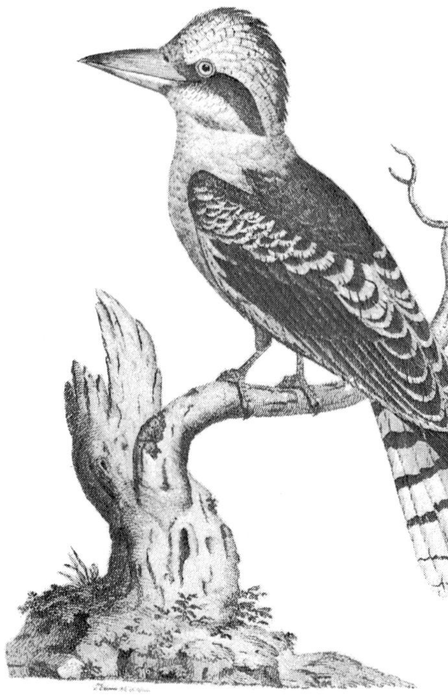

This engraving of the 'Great Brown Kingfisher' (above) is from *The Voyage of Governor Phillip to Botany Bay* by Governor Phillip, published 1789.

The first recorded illustration of a kookaburra: from Pierre Sonnerat's *Voyage à la Nouvelle Guinée*, published 1776 (opposite page)

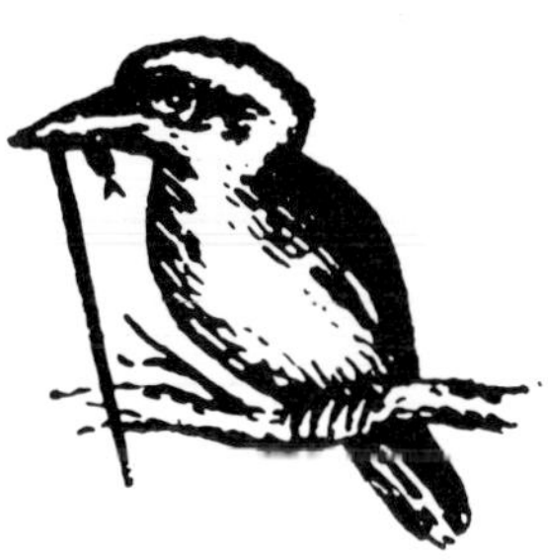

kookaburra accurately but claims he saw it in New Guinea, where it does not occur. He makes no mention of the famous laugh, which suggests he was dealing with skins, not live birds. Scholars have suggested that either Sonnerat described birds brought back to New Guinea by native fishermen or traders from Australia, or, even more intriguingly, that he obtained a specimen of the kookaburra from Sir Joseph Banks, whom he met at the Cape of Good Hope in 1770, and claimed that he had found it in New Guinea. Another scientist read Sonnerat's book and registered the name *Dacelo novaeguineae*. So a misleading name, because it was the first registered, is by the law of priority the legal name, and our all-Australian bird is flying false colours. As A. J. Campbell, a leading Australian ornithologist of the time, writing against this sort of foolishness in *The Emu* in 1908 said: 'On the so-called law of priority, why should not the Commonwealth of Australia be called "New Holland" and Tasmania "Van Diemen's Land"?'

'EVEN THE BIRDS MOCK OUR MISERY'

Governor Phillip and his convict fleet arrived at Port Jackson to settle this continent in January 1788. The little colony was on the brink of starvation for the first few years. One poor convict wrote, 'Even the birds mock our misery'; perhaps this was a reference to the kookaburra's laugh.

Governor Phillip's account of the settlement, published in 1789, included an illustration of the 'Great Brown Kingfisher'. Phillip also notes the Aboriginal name, 'kookaburra'. He describes exploratory forays into the bush around Port Jackson and the enthusiastic shooting and eating of the native birds by hungry British officers, but no mention is made of the kookaburra's laugh. We can be grateful for the lack of details about preparing kookaburras for the pot, but puzzled by the omission of the famous laugh.

John White, Surgeon-General to the First Fleet, published his *Journal* in 1790. This contained 65 natural history plates, including one of the 'Great Brown Kings Fisher'. Both

Governor Phillip and White took as their reference a book published in 1782 by Dr John Latham, *General Synopsis of Birds*, Volume II. White states, 'The bird is not uncommon in New Guinea from whence Latham took his example'. Presumably Dr Latham had been misled by Sonnerat's report.

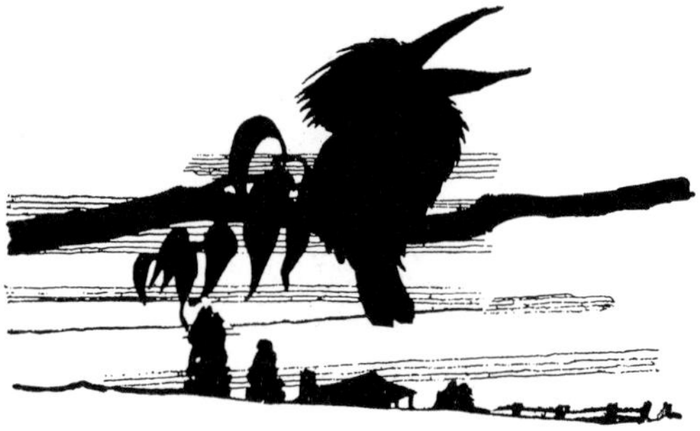

THE LAUGHING JACKASS

No one has been able to explain quite how the kookaburra, the herald of the dawn, had his wings metaphorically clipped and was burdened with his new and unappealing title of the Laughing Jackass. But we know that before the eighteenth century drew to a close the European settlers had bestowed this title on him.

It is mentioned in some notes by Thomas Watling who was transported to Australia. Having gone AWOL for several years in Capetown, Watling finally reached our shores, a most unwilling and ungracious guest, in 1792. When he received a pardon in 1797 he left as soon as he could, having done some very valuable work recording the local topography and its flora and fauna.

Some early white settlers found the kookaburra's laugh unnerving in the solitude of the bush. Our kookaburra was known by some as 'the cynic of the bush', and his laughter reminded them of the braying of a jackass.

Many explanations have been advanced of how our hero gained this name. One writer suggested that it came from the French word jacasse, but the dictionary reveals that jacasse means magpie.

In 1931, E. A. Vidler wrote in *Our Own Birds*:

> . . . some people think that it came from the aborigines who, it is said, when they first made acquaintance with a laughing gold-digger, called him 'Chaka'chaka' in imitation of his hilarious noise. The miners transferred the name to the bird the natives called 'Kookaburra' and gave the bird the name of 'Chaka', which became corrupted into 'Jackass'.

As he had been called the Laughing Jackass for some sixty years before gold was discovered, this ingenious explanation seems a little unlikely!

THE SETTLER'S CLOCK

Another title bestowed early on the kookaburra was a more friendly one, the Settler's Clock or the Bushman's Clock. As early as 1802, the explorer and naturalist George Caley wrote that he had heard the kookaburra referred to as the Hawkesbury Clock. What makes the name so pertinent is Caley's assertion that there was not a single clock (of the mechanical variety) in the entire Hawkesbury settlement. It was in 1802 that the Governor of the colony of New South Wales, Philip Gidley King, introduced cedar-cutting licences because he was concerned about the cedar traffic on the Hawkesbury. Many cedar cutters must have lain in their tents waiting for the kookaburra to signal that it was time to rise and renew their efforts to roll logs to the river.

Early literature commonly refers to the kookaburra as the bushman's or settler's clock, and in *Bush Wanderings* by An Old Bushman, published in 1861, we read:

> About an hour before sunrise the bushman is awakened by the most discordant sounds, as if a troop of fiends were shouting, hooping and laughing round him in one wild chorus; this is the morning song of the Laughing Jackass, warning his feathered mates that daybreak is at hand. At noon the same wild laugh is heard and as the sun sinks into the west, it again rings through the bush.

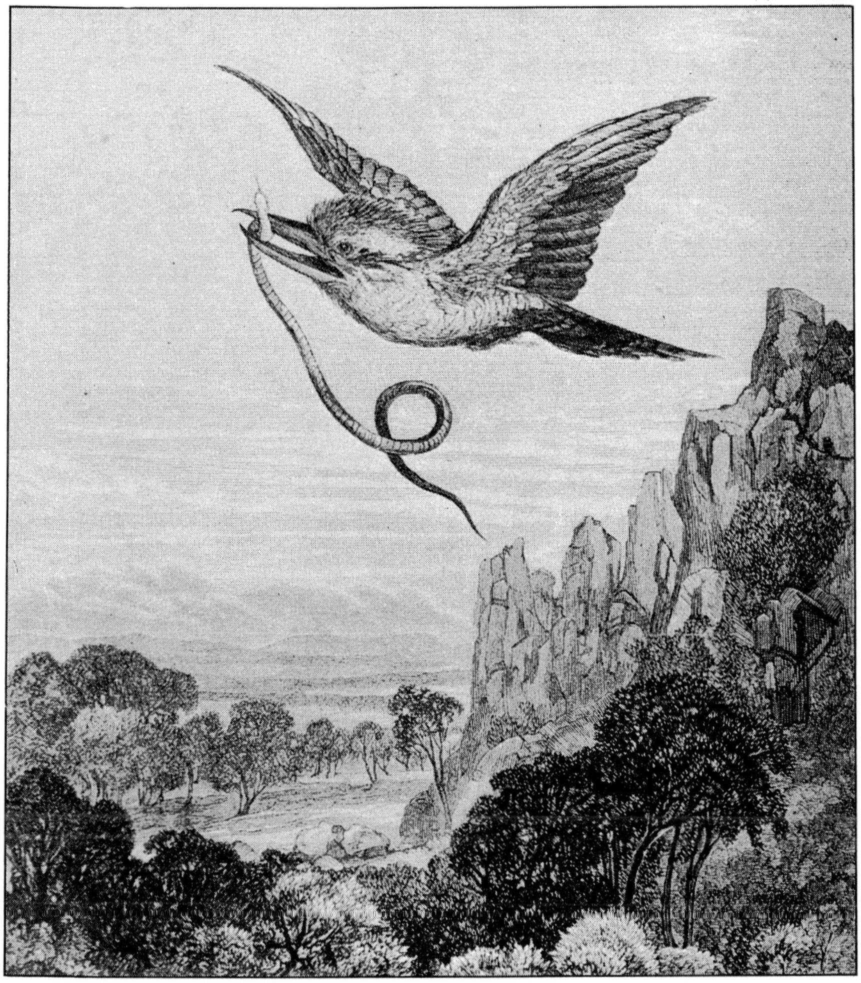

The kookaburra was also known as the Snake Destroyer, as an issue of the *Illustrated Australian News* pictured him on 27 December 1888

THE SNAKE CATCHER

Once the early settlers in Australia recovered from their initial shock at the uncouthness of our larrikin friend and became accustomed to his rollicking laughter, the bird quickly established himself as a 'goody' of the bush. One of the reasons for this was his celebrated role as a snake catcher. Many Australian birds are efficient despatchers of snakes, but for some reason it is Jolly Jack whose prowess has always been most admired. Perhaps it's something to do with the sheer pluck of a kingfisher taking on such a dangerous job without using his claws as a bird of prey would do. His claws are not strong enough to hold a reptile, so he has to

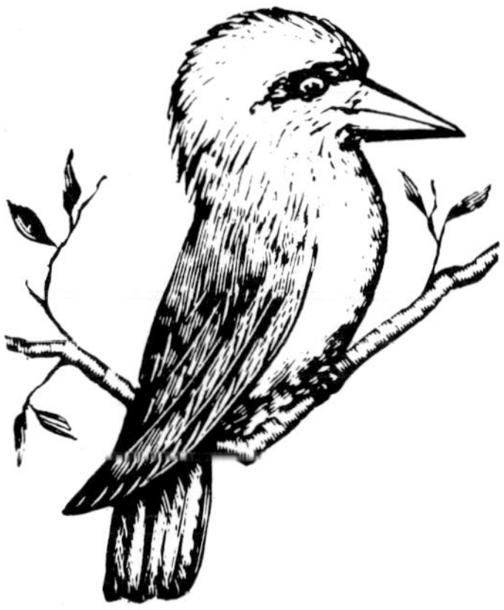

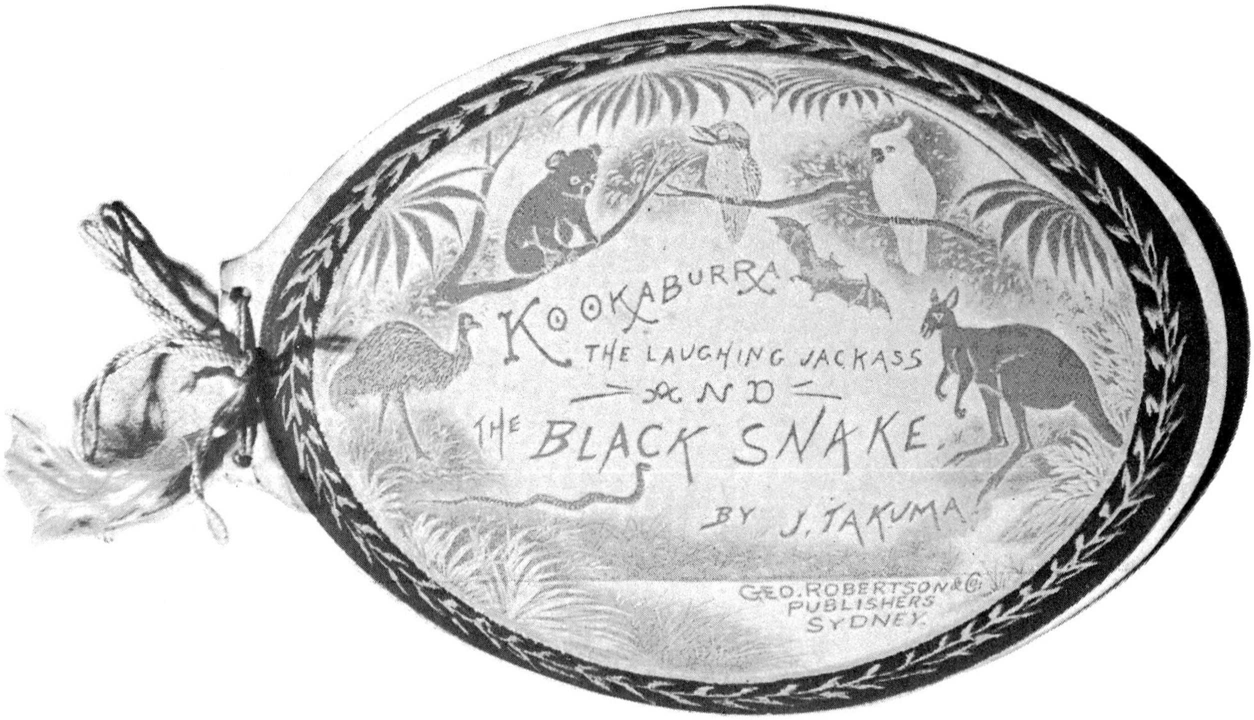

A book shaped like an emu's egg tells the fable of the kookaburra and the black snake. The author is Japanese-born J. Takuma, a noted nineteenth-century carver of emu eggs. Several eggs carved by Takuma in the style of the illustrations in the book are in Sydney collections.

swoop down and seize his quarry in his beak. Instinct suggests that behind the snake's head is the safest spot.

The kookaburra then flies to a tree and vigorously shakes his head from side to side with an air of desperate frenzy, whipping the snake like a stockwhip, and beating its head against a tree branch. Another less frequent but more publicised technique is for the kookaburra to swoop high into the air, dropping the snake from a great height on to rocks or hard ground.

Imagine the aerodynamic problems of balance at take-off! On some occasions disaster strikes – crash landings, snakes and all, have been observed.

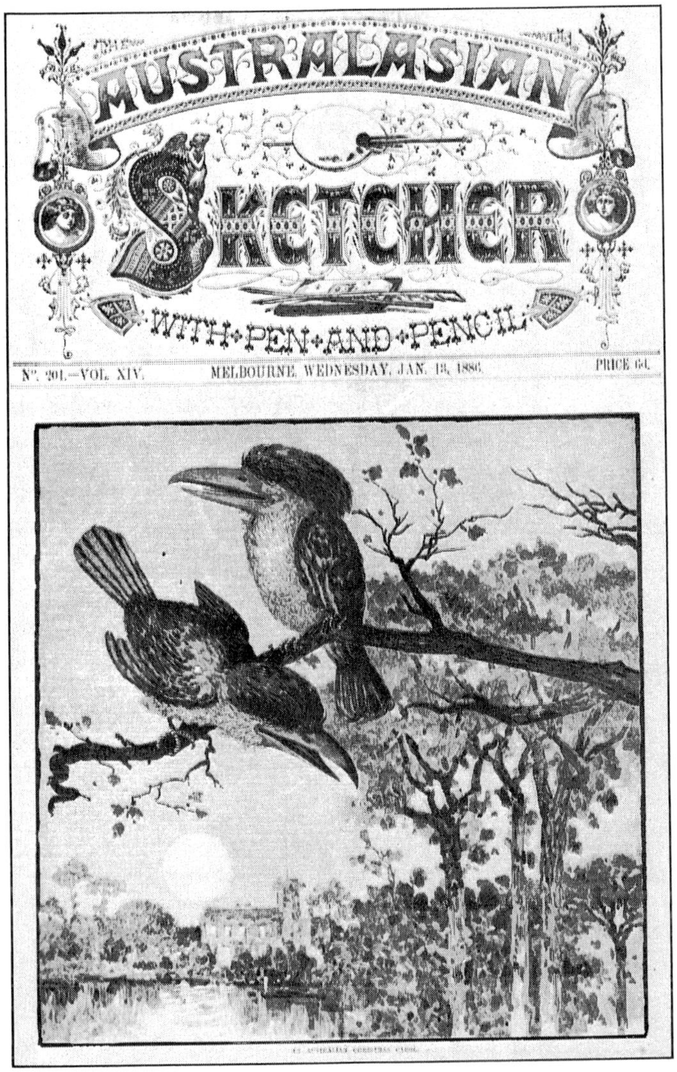

The colonists of the Victorian era were in dread fear of snakes, so the 'Snake Destroyer' was given hero status, as the illustration from an 1888 *Illustrated Australian News* depicts (see page 23). The Snake Destroyer was a valued companion of the bushman and the settler. His exploits were written into children's stories, cast into iron as a decorative element of hallstands, carved on emu eggs and celebrated in poetry and art. After Federation in 1901, when the kookaburra's position in popular art became so prominent, the snake catcher was to be the inspiration for the brand name of several commercial products that featured some sort of snake-like characteristic.

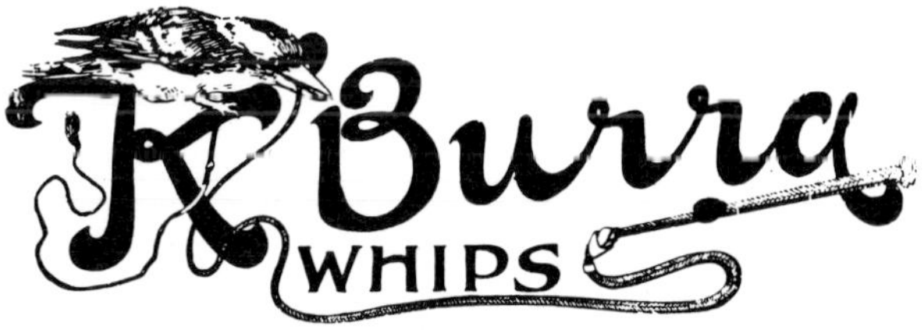

'An Australian Christmas Carol', from the *Australasian Sketcher*, 13 January 1886 (top)

The trademark for K'Burra whips was registered in 1922 by Walther and Stevenson

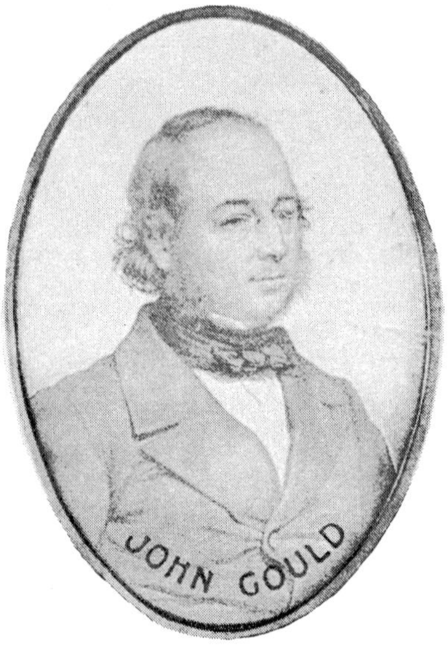

This portrait of John Gould comes from an old Gould League of Bird Lovers' certificate

OBSERVATIONS FROM EARLY DAYS

John Gould, who visited Australia from 1838 to 1840, was the ornithologist and entrepreneur who put Australia's bird life 'on the map'. He had the following to say about our friend:

> The *Dacelo gigas* is a bird with which every resident and traveller in New South Wales is more or less familiar, for, independently of its large size, its voice is so extraordinary as to be unlike that of any other bird. In its disposition it is by no means shy, and when any new objects are presented to its notice such as a party traversing the bush or pitching their tent in the vicinity of its retreat, it becomes very prying and inquisitive, often perching on the dead branch of some neighbouring tree, and watching with curiosity the kindling of the fire and the preparation of the meal; its presence, however, is seldom detected and until it emits its extraordinary gurgling, laughing note, which generally calls forth some exclamation according with the temper of the hearer, such as 'There is our old friend the Laughing Jackass', or an epithet of a less friendly character.

So remarkable are the sounds emitted by the bird that they have been noted by nearly every early writer on New South Wales.

George Caley wrote, '[the kookaburra's] loud noise, somewhat like laughing, may be heard at a considerable distance, from which circumstance, and its uncouth appearance, it probably received the extraordinary appellation given to it by the settlers on their first arrival in the colony'.

Captain Sturt wrote, 'Its cry, which resembles a chorus of wild spirits, is apt to startle the traveller who may be in jeopardy, as if laughing and mocking at his misfortune'.

Mr Bennett in his *Wanderings* wrote:

> Its peculiar gurgling laugh, commencing in a low, and gradually rising to a high and loud tone, is often heard in all parts of the colony, the deafening noise being poured forth while the bird remains perched upon a neighbouring tree; it rises with the dawn, when the woods re-echo with its gurgling laugh; at sunset it is again heard; and as that glorious orb sinks in the west, a last 'good night' is given in its peculiar tones to all within hearing.

In 1888, W. F. Morrison wrote in *The Aldine History of N.S.W.*:

> But the most wonderful specimen of this tribe (the Kingfishers) is the Laughing Jackass (*Dacelo gigas*), or the Gogabera of the natives. It is a marvellous bird. Why it is called by such a repulsive name is not difficult to understand when one becomes better acquainted with its nature and habits. It is one of the oddest of the winged tribe in the Australian continent. It is a Kingfisher of great size, almost as large as a crow. It is of a brownish hue, and has a remarkably large head and long heavy beak. Its chief delight is to pounce down upon a snake, or other reptile, and carry it by the neck to the branch of some neighbourhood tree, where he is joined by his mates, sometimes by a great number of them. They delight in biting their prey, and amusing themselves by dropping it on the ground and picking it up again, and repeating the amusement amid the clatter of a general din. As the traveller passes near them, they seem to take great delight in joining in a most hideous exhibition of their vocal organs, that

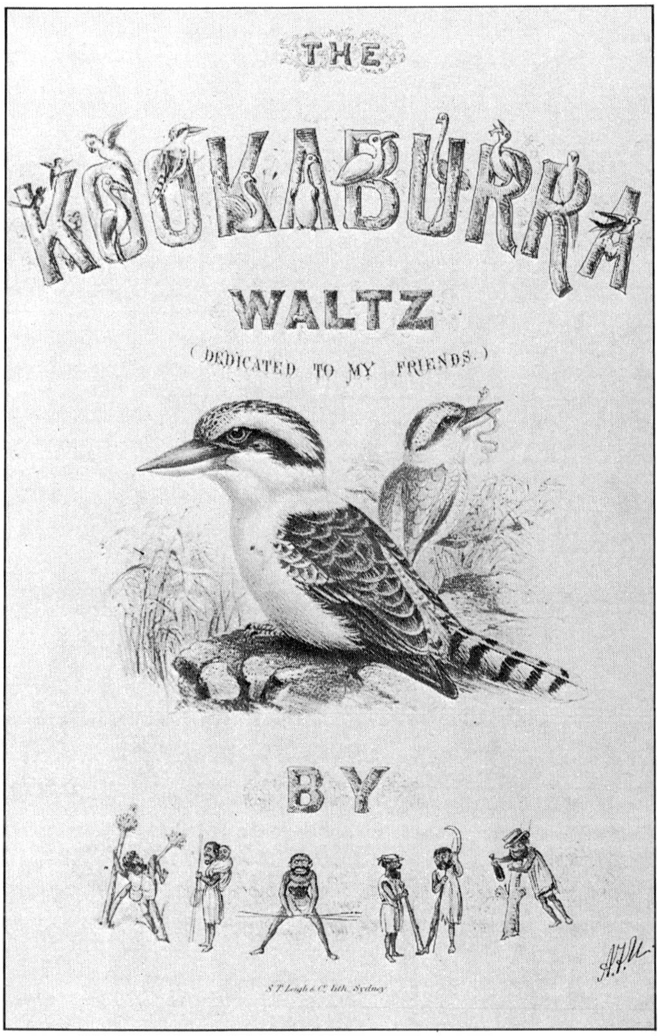

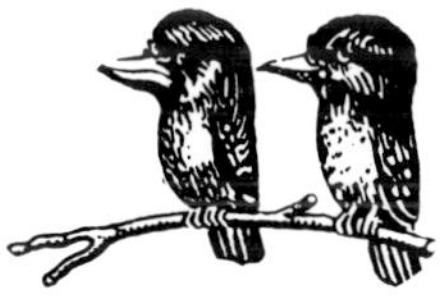

A charming nineteenth-century music cover—'The Kookaburra Waltz' by Krama

reminds one very much of the braying of an ass, when many of them are together.

They provoke laughter by the ridiculous tones they make in concert, ludicrous in the extreme, and contagious in effect. It is very easily tamed, and seems very much pleased with the advance of civilization, for he has a jollier time of it under the new conditions of life that are thus thrust upon him.

Early accounts of the kookaburra are usually written with warmth, never with indifference. Always a prominent creature in the bush, Jack was an identifiable Australian character.

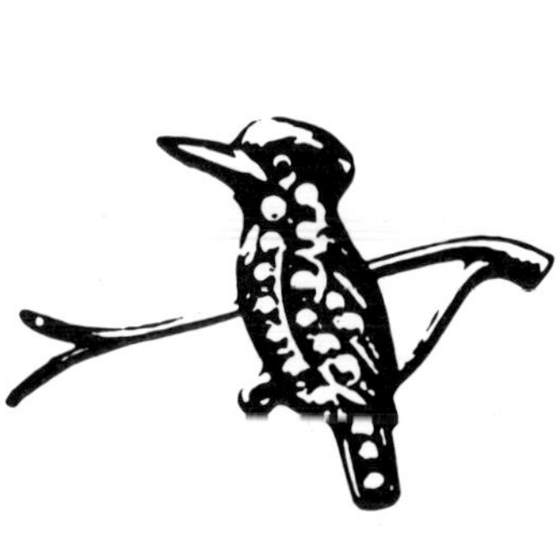

-3-
Family Life

Kookaburras have an interesting and highly developed family life. They live in an extended family situation with a breeding pair and lots of older brothers and sisters who all contribute to the feeding and protecting of the young. The breeding pair remain faithful to each other and live in one territory unless some serious upheaval dislocates them. Because they remain permanently mated they don't need the differentiation in plumage that one-time breeders need, so there is little difference in the plumage of males and females.

The Laughing Kookaburra is a native of eastern Australia from Adelaide around to Cairns. It was introduced to Tasmania and Western Australia about eighty years ago. The Blue-winged Kookaburra, which does not live in southern Australia, is called *Dacelo leachii*. It is not as famous because it doesn't laugh.

A most extensive study of the kookaburra was made by a young American, Veronica Parry, who came to Australia in the 1960s to do her Master of Science thesis on the kookaburra. This was published by Lansdowne Press in 1970, entitled *Kookaburras*. She studied the extended family situation of the kookaburras and their system of territories, each of which ranges from three to eight acres, depending on the numbers in the family and their ability to defend it.

A good territory needs a hole in a tall gum tree or a hollow log in dense bush where the female kookaburra lays about three pearly white eggs. It should also have dense bush for refuge

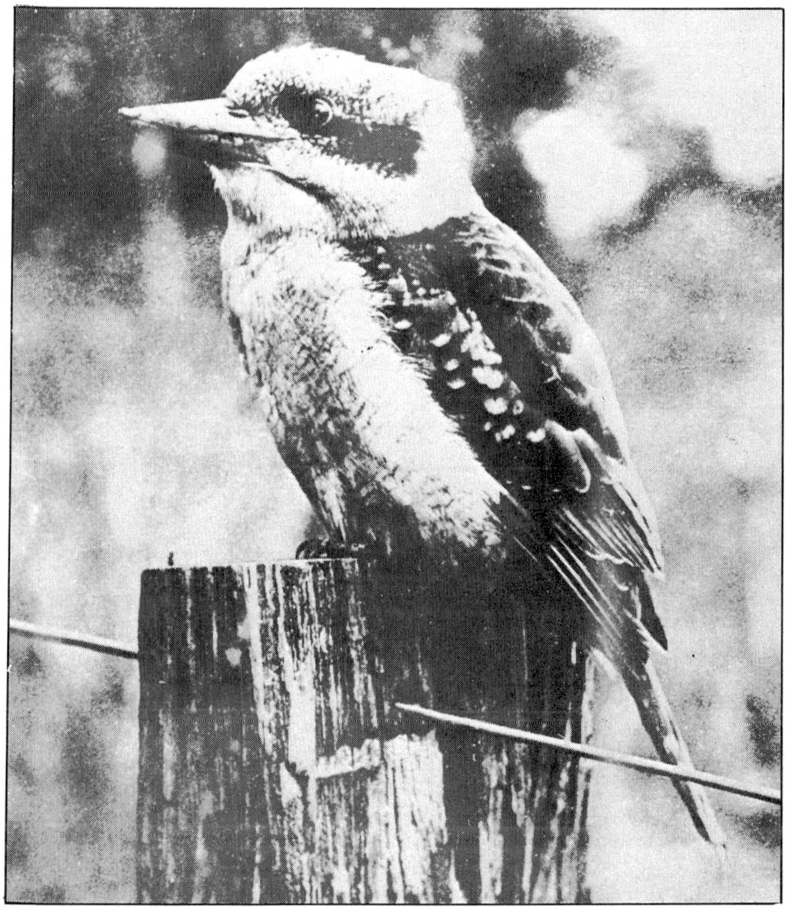

An old photograph of Jack sitting on a fence post

for the fledglings. An open area for hunting snakes, lizards, and other food is the final requirement for A grade kookaburra real estate.

As anyone who has lived near a family of kookas well knows, they are very friendly birds, not at all averse to receiving handouts of juicy chopped meats from humans. In fact they can be rather a nuisance when they line up on the verandah rail at six o'clock in the morning, tapping their beaks and letting everyone know that a spot of rail service would be in order. However, a friendly human is not a necessary part of a good territory.

When the eggs hatch in October, the whole family work diligently to supply food for the new arrivals and to protect them from predators.

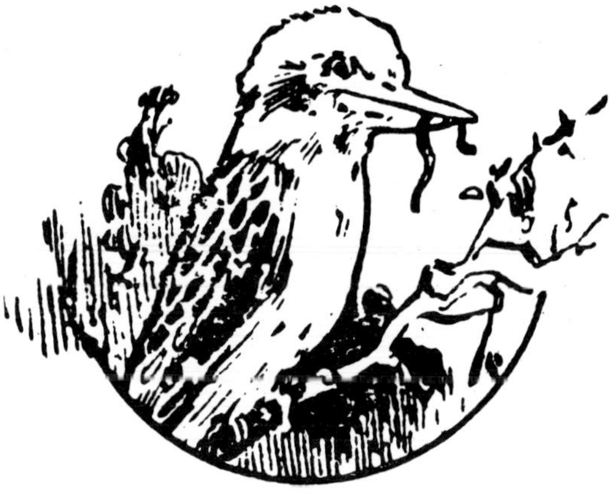

If a predator is spotted near the nest, the bomber squadron is alerted and intruders are bombarded by the family in turn. Because of the extended family situation, the kookaburra fledglings are very well protected and mortality rates are low. It is a grand sunrise when the youngsters have mastered their singing lessons and join the chorus!

A meal of baby snakes is a great delicacy, and one enjoyed by the whole kookaburra family, much to the grief of the mother snake. The feast is often celebrated with a rousing and merry chorus. Larger snakes may be swallowed head first. A disconcerting sight is that of an over-replete Jackass, with a foot or so of snake he just can't manage hanging out of his mouth. Alternatively, larger snakes may be the object of a jolly good tug-of-war back home with the entire family joining in. The snake usually is pulled into a number of parts, making digestion more agreeable.

The kookaburra does not require a river, pond or dam in his territory because he does not drink. In our dry continent, he extracts all the moisture he needs from his food.

Of course, the natural breeding areas of the kookaburra have been seriously reduced since the advent of the European settlers. As more and more bush is cleared, the familiar laugh is heard much less frequently.

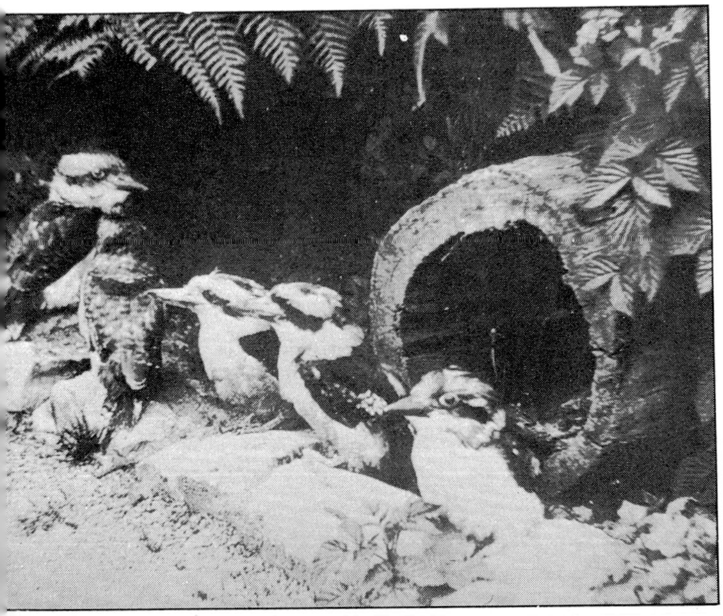

'GIVE A BIRD A BAD NAME'

In the early 1980s there were rumblings from some farmers in Western Australia that kookaburras were raiding nests of other small native birds in the state and reducing their numbers. Because of this the farmers wanted kookaburras stripped of their protected classification and declared vermin. In the words of one anti-kookaburra person: 'Farmers should be able to pot kookas like wild cats'. This, of course, brought howls of protests and denials from the kookaburra lovers.

The truth of the matter is hard to determine. Kookaburras are an introduced species to Western Australia – their native habitat is in the east. They were first taken to Western Australia in about 1898. *The Story of Kurri Kurri the Kookaburra* by Leslie Rees (first published by John Sands in 1948) is a children's story telling about the abduction of two little kookaburras. Without their natural predators (like the lace goanna, a strong tree climber), kookaburras have flourished in the west, but their role as reducers of the small native bird population seems disproved by two pieces of research.

Veronica Parry spent two years in the Victorian Dandenong Ranges studying the kookaburra in the field. She observed that the kookaburra's diet consisted of about one-third snakes and lizards, one-third insects, and the remainder earthworms, shellfish, kitchen titbits and small rodents. She did not observe the kookaburra eating other small birds and decided that when other food was plentiful, birds did not constitute part of the kookaburra's diet.

Kookaburras do a good job, especially in time of plague, in keeping the insect population under control. In a scientific study carried out under the auspices of the Agricultural Protection Board of Western Australia, 43 kookaburras were examined. Ninety-nine per cent of all food items were invertebrates – ants, wasps and so on. Birds formed 0·23 per cent of all food items (that is, 1 out of 428 items). Dr Ian Rooke, the researcher, has concluded that

Fledglings obtain instructions outside their nest

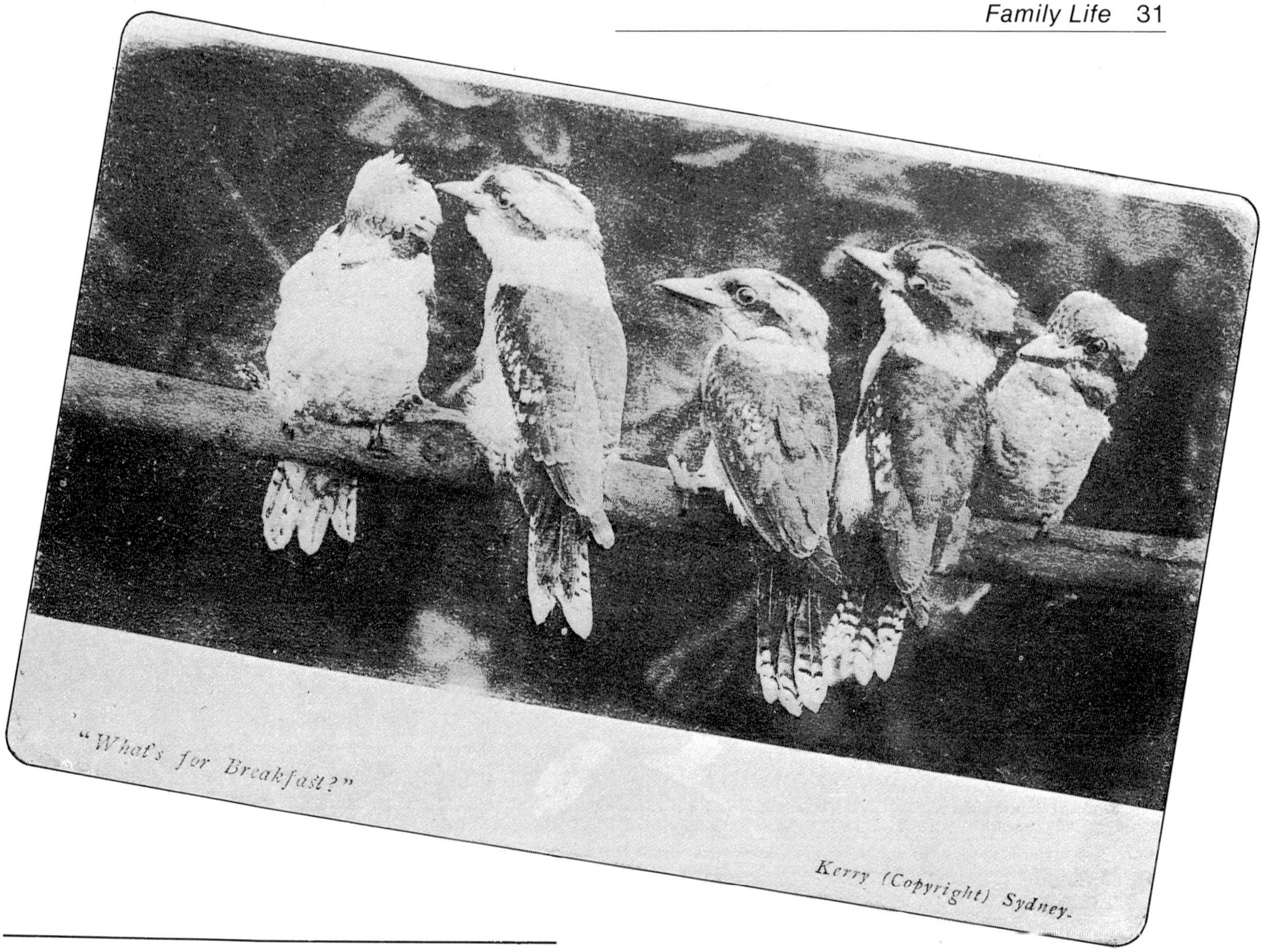

'What's for Breakfast?' An old postcard reproducing a photograph by Charles Kerry

kookaburras are not a threat to small native birds.

Kookaburra fledglings are sometimes eaten by butcherbirds – so the laws of nature do prevail.

WHAT'S THE JOKE?

Why does the kookaburra laugh? Legends, poems and stories all try to explain how he got his laugh, and they attribute human qualities to what is, after all, simply a bird's natural song that happens to resemble wild human laughter.

The kookaburra chorus takes place at dawn and at twilight. All the birds in the family sit on their roosting perch and laugh their familiar song. Veronica Parry, after carefully studying this aspect of kookaburra behaviour, concluded that the song is a declaration of territorial rights. Neighbouring families will take it in turns to chorus. The song intensifies in the three months before breeding takes place, as

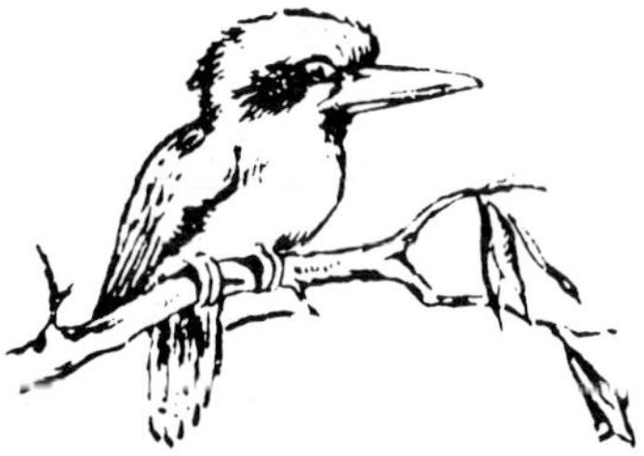

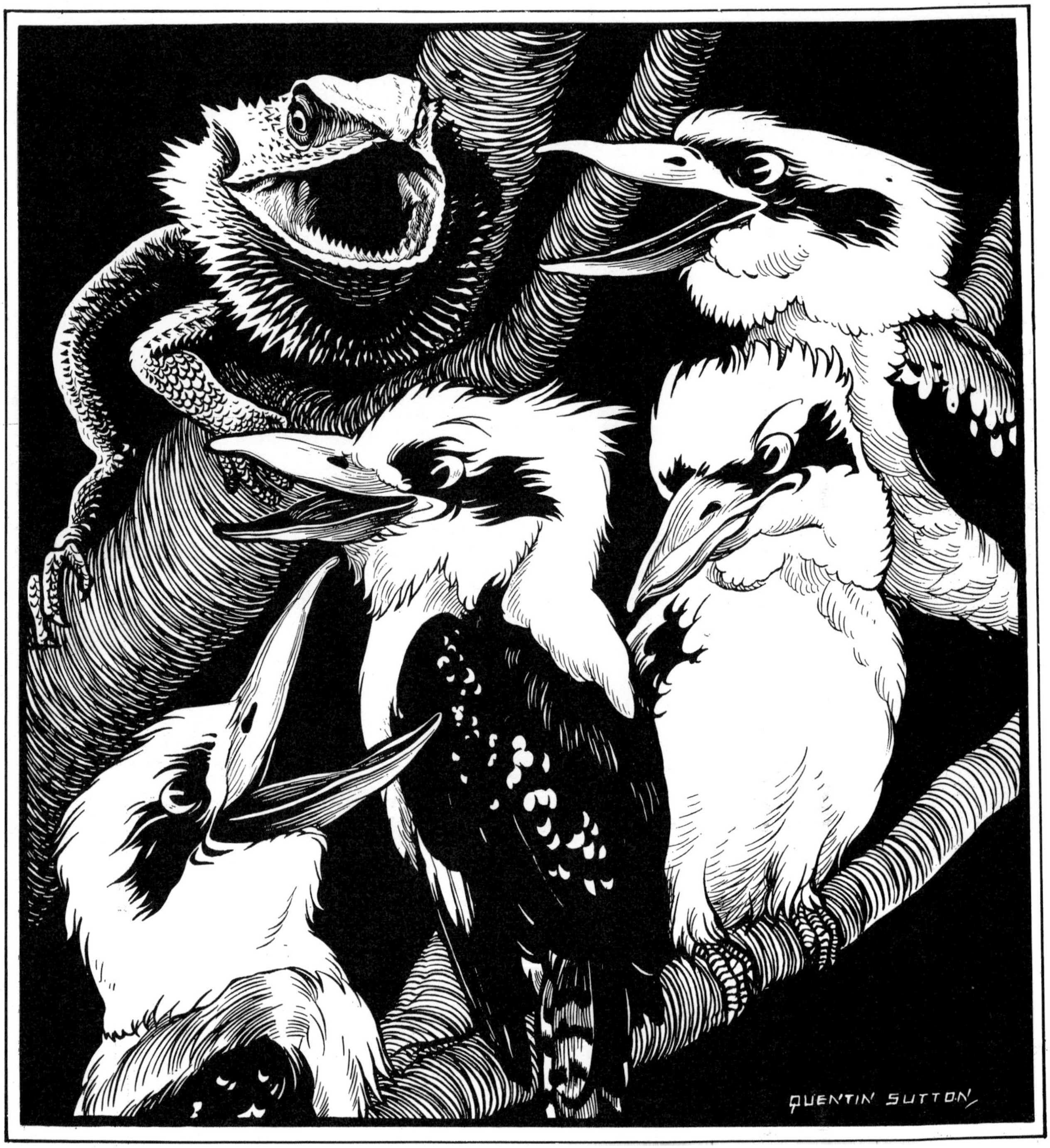

'What's the joke?' asks the puzzled frill-necked lizard from *A Jackeroo's Jingles* by Alan Edmunds

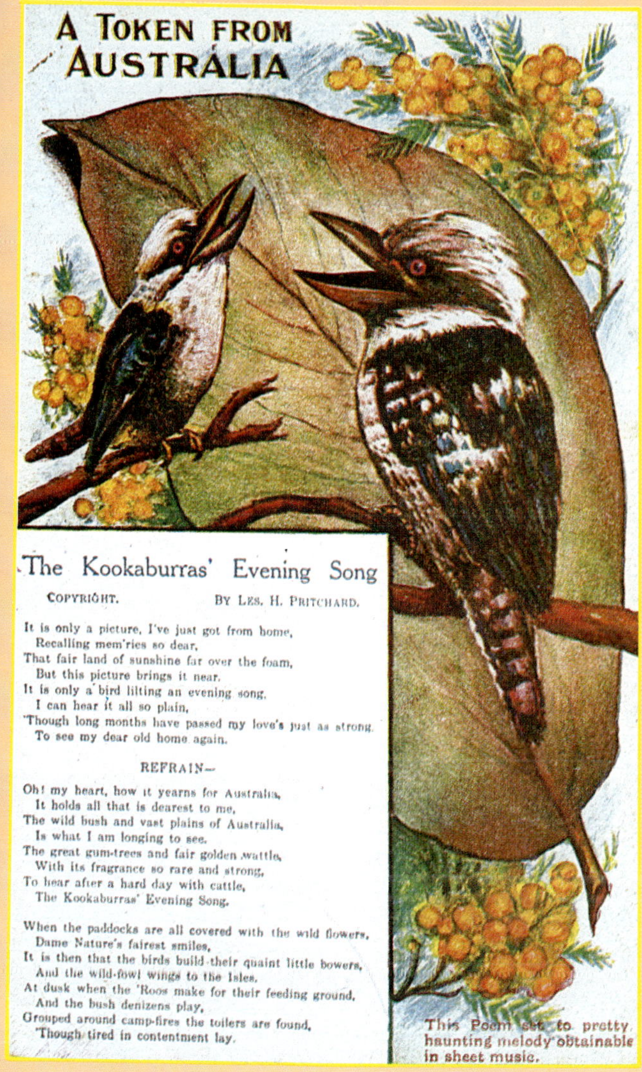

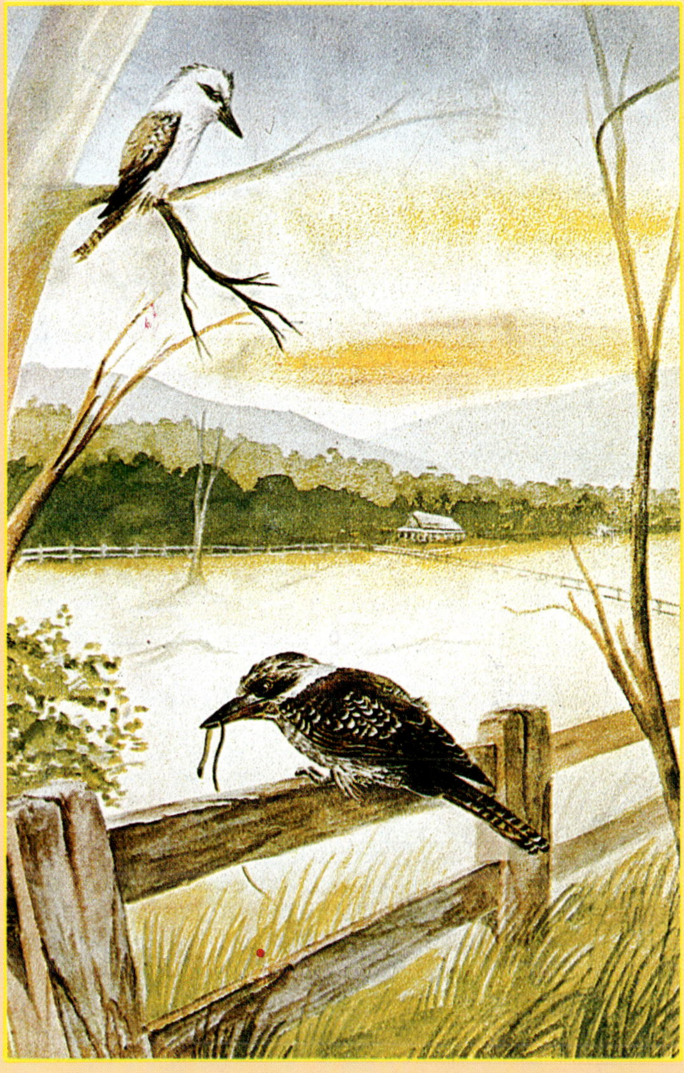

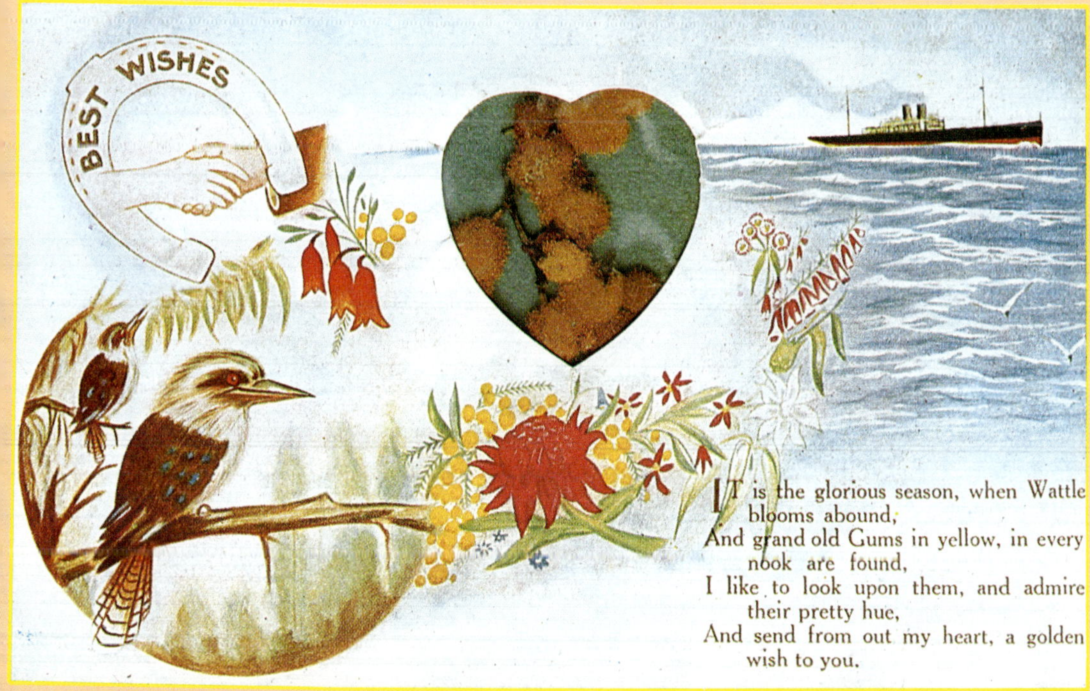

A token from Australia (above left)

A nostalgic postcard by Oscar Stahl (above right)

A chuckle across the waters (left)

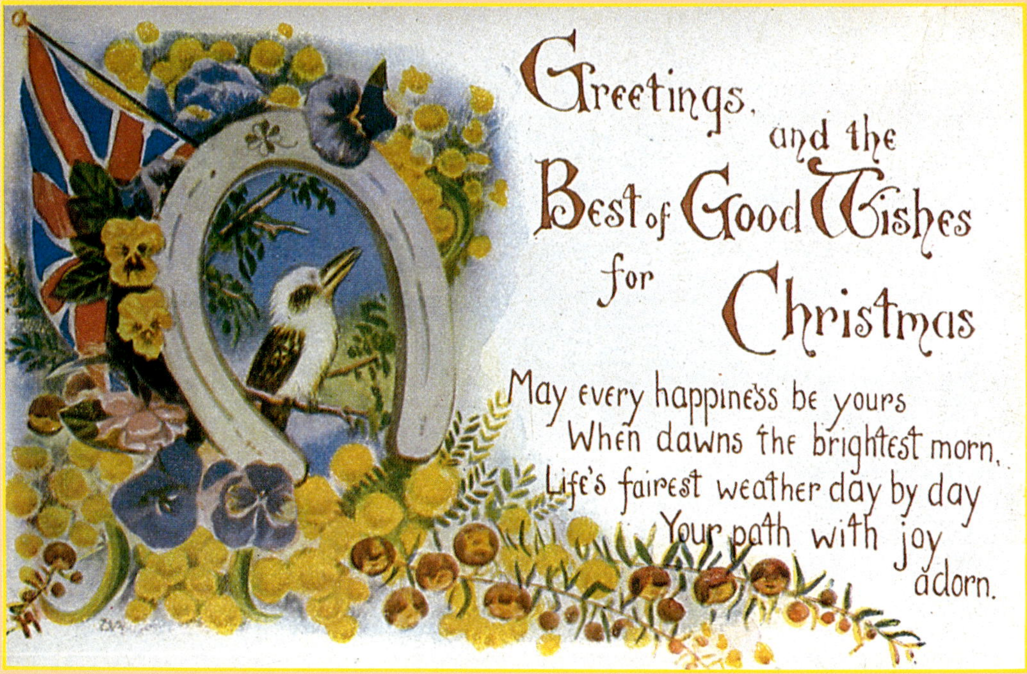

A cheerful Christmas card (left)

Another kookaburra greeting (below left)

A striking depiction of the snake catcher on a J. M. Cantle postcard *c.* 1908 (below right)

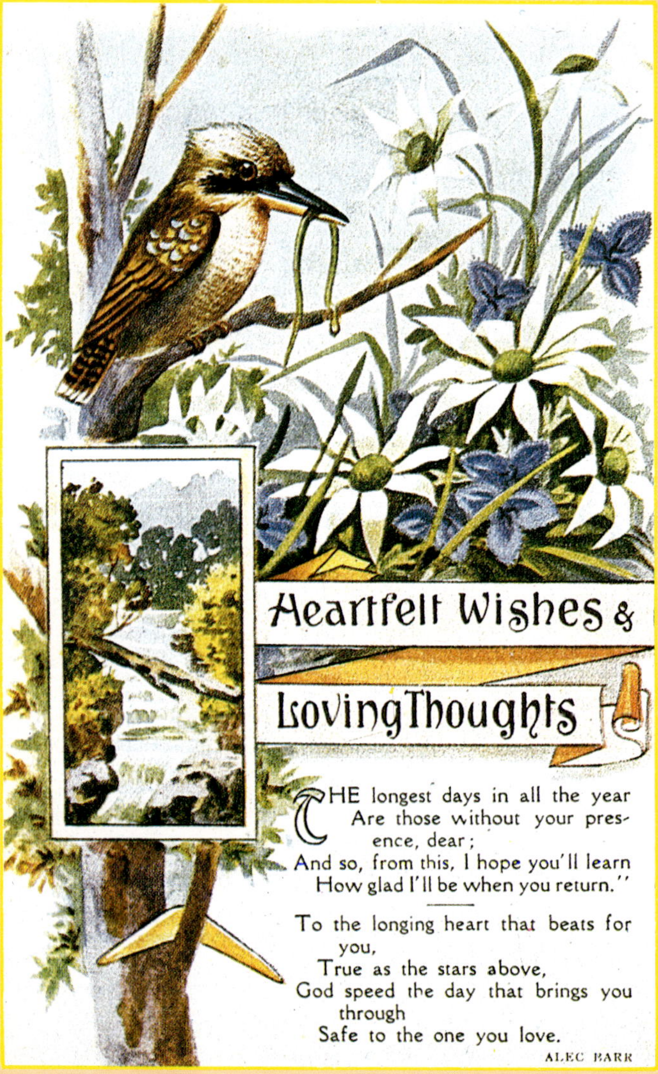

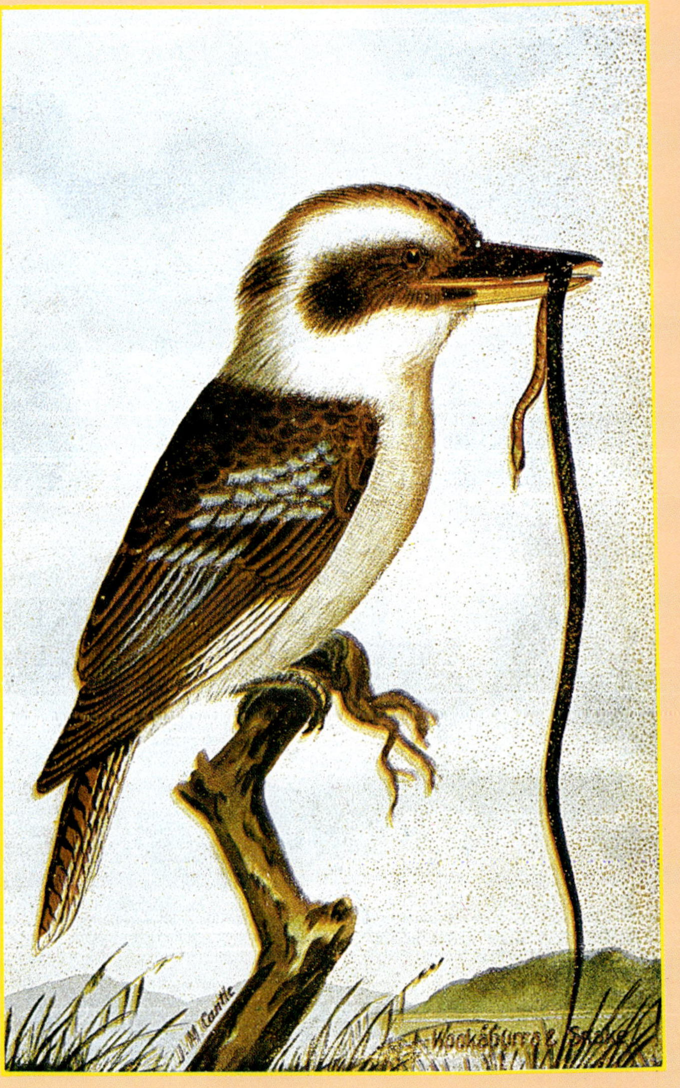

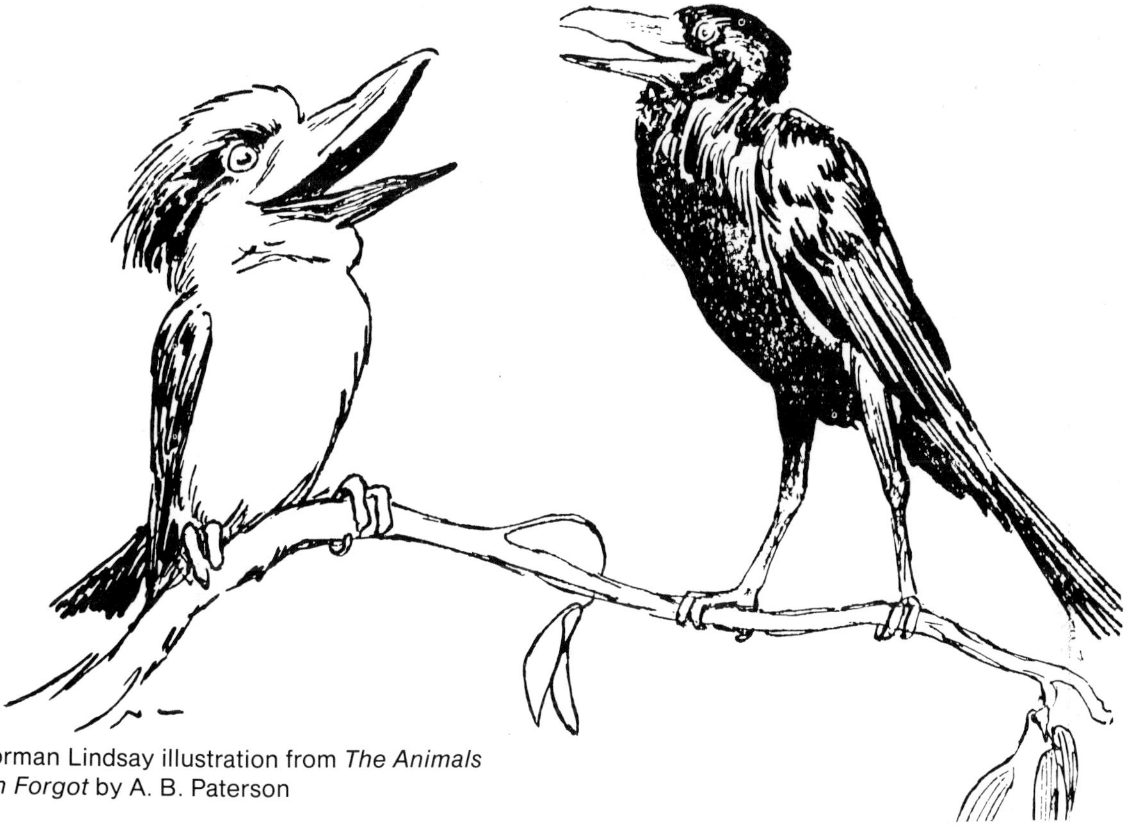

A Norman Lindsay illustration from *The Animals Noah Forgot* by A. B. Paterson

territorial boundaries are redetermined depending on the fluctuating strengths of various family groups. Apart from this territorial aspect, the chorus provides the kookaburra with an opportunity for group interaction and solidarity. Other times for laughter are after some tense or exciting event, like the capture of a large snake or the successful first flight of the baby birds.

There is a charming Aboriginal story with a most ingenious explanation of the famous laugh. It relates to the time long ago when the kookaburra's staple fare was tadpoles. One young kookaburra girl who did not like tadpoles boasted to an admirer that she preferred to eat spitfires, those writhing clumps of caterpillars. The admirer ungallantly demanded proof.

After one beakful of spitfires, her throat and chest aflame, she dive-bombed the creek. Now for the irony of the Aboriginal story. In her anxiety to take a mouthful of water, she swallowed a tadpole. She couldn't decide which was worse: the burning of the spitfires or the feeling of a slippery tadpole in her throat. First she tried to throw the tadpole up, then she tried to swallow the water. The result: 'Ooh ooh ooh ooh aah aah aah aah aah!' – the first kookaburra laugh. Her friends and relations so admired the aria that they all demanded laughing lessons.

Banjo Paterson, in his book for children *The Animals Noah Forgot*, has another explanation of why the kookaburra laughs. He laughs whenever he sees a crow because he remembers how he outwitted the Boastful Crow. The Boastful Crow was telling of his prowess as a traveller and hunter throughout the country. The Laughing Jack made a bold bet of 100 mice that the Boastful Crow would not dare to migrate with the little green bee birds, who fly to Japan every winter. Naturally he won the bet, and Laughing Jack still laughs whenever he sees a crow.

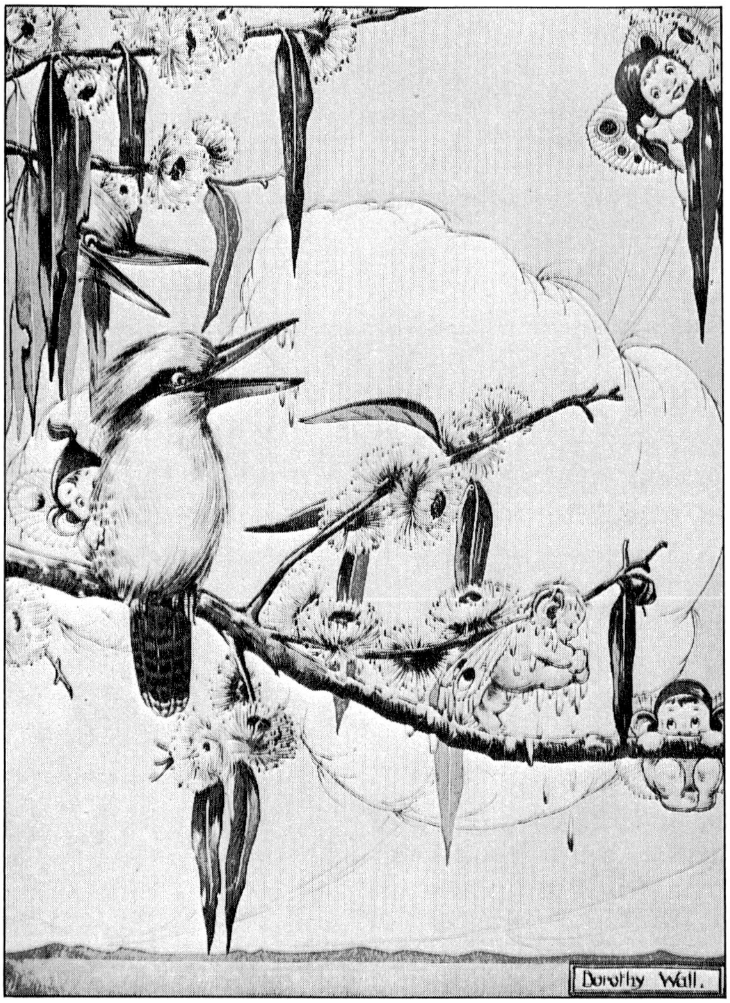

The Little Grey Man of J. J. Hall's *The Crystal Bowl* gives a further explanation of why the kookaburra laughs. One day, a brownie was leaning over the edge of a honey pot when one of his mates crept up behind him and pushed him in. Luckily our Jackass was nearby. He was able to fish out the brownie before he drowned. The sight of the brownie dripping with honey and staggering along the gum tree branch was too much for the Jackass, and his mirth and jolly laughter were heard throughout the bush.

So whenever you hear the kookaburra laughing, you'll have to choose which story to believe.

'The Jackass thought that he had never seen anything so funny.' A Dorothy Wall illustration (above) from *The Crystal Bowl* by J. J. Hall. This children's book was first published in Melbourne in 1922

John Jackass (opposite page) is from another children's book of 1922, *Kangaroo Rhymes* by Stephen Grey

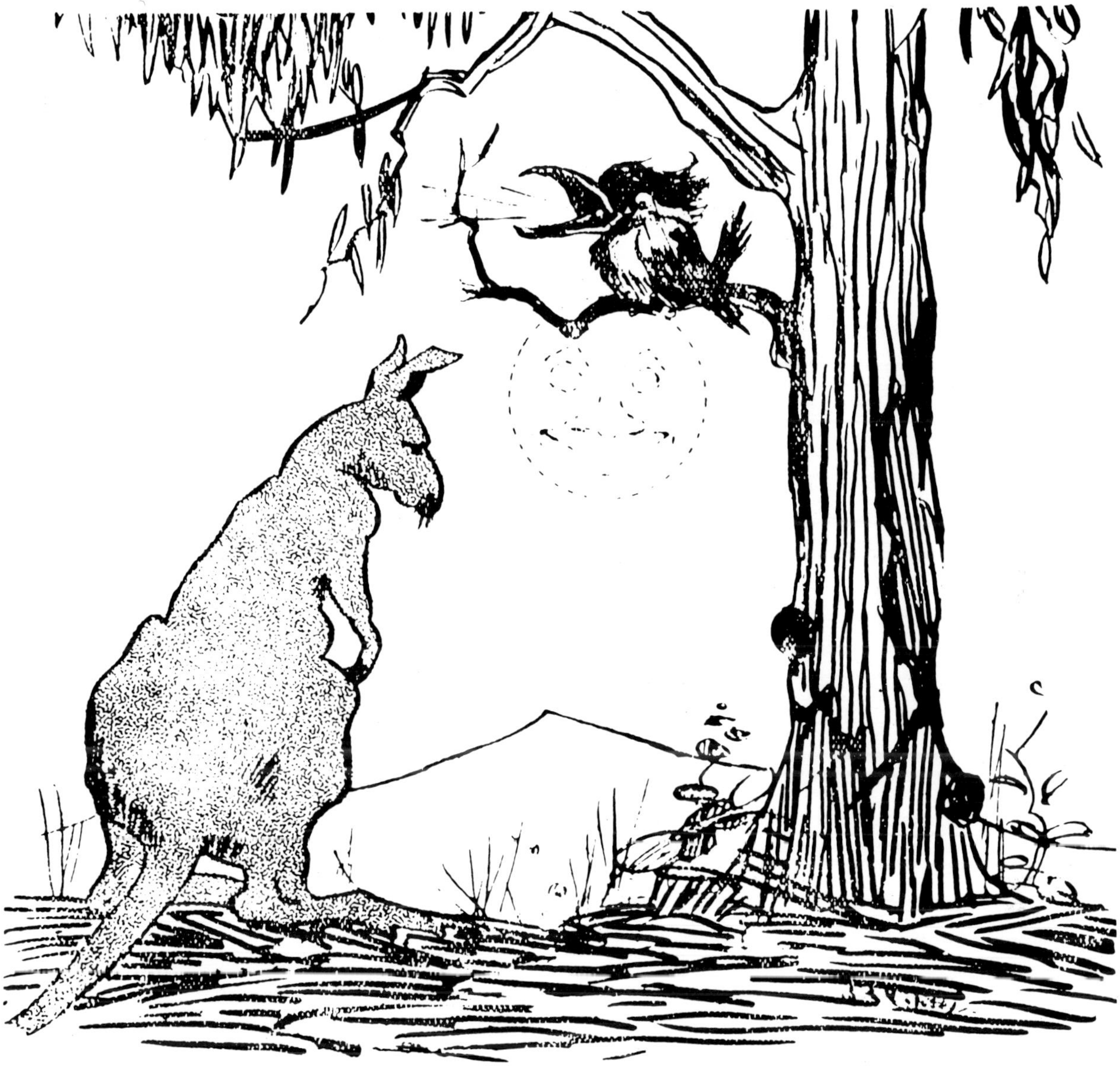

John Jackass

Old Man Kangaroo, hopping through the grass,
Kookaburra on a tree waits to see him pass;
Poor old Kangaroo trips and hurts his toe;
He-he! Ha-ha! HO-HO-HO!

-4-
Official Kookaburras

As an Australian symbol, the kookaburra is a twentieth-century phenomenon. The kangaroo and the emu were used constantly throughout the nineteenth century to support numerous official coats of arms. By the time Federation occurred and an official coat of arms was granted in 1908, the kangaroo and emu had established indubitable claim to the honour of star billing. One whimsical displacement of the emu occurs on the little gold brooch illustrated on page 37: on this occasion our merry friend has supplanted him.

However, the kookaburra motif has been used officially on many occasions. The 'borough 'burra' appears on the crests of coats of arms of two cities and a country shire. The kookaburra appeared on our third national postage stamp and was used on the famous trial square penny and halfpenny coins. A most appropriate official

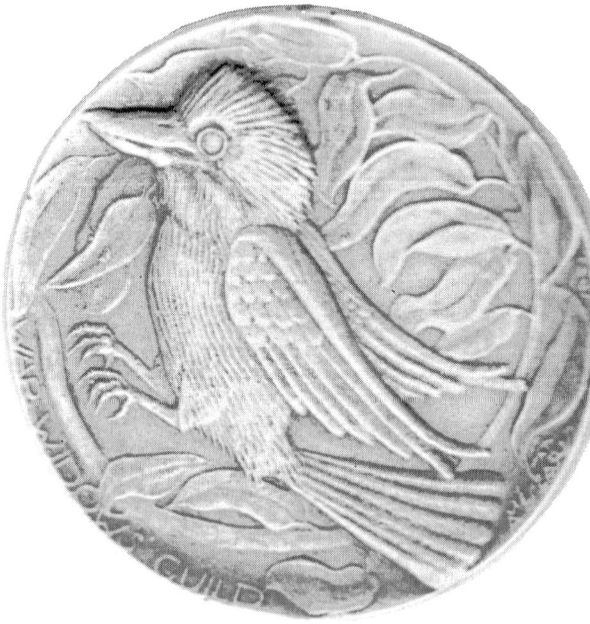

The kookaburra was chosen as the emblem of the War Widows' Guild brooch

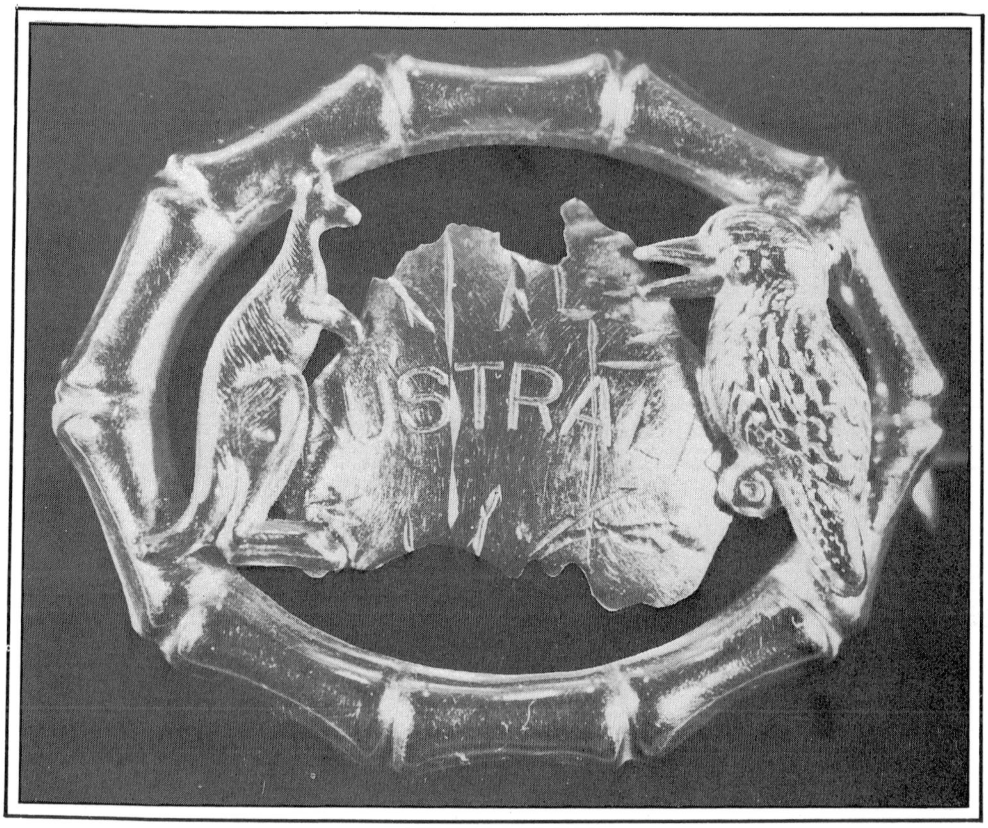

use of the kookaburra was as the symbol of various Australian bombing squadrons during the two world wars. As well, the Army and Navy used the kookaburra on their signs and badges.

We can but surmise that the merriment of the kookaburra filled many a bureaucratic heart earlier this century, inspiring a number of designers to choose the Laughing Jackass as their representative symbol. Specific uses are described in this chapter.

THE BOROUGH 'BURRA

The Shire of Korumburra in Victoria features two kookaburras on its crest. Originally called the Shire of Poowong and Jeetho in 1891, the name was changed to Korumburra in 1922 and the current crest was adopted. The shire's motto is 'Courage conquers the wilderness'.

This little gold brooch (above) must have been made before 1911 because on the map the Northern Territory is not separated from South Australia.

Kookaburras reign supreme on the Korumburra Shire crest (below)

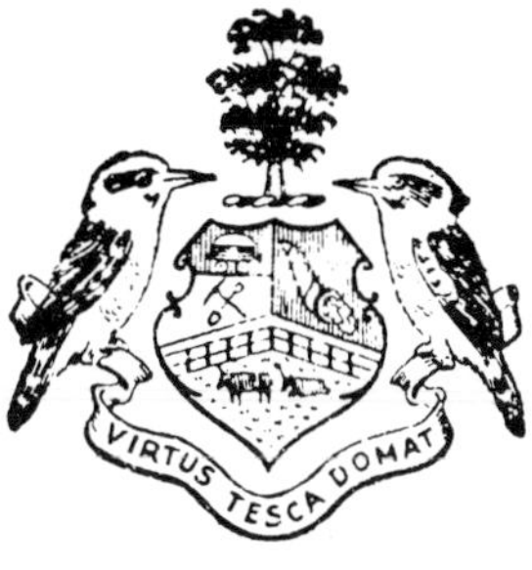

SHIRE OF KORUMBURRA

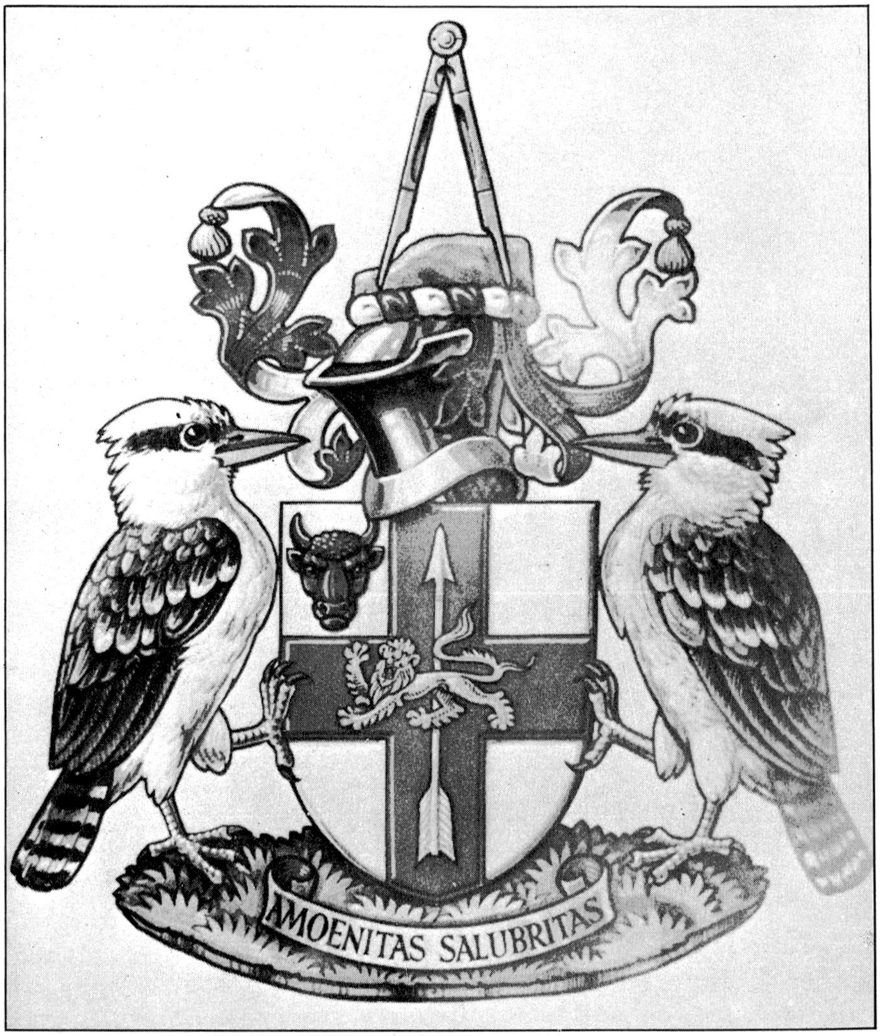

Coat of arms of the Municipality of Bowral

In 1925 the city of Ringwood in Victoria (then the Borough of Ringwood) adopted the crest of her English sister city Ringwood. The kookaburra took the place of the English blackbird and was chosen because 'the bird denotes progress by his beauty, speed, courage and strength'.

Another city that enjoys the service of the borough 'burra is Bowral in New South Wales, whose crest features two handsome kookaburras supporting the city's coat of arms. The municipality of Bowral was granted a coat of arms in 1957.

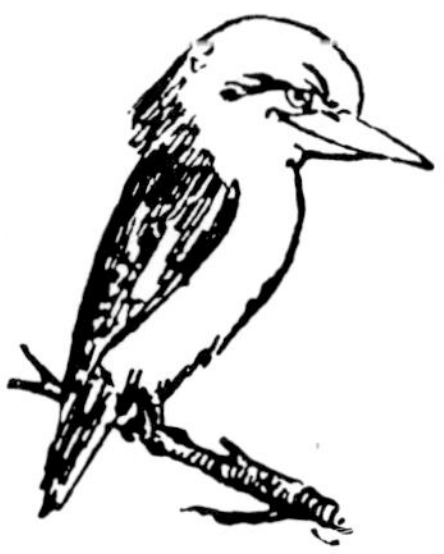

AIRFORCE USES OF THE KOOKABURRA SYMBOL

The laughter of the kookaburra is believed to be territorial. If the territory is encroached upon by neighbouring kookaburras or if fledgling birds are attacked by other birds or goannas, the entire kookaburra family commence a most extraordinary bombing operation. Emitting raucous cries, the family carry out a disciplined and terrifying attack on the intruder. Frantic flapping of wings takes place as a figure-of-eight dive-bombing action proceeds. The kookaburra family in turn bombard the luckless enemy and attempt to chase it from the territory. After each bombing dive, the kookaburra climbs high and swoops again from the other direction.

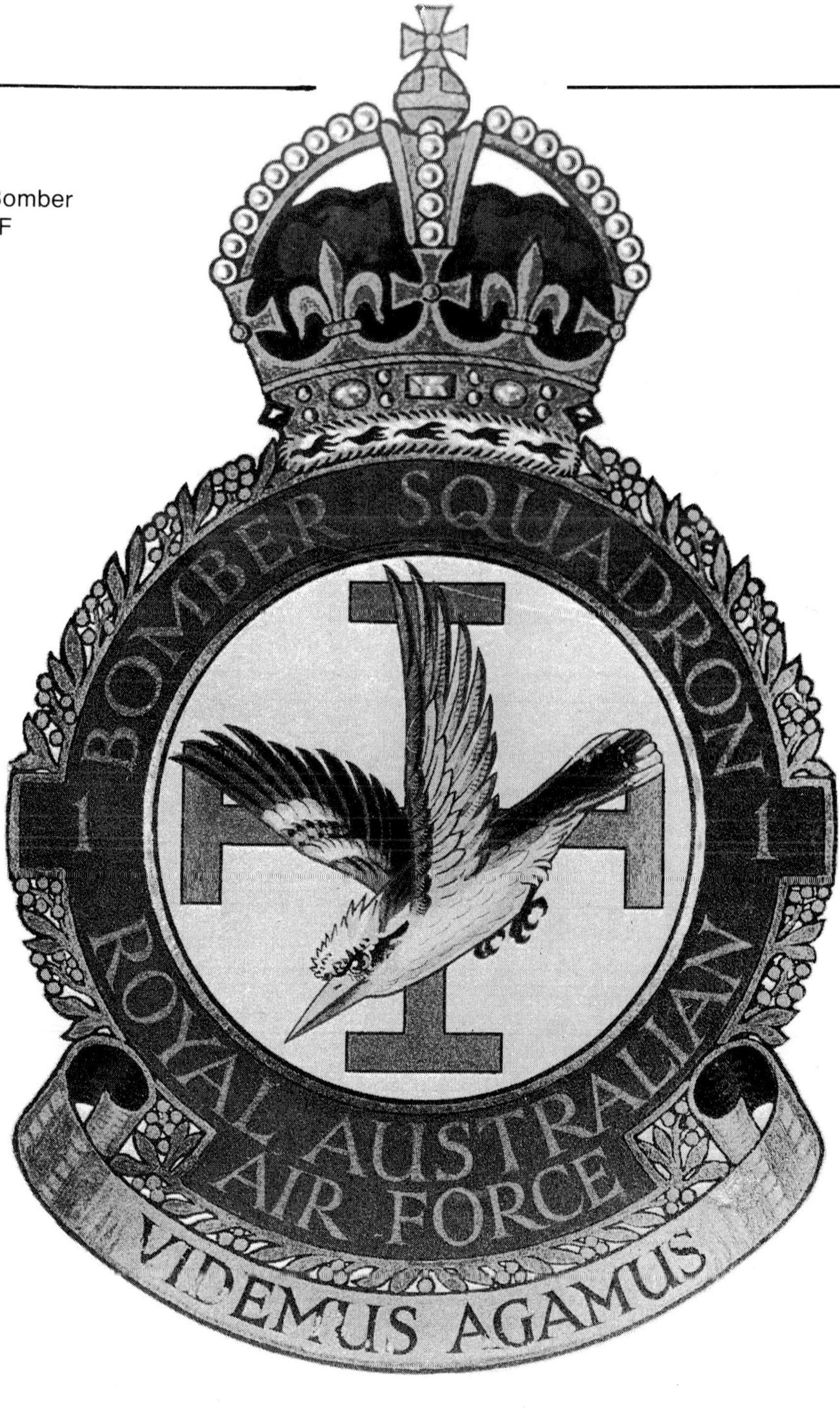

Crest of No. 1 Bomber Squadron, RAAF

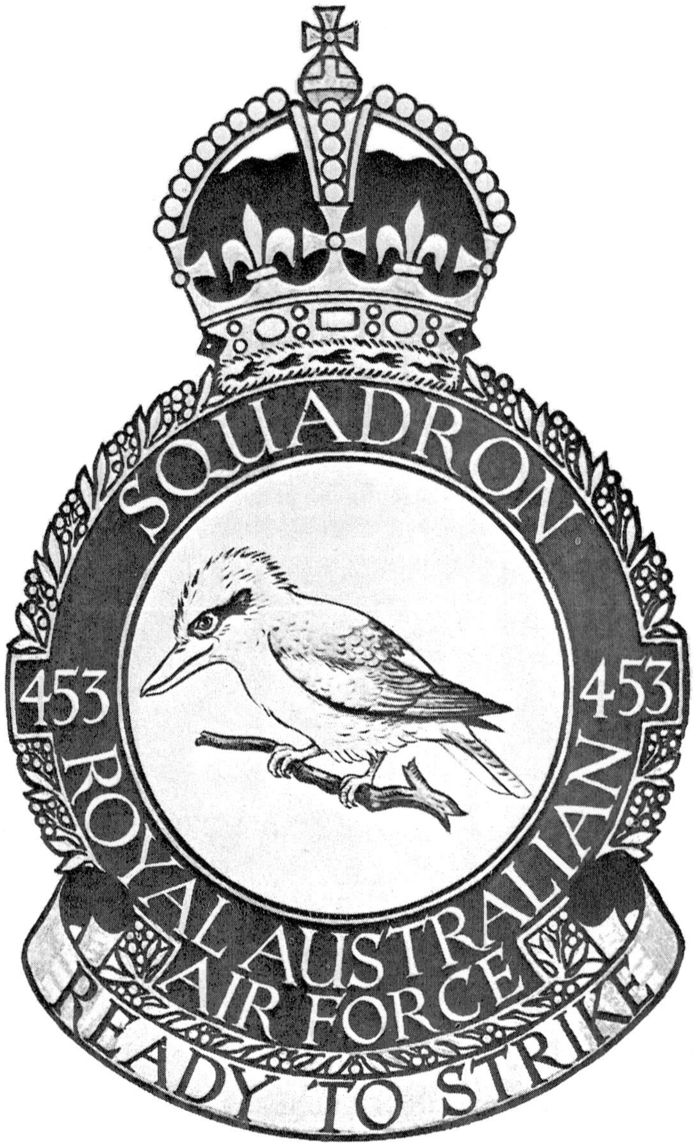

Crest of No. 453 Bomber Squadron, RAAF

Given the kookaburra's considerable experience in bombing tactics in defence of his own family and territory, he was an appropriate choice for the unit badge of the royal Australian Airforce No. 1 Bomber Squadron. The No. 1 Squadron dates from the foundation of the Royal Australian Air Force, having been formed as a squadron of the then Australian Flying Corps (a corps of the Australian Army) at Point Cook, Victoria, in December 1915. The No. 1 squadron has a long and distinguished history.

The squadron's very striking badge was approved by the late King George VI in May 1940, the badge then carrying the wording 'Bomber Squadron'. In October 1949 the wording was shortened to 'Squadron'.

The kookaburra was also chosen for the unit badge of the No. 453 Squadron, a World War II squadron that was formed at Bankstown, New South Wales on 23 May 1941 and finally disbanded at Wunstorf, Germany on 21 January 1946. This squadron flew Buffalo aircraft in Malaya and Sumatra for some ten months and then re-formed in the United Kingdom where it flew Spitfires in the UK, France and Germany. The kookaburra in the squadron's badge certainly looks 'ready to strike' – the squadron's motto.

The kookaburra also features in the unofficial badge of the No. 467 Squadron.

THE ILL-FATED KOOKABURRA

Although the plane concerned was not part of the airforce, it is perhaps appropriate to mention another kookaburra famous in aviation circles. *Kookaburra* was the name of the plane flown by Keith Anderson and Bob Hitchcock and lost in the Tanami Desert in 1929 on a gallant search for Smithy (Charles Kingsford Smith) and Charles Ulm, who had disappeared. Ironically, Smithy and Ulm were found alive and well, but the searchers perished. The bodies of those brave pioneer aviators were recovered in 1929, but the wreck of the little *Kookaburra* was lost in the desert for forty-nine years until it was found by an expedition led by Dick Smith in 1978.

MILITARY KOOKABURRAS

In 1930, two battalions – the 51st Battalion of the Far North Queensland Regiment and the 20th Battalion of the Parramatta and Blue Mountains Regiment – adopted badges featuring the kookaburra.

During World War II, the kookaburra saw active service as the formation sign or emblem of the famous 7th Division of the A.I.F.

KOOKABURRAS COURAGEOUS

In keeping with his sea-faring ancestry, the kookaburra has also seen service in the Royal Australian Navy on the badge of HMAS *Yarra*, which has been a destroyer escort in the RAN fleet.

As a tribute to its bravery, industriousness, home-making abilities and cheerfulness in the face of adversity, the kookaburra was chosen by Mrs Jessie Vasey, founder of the War Widows' Guild, as the Guild's emblem. The handsome brooch of the Guild was designed by the Melbourne sculptor Andor Meszaros.

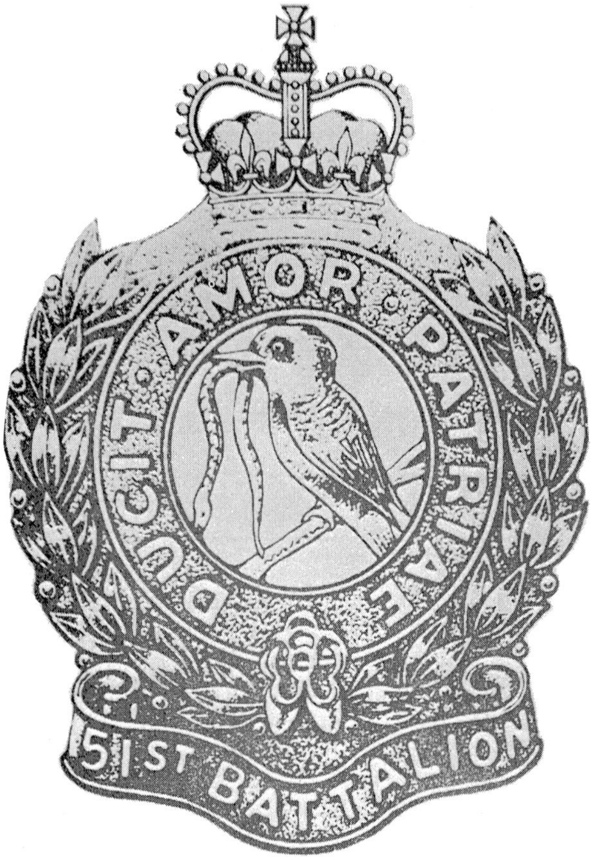

Hat badge of 51st Infantry Battalion, Far North Queensland Regiment

Badge of HMAS *Yarra*, destroyer escort in the RAN fleet (below)

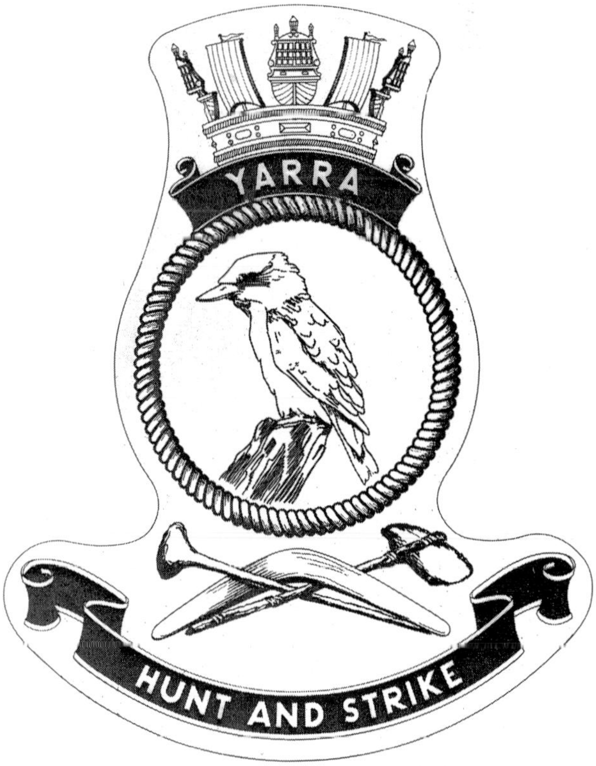

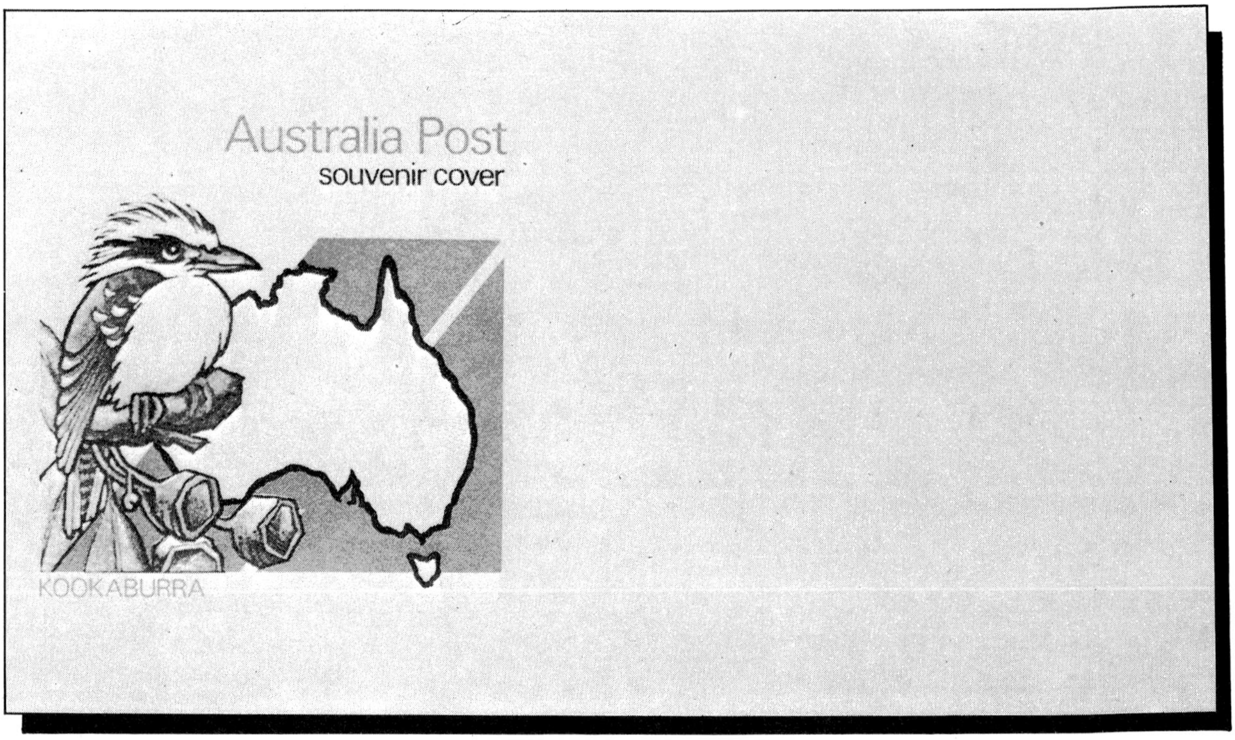

STAMPS

Other official uses of the kookaburra motif have been for stamps and coins.

It was not until 1913, twelve years after Federation, that the first Australian Commonwealth postage stamps were issued. The Post Office was not responsible for this delay. There was a political disagreement between the royalists and the republicans of the day as to whether the Monarch's head should be included. Considerable anti-royalist sentiment existed in the Australian Fisher Government of the time and the kangaroo set in a map of Australia was chosen for the first stamps. Later in 1913, when Joseph Cook led the conservatives to victory over Andrew Fisher at the elections, one of the first acts of the new Government was to introduce a full range of George V stamps, which were used concurrently with the kangaroo stamps.

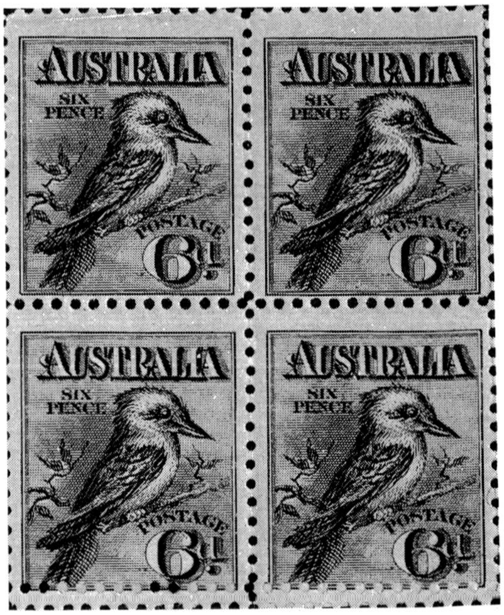

1977 Australia Post souvenir cover (top) and a corner block of sixpenny claret-coloured kookaburra stamps issued in 1914 (above)

1919–21 cupro-nickel kookaburra trial penny and halfpenny (opposite page, left and right), while at the top of the page are some threepenny blue kookaburra stamps of 1928

The next stamp, issued on 26 August 1914, was the sixpenny claret-coloured Australian Commonwealth stamp featuring a kookaburra on the branch of a gum tree. No further stamps were issued for another thirteen years. An unused mint condition sixpenny claret kooka is worth about $150 today.

Other philatelic kookabarras are:

1928 threepenny blue
1932 sixpenny brown
1937–56 sixpenny brown

The kookaburra motif was used again for the 1978 National Stamp Week Commemorative Issue, which reproduced the threepenny blue. A different kookaburra image was used in the same year for the Australia Post pre-stamped envelopes.

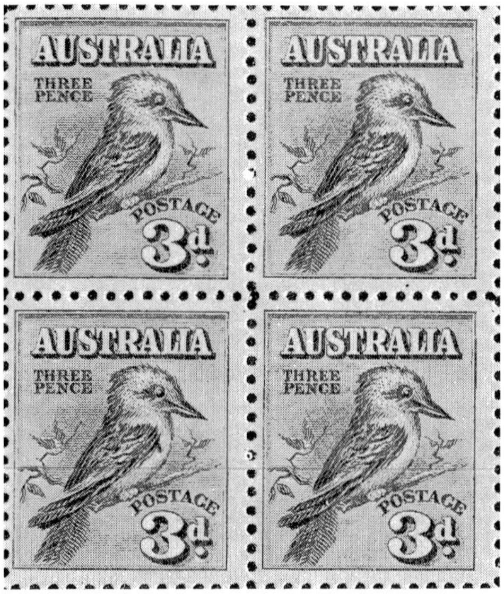

COINS

The kookaburra was used on the trial square penny and halfpenny in cupro-nickel from 1919 to 1921. These experimental coins were produced in an attempt to get away from the heavy bronze pennies and halfpennies of the time.

Nickel was the same colour as the silver coinage, so to avoid confusion, the kookaburra coins were made square. This turned out to be one of the main reasons they were not adopted, for they would not fit into the slot machines of the day. Bowing to the then considerable technical problems of minting cupro-nickel coins, Australia continued to use its old bronze pennies and halfpennies for some years. Kookaburra trial pennies and halfpennies are rare and expensive birds today.

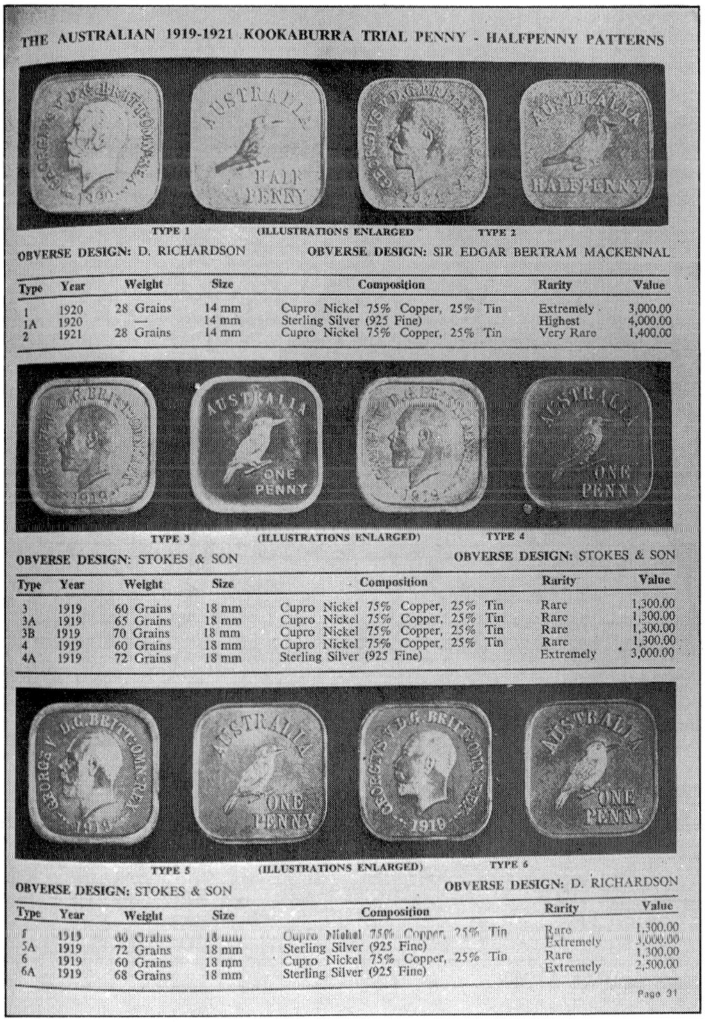
THE AUSTRALIAN 1919-1921 KOOKABURRA TRIAL PENNY - HALFPENNY PATTERNS

TYPE 1 (ILLUSTRATIONS ENLARGED) TYPE 2

OBVERSE DESIGN: D. RICHARDSON OBVERSE DESIGN: SIR EDGAR BERTRAM MACKENNAL

Type	Year	Weight	Size	Composition	Rarity	Value
1	1920	28 Grains	14 mm	Cupro Nickel 75% Copper, 25% Tin	Extremely	3,000.00
1A	1920	—	14 mm	Sterling Silver (925 Fine)	Highest	4,000.00
2	1921	28 Grains	14 mm	Cupro Nickel 75% Copper, 25% Tin	Very Rare	1,400.00

TYPE 3 (ILLUSTRATIONS ENLARGED) TYPE 4

OBVERSE DESIGN: STOKES & SON OBVERSE DESIGN: STOKES & SON

Type	Year	Weight	Size	Composition	Rarity	Value
3	1919	60 Grains	18 mm	Cupro Nickel 75% Copper, 25% Tin	Rare	1,300.00
3A	1919	65 Grains	18 mm	Cupro Nickel 75% Copper, 25% Tin	Rare	1,300.00
3B	1919	70 Grains	18 mm	Cupro Nickel 75% Copper, 25% Tin	Rare	1,300.00
4	1919	60 Grains	18 mm	Cupro Nickel 75% Copper, 25% Tin	Rare	1,300.00
4A	1919	72 Grains	18 mm	Sterling Silver (925 Fine)	Extremely	3,000.00

TYPE 5 (ILLUSTRATIONS ENLARGED) TYPE 6

OBVERSE DESIGN: STOKES & SON OBVERSE DESIGN: D. RICHARDSON

Type	Year	Weight	Size	Composition	Rarity	Value
5	1919	60 Grains	18 mm	Cupro Nickel 75% Copper, 25% Tin	Rare	1,300.00
5A	1919	72 Grains	18 mm	Sterling Silver (925 Fine)	Extremely	3,000.00
6	1919	60 Grains	18 mm	Cupro Nickel 75% Copper, 25% Tin	Rare	1,300.00
6A	1919	68 Grains	18 mm	Sterling Silver (925 Fine)	Extremely	2,500.00

Page 31

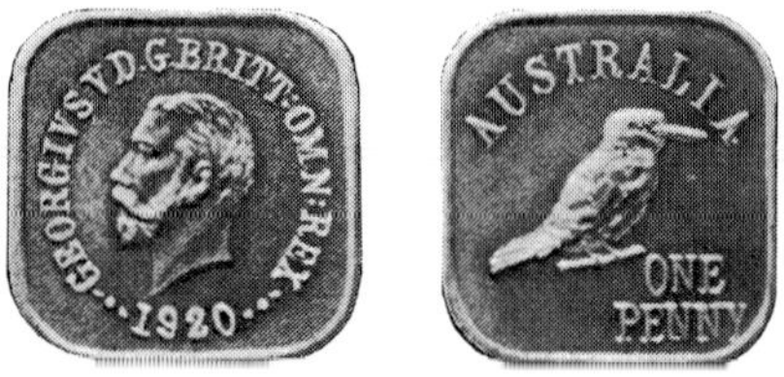

-5-
AUSTRALIA CALLING

Prior to the beginning of World War I in 1914, the kookaburra became established as a favourite emblem on the postcard, a most convenient form of communication for that period. Greeting cards, get-well cards and Christmas cards also combined the kookaburra and expressions of sentiment. The kookaburra became a symbol of goodwill, especially for Australians sending cards to those abroad. Many Britons received a chuckle across the waters in the form of a kookaburra postcard bearing a cheerful message or a jingle. Links with the 'mother country' were still strong in those days and people in the postcard business must have done a roaring trade. As families dispersed to the winds perhaps the huge barrier of distance encouraged what became a general craze.

The sort of message Jack sent back to England was:

> Greetings sincere I send, and true,
> To let you know I am thinking of you;
> I wish you all you wish yourself,
> Plenty of love and the best of health,
> And LAUGHING JACK will my message take,
> With all that is best for 'OLD TIMES SAKE.'

Another quaint card reads:

> Oh! ye strange wild bird, will ye bear a Greeting
> To the Folk that live in the 'Way Beyond?'

Some of the kookaburra postcards bore reproductions of paintings by important bird artists. The best known is Neville Cayley senior,

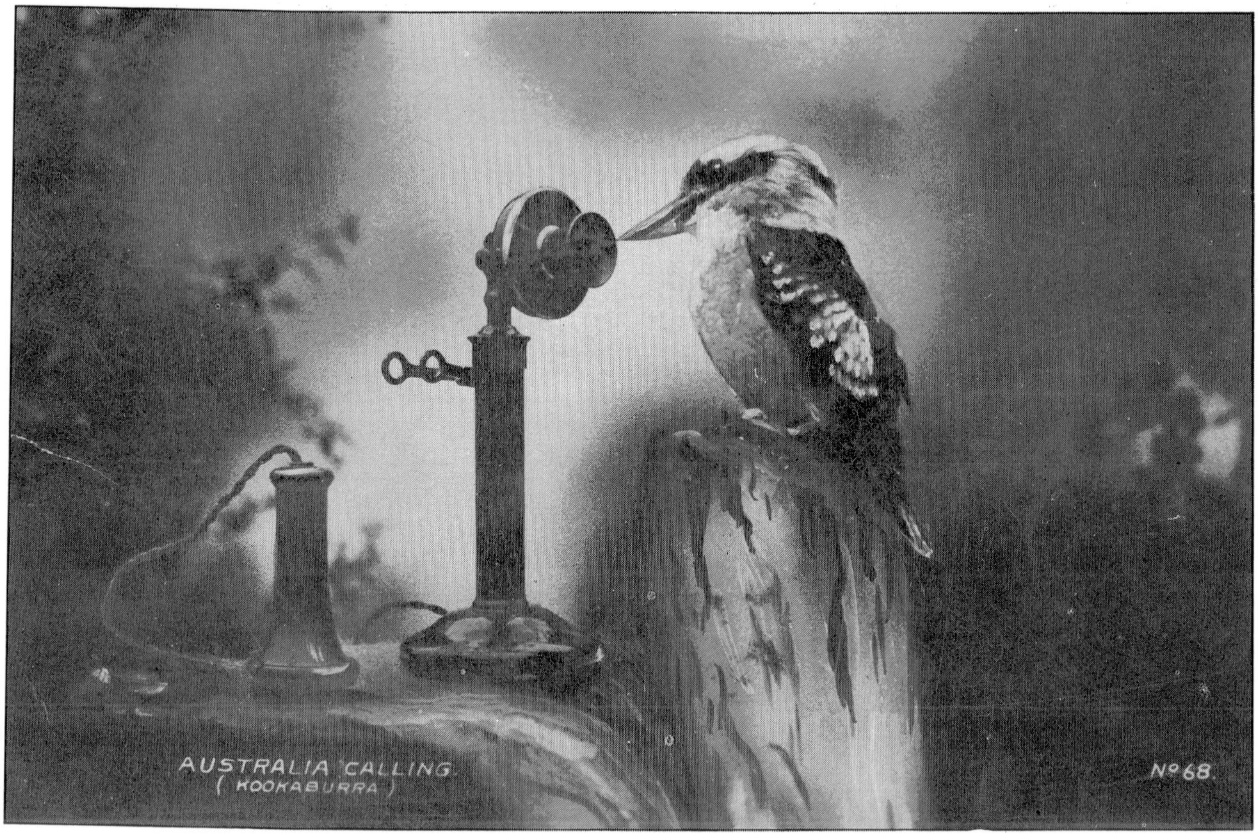

Postcard by Valentine, printed in Great Britain

who painted more kookaburras than any artist before or since. Cayley did not design works specifically for the postcard; he died in 1903 before the postcard craze had fully developed here.

Another well-known bird artist was John Mitchell Cantle. Between 1905 and 1907 he designed bird paintings specifically for the postcard. Among them are kookaburras, looking rather better groomed than those by Cayley.

A number of illustrations of kookaburras by Hal Gye, the caricaturist, famous for his illustrations in the books of C. J. Dennis, were produced as postcards. Other illustrations, including cuddly kookaburras from some of Ida Rentoul Outhwaite's fairy books, also appeared as postcards. All these artists increased the public's awareness of Laughing Jack until by the

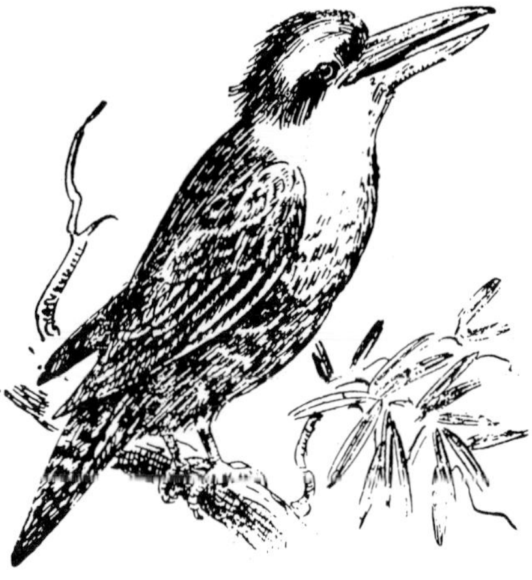

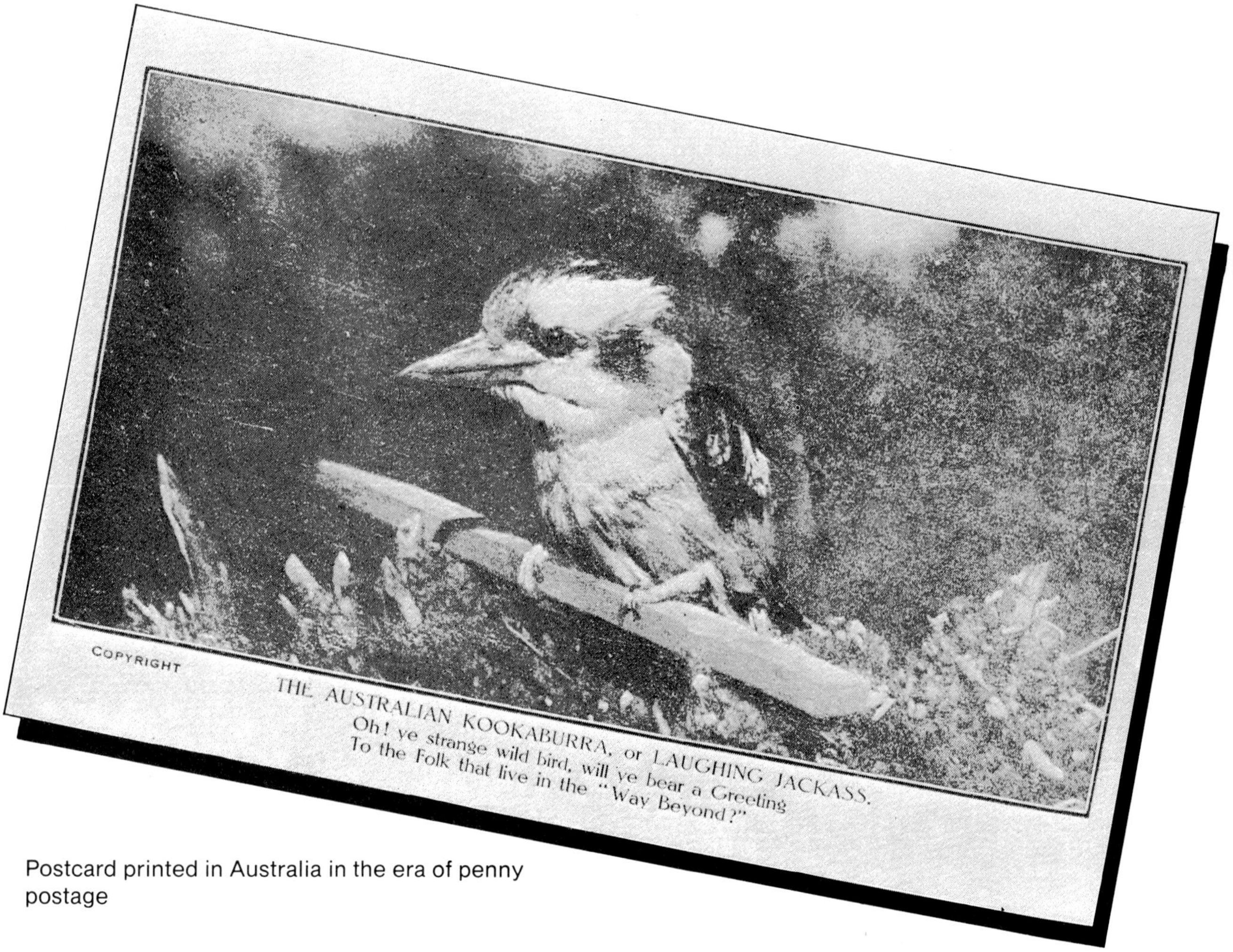

Postcard printed in Australia in the era of penny postage

beginning of World War I he was generally accepted as an integral part of national folklore.

War broke out in Europe and brave Australian volunteers established the Anzac tradition in the trenches of Gallipoli and Europe. Postcards depicted native fauna and flora, often with a map of Australia, an Australian flag or a typical bush scene. These symbolised the most nostalgic memories of home at the time and many a card was sent by a tearful mother or loving bride. Now, the

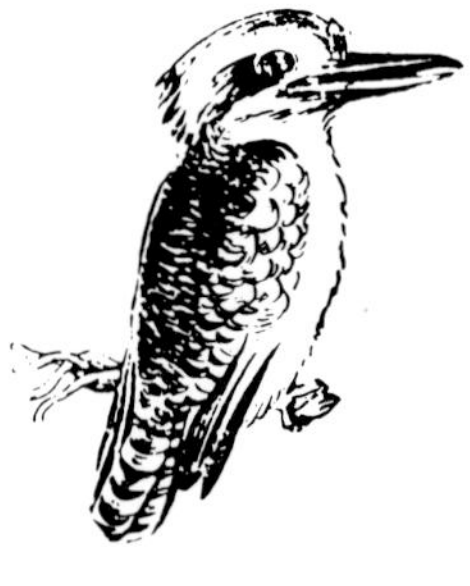

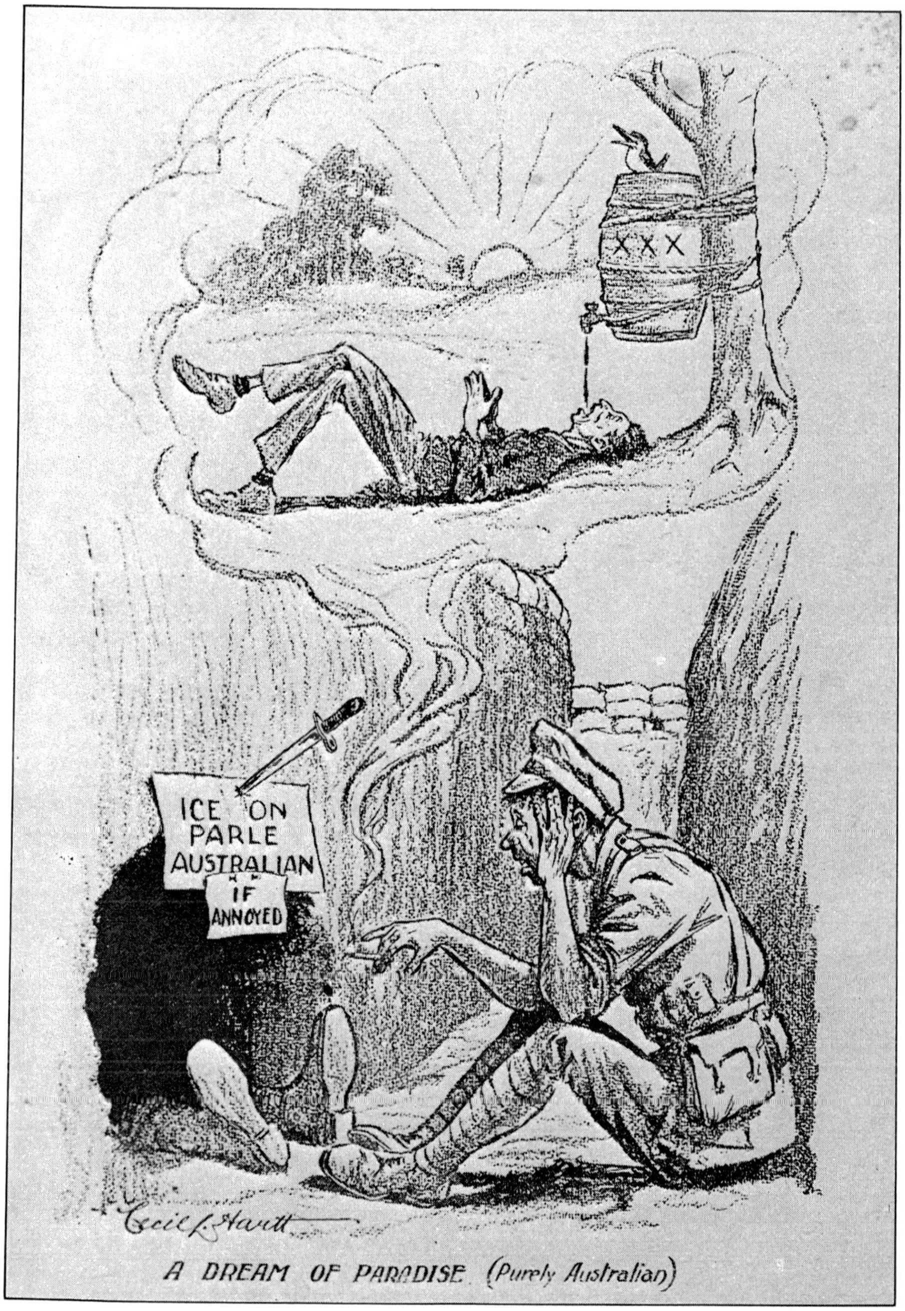

This illustration by Cecil L. Hartt appeared in *Humorosities*, circulated during World War I. *Humorosities* was published in Sydney after the war and sold 60 000 copies

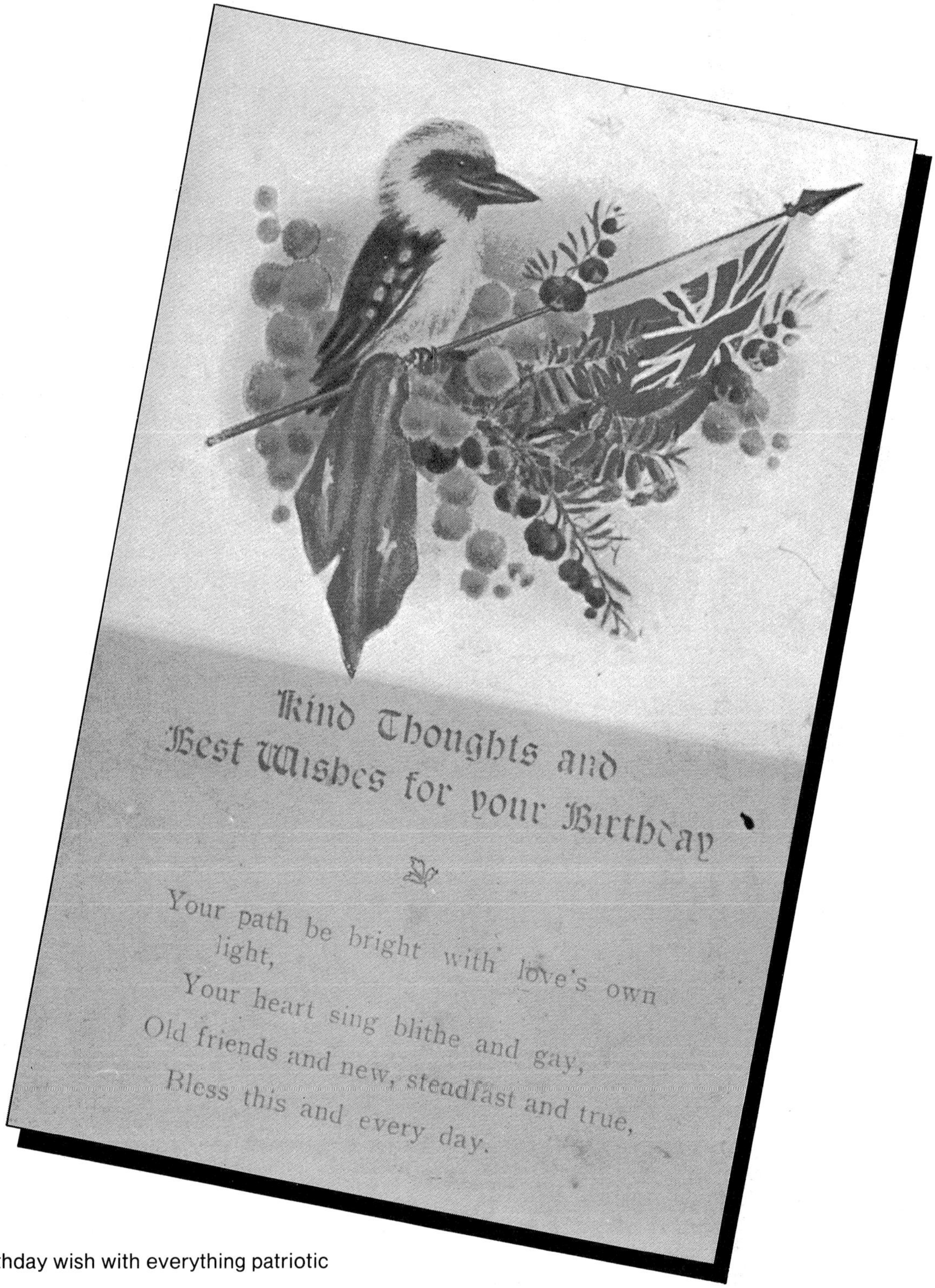

A birthday wish with everything patriotic

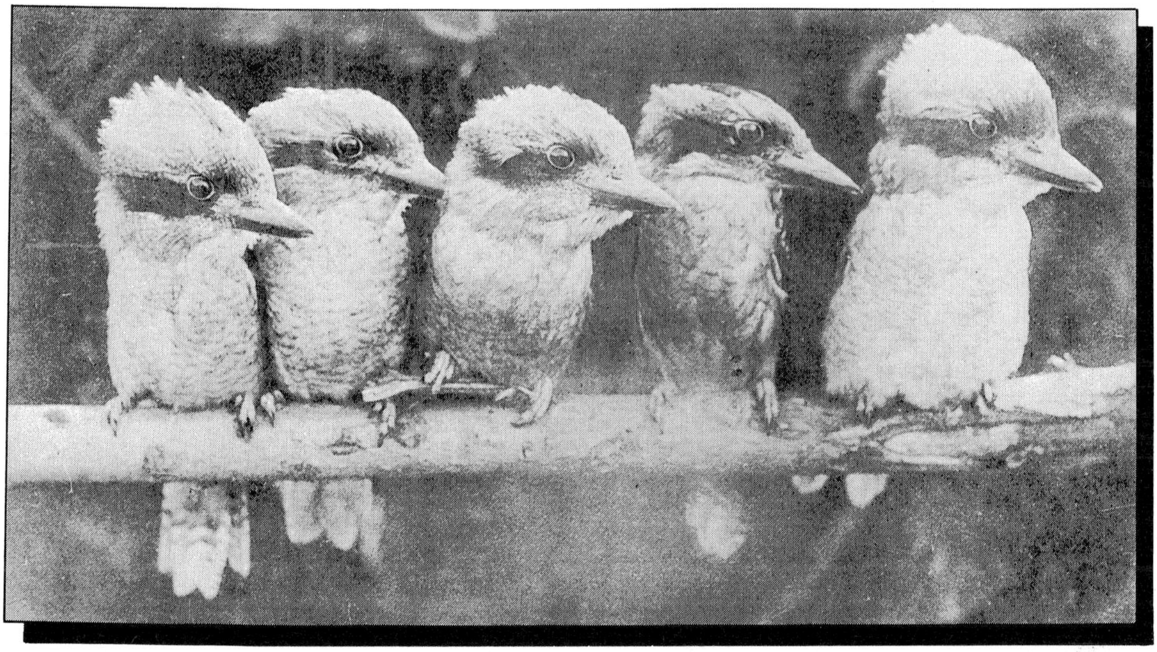

'Who said snakes?'

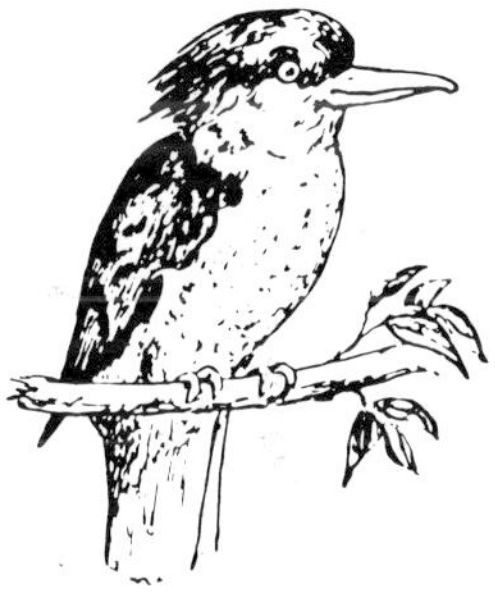

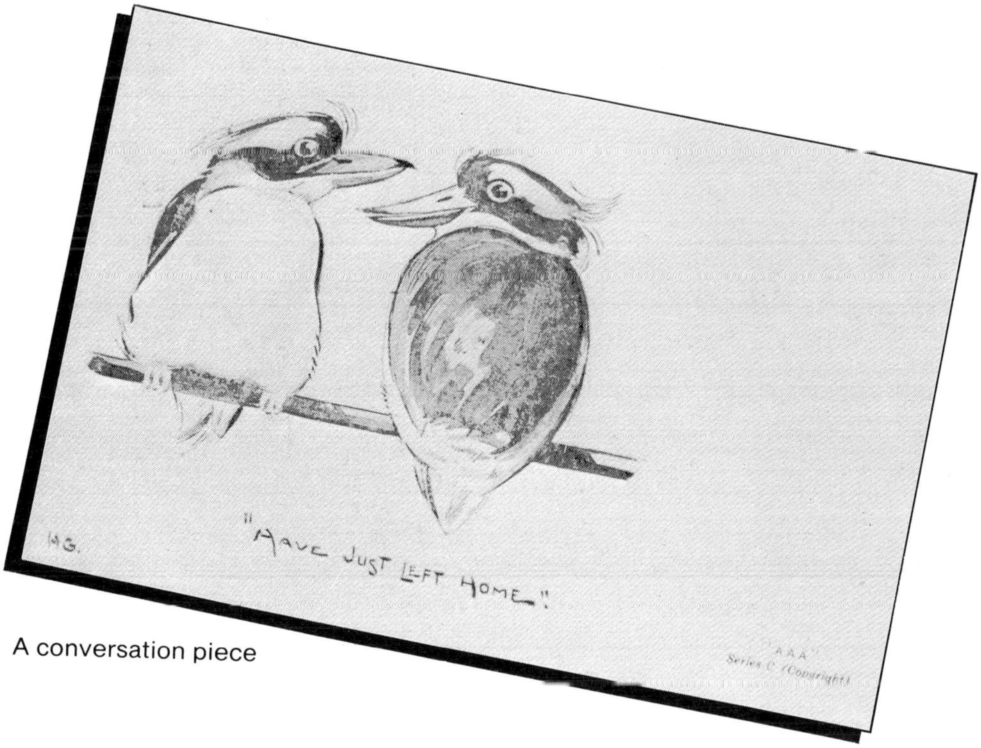

A conversation piece

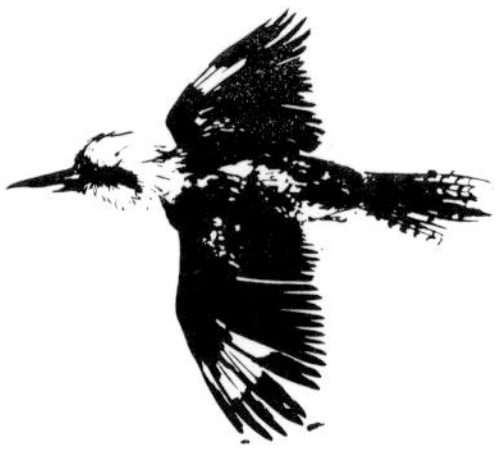

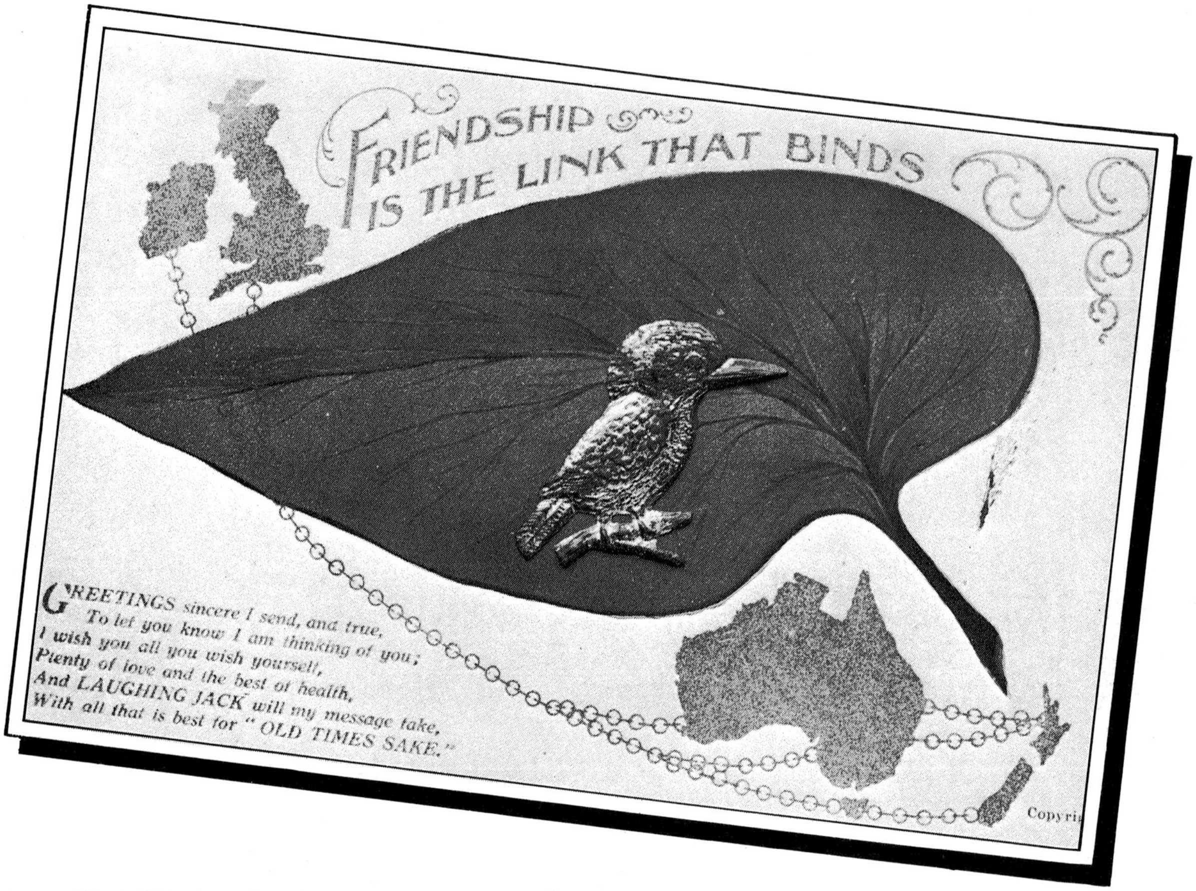

This pre-World War I postcard conveys a message of goodwill

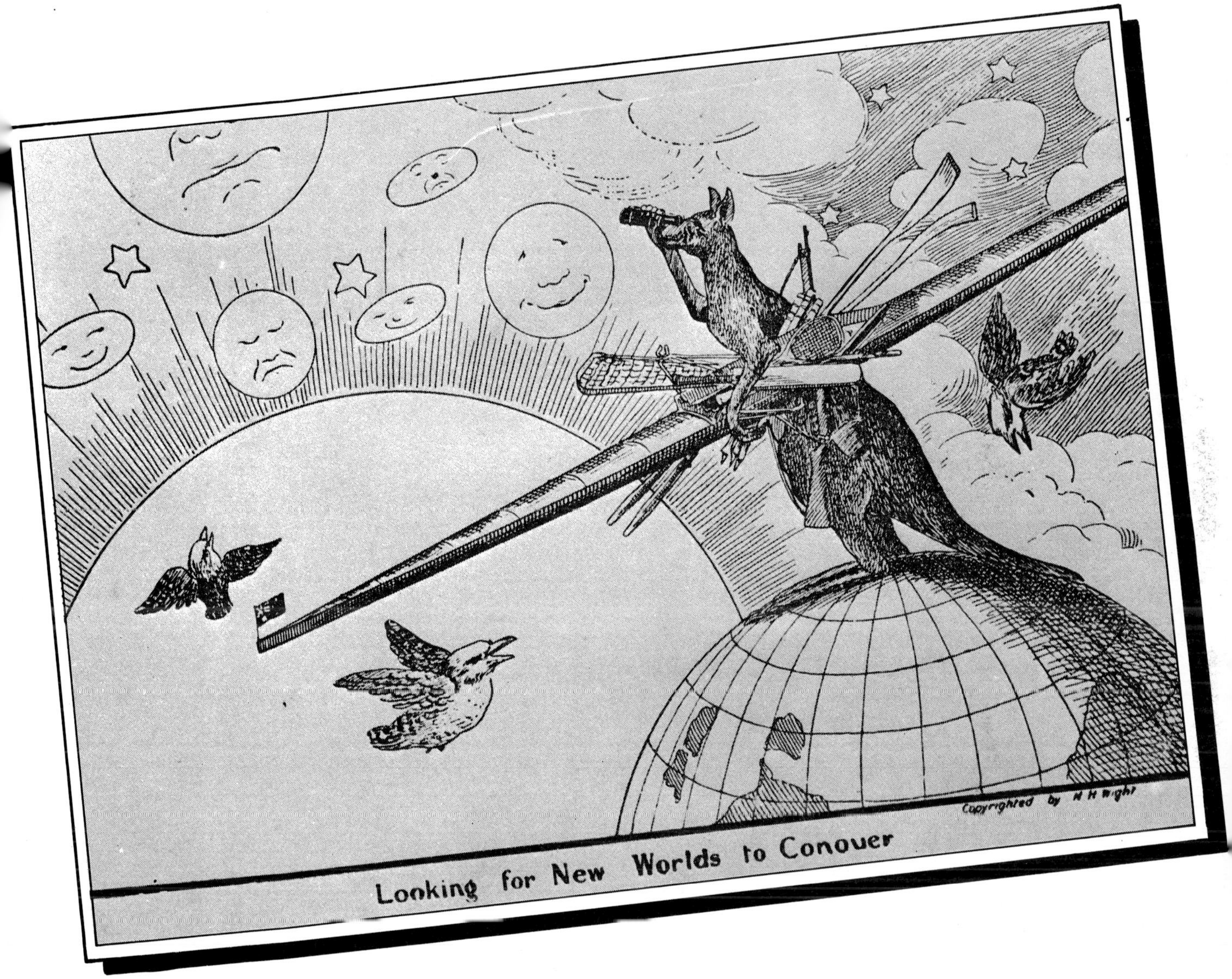

'Looking for New Worlds to Conquer.' Old postcard postmarked 1907

kookaburra also emerged in the role of a digger, and appeared on postcards as a sturdy and invincible 'Diggaburra', dressed in army, navy or airforce headgear.

The kookaburra became a cherished memory for the boys as well as a good luck symbol. The drawing by Cecil L. Hartt illustrates this nostalgia felt by the troops abroad. A fervent message from Diggaburra on one wartime postcard reads:

> Hear the kookaburra shouting,
> While his men are nobly scouting,
> Hear him say Good Luck I send you,
> And may Heaven above defend you.

Another kookaburra card was 'A coo-ee from Australia', which was posted by a loving mother to her 'dear Edward' on 27 October 1918. With only fourteen days of the slaughter remaining, we can't help hoping that she was able to see her son come back safely to her from 'far across the deep blue sea'.

The war over, Diggaburra was not forgotten. In 1922 he became the trademark for the Queensland Digger Tea Supply Company.

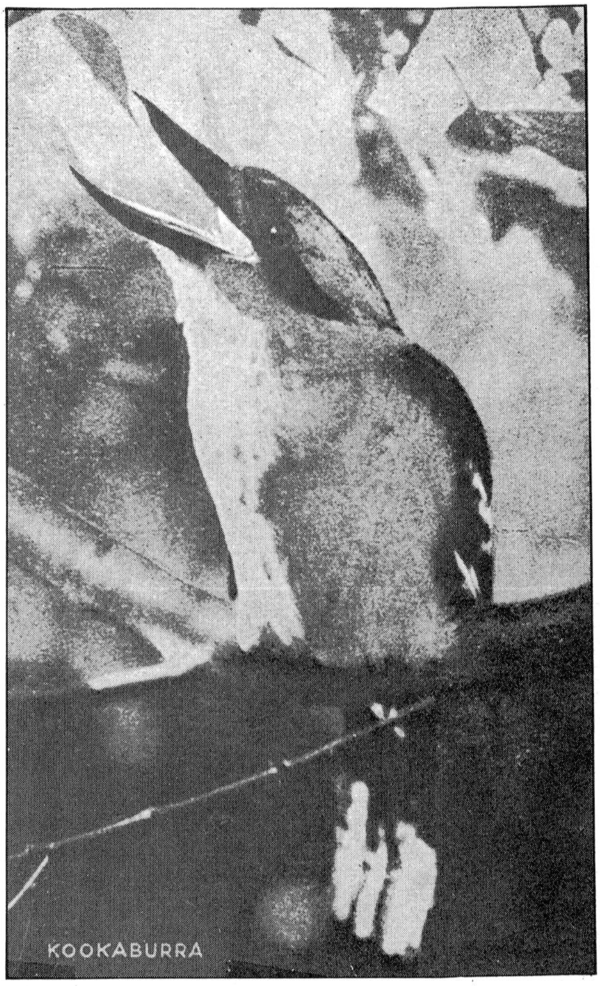

Postcard *c.* 1920

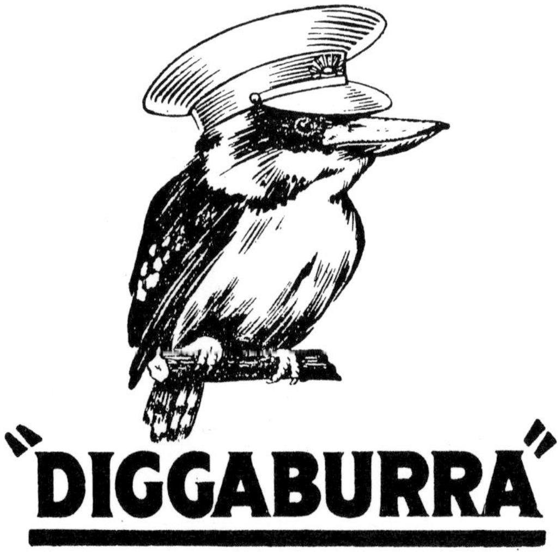

Diggaburra was the symbol of the Queensland Digger Tea Supply Company, registered in 1922

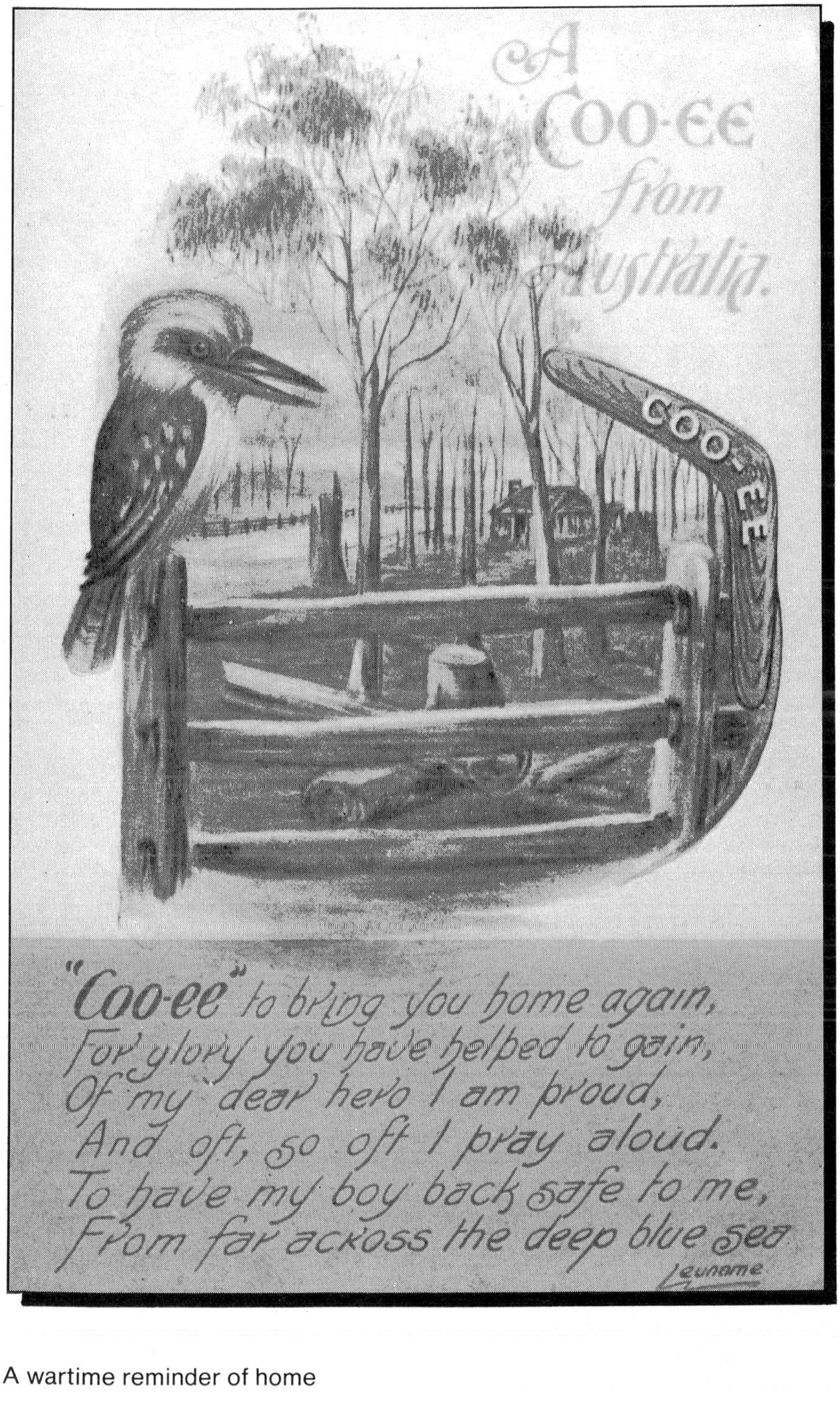

A wartime reminder of home

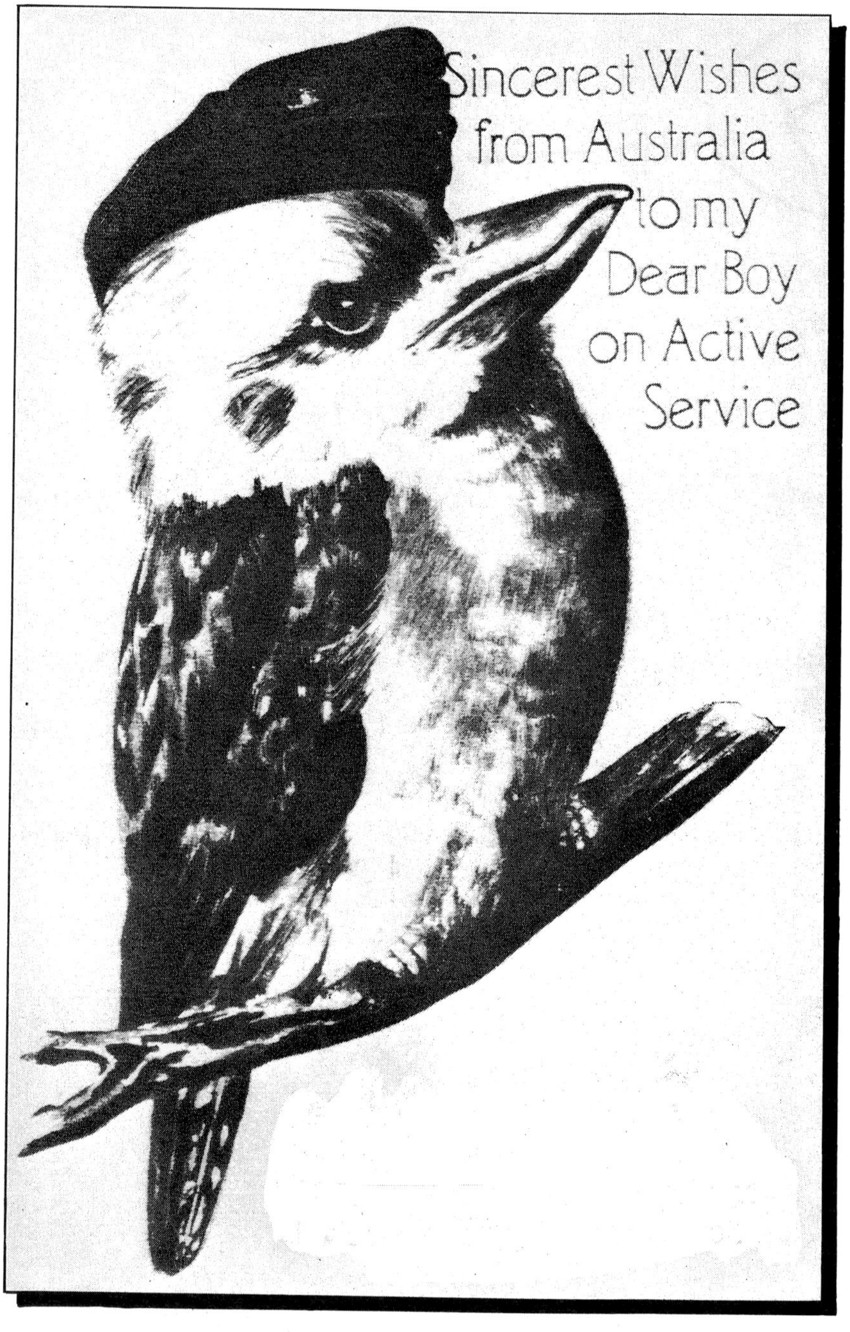
Sincerest Wishes
from Australia
to my
Dear Boy
on Active
Service

Wartime postcards show the kookaburra dressed for action

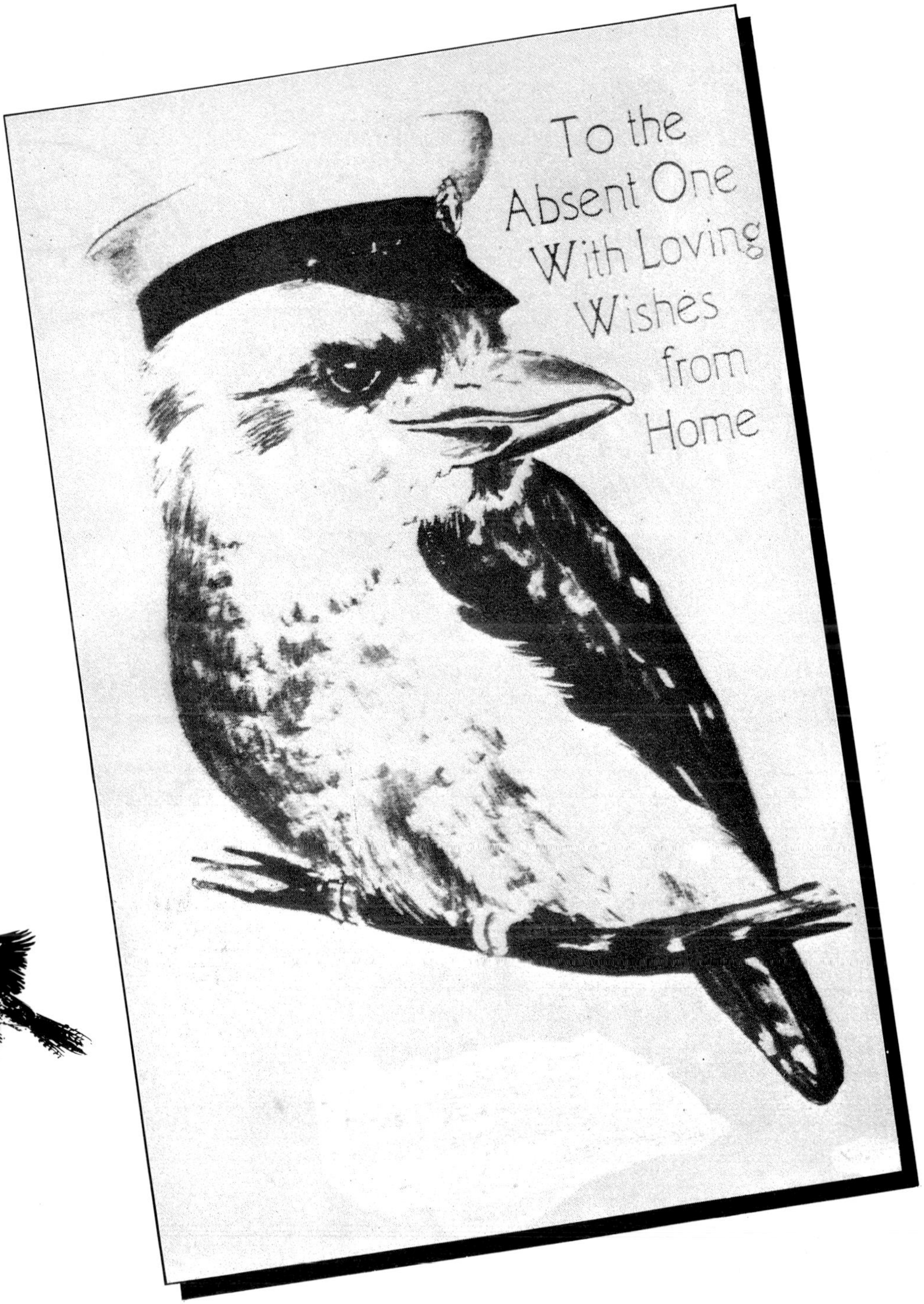

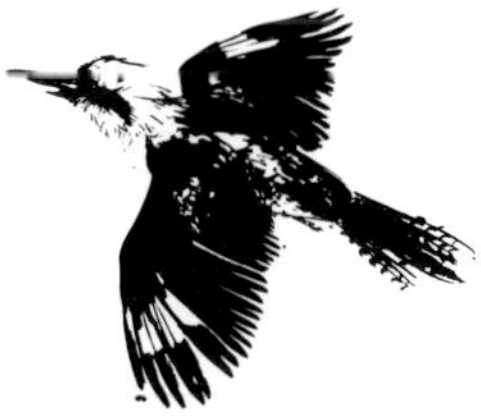

-6-
Kookaburra Trademarks

The kookaburra motif has been prominent in the world of commerce and marketing in Australia. In the early years of this century, a period of emerging national consciousness, the kookaburra lent its image to an extraordinary range of products. We include at the end of this chapter a full list of kookaburra trademarks from Mimmo Cozzolino's book, *Symbols of Australia*.

World War I confirmed the sense of Australian identity and the 1920s saw the registering of many more kookaburra trademarks. The number of registrations declined during the 1930s and after World War II the kookaburra motif fell from favour. Marketing became internationalised and although some steadfast firms hung onto their kookaburra trademarks, the kookaburra found himself somewhat old-fashioned and out of date among the slick new marketers. But later there were signs that the wheel of marketing fashion was again turning: a new nationalism emerged, and the kookaburra steadily gained satisfied converts. One very effective use of kookaburra symbol was by the Victorian Savings and Loan Society of Ballarat, Victoria, who adopted a kooka logo in 1973 to complement their advertising slogan 'Join the happy people'. The Society's theme in the early 1980s was 'Wake up each morning a little richer', which was very appropriate for a place where many clients would hear the kookaburra each morning.

A few years ago Coca-Cola adopted the kookaburra – rechristened 'Kickaburra' – as a

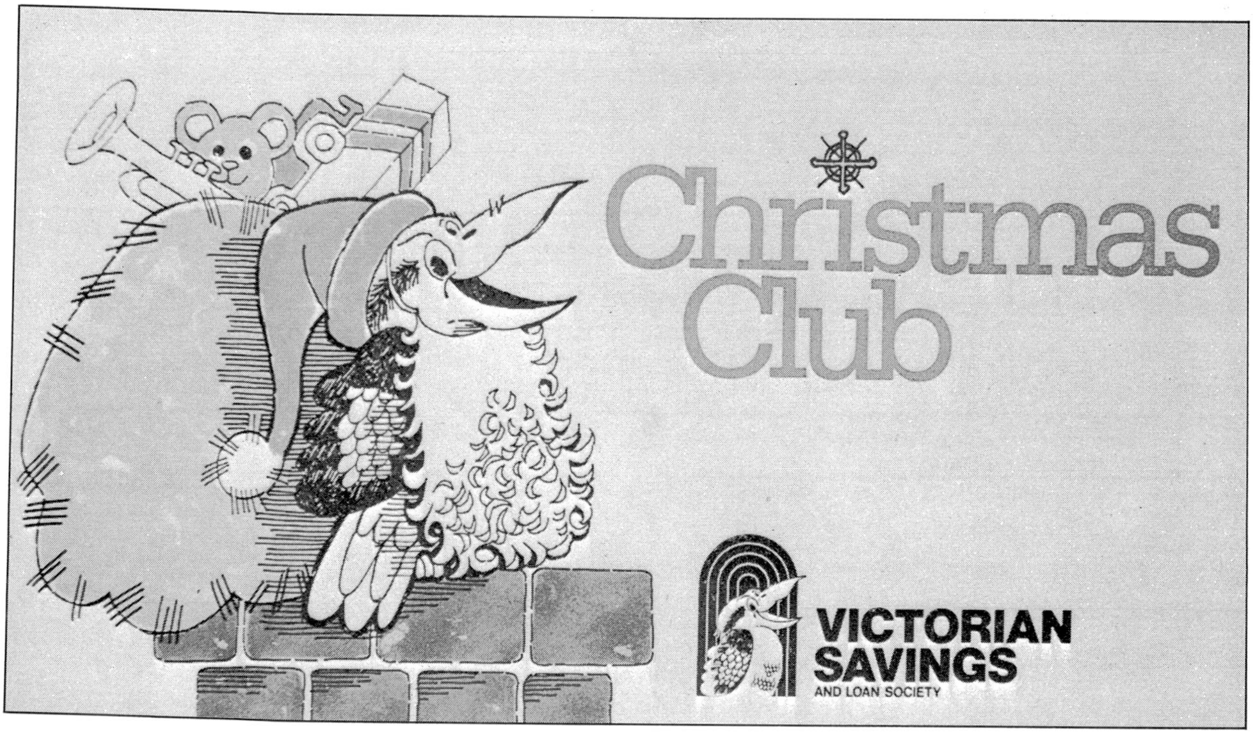

An advertising kookaburra working for the Victorian Savings and Loan Society, Ballarat, Victoria (above). Below is the hosiery trademark registered by the Australian Knitting Mills in 1913

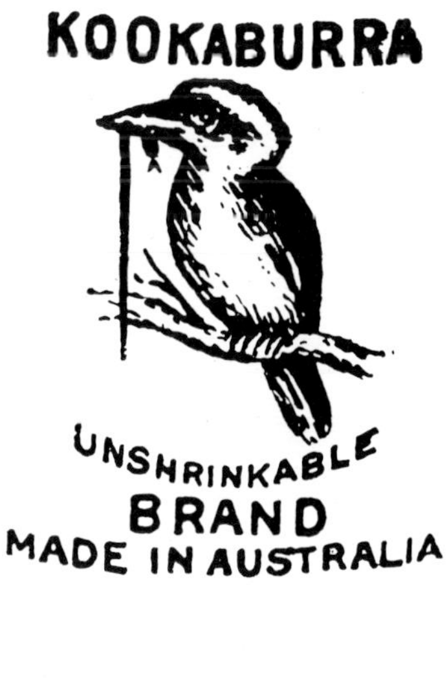

sporting symbol in its promotions. Kickaburra was used as the mascot at the World Youth Soccer Championships in Melbourne in September 1981 and a young lady in a Kickaburra costume was seen at the 1982 Test and one-day cricket matches.

SNAKE-LIKE MOTIFS

A number of marketers took advantage of the association in many people's minds between the kookaburra and the snake. An interesting early use of the motif was registered in Melbourne in 1913 by the Australian Knitting Mills Ltd for unshrinkable ladies' hosiery . . . The snake might not like the comparison! Another clever snake association occurs in the advertising device for Kookaburra Fadeless Blinds registered in 1936 by Duval. Other products in this category included whips (1922), ropes (1925), shoelaces and spaghetti.

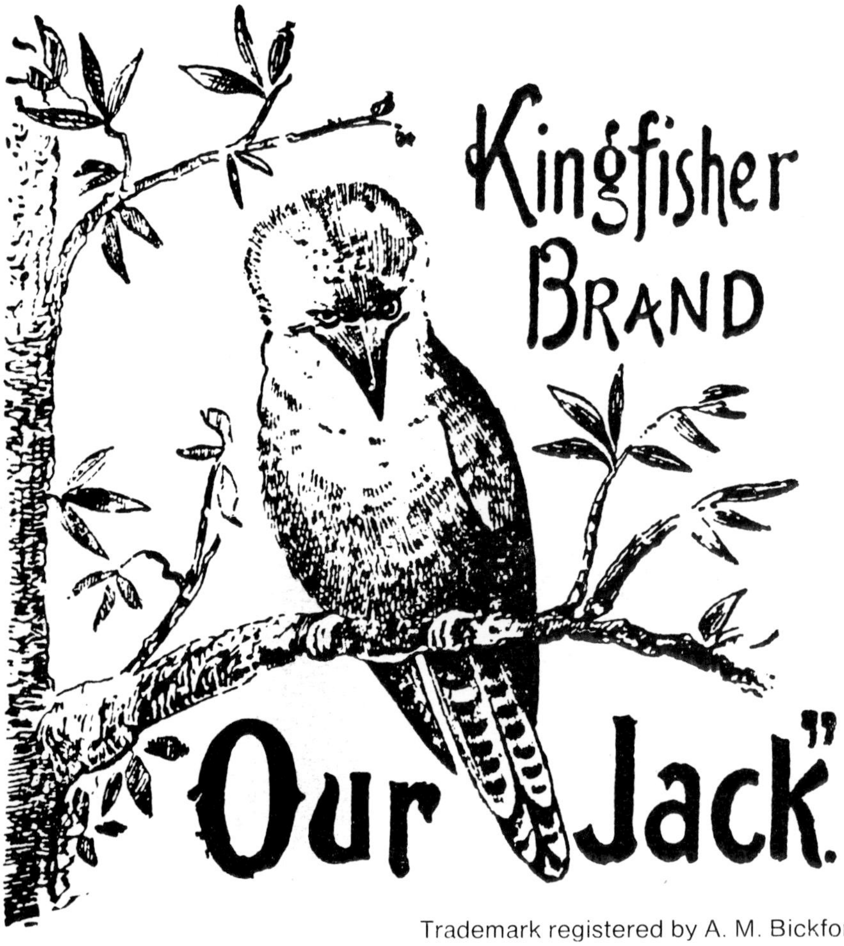

Trademark registered by A. M. Bickford & Sons, 1899

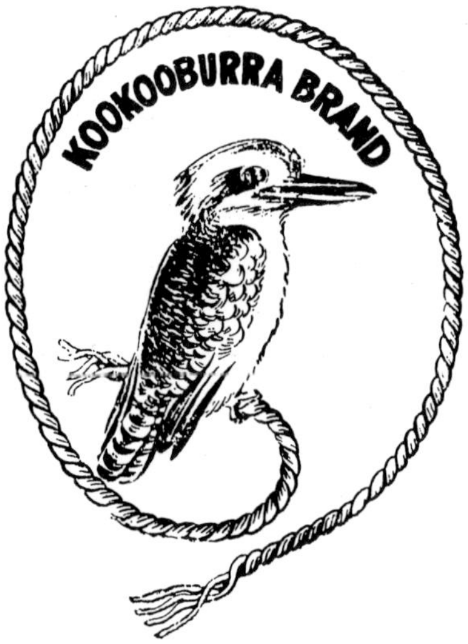

Kookooburra Brand ropes, registered by A. Forsyth & Co. Ltd, Sydney, 1925

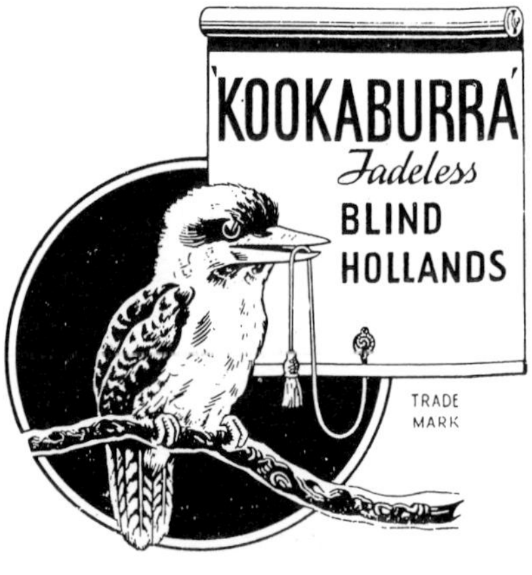

A clever trademark registered in 1936 by Duval

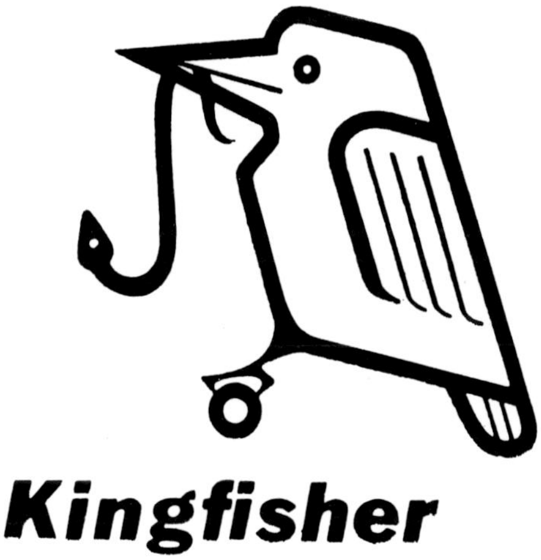

R. Fisher Pty Ltd (shelving racks and storage) registered their Kingfisher trademark in 1956

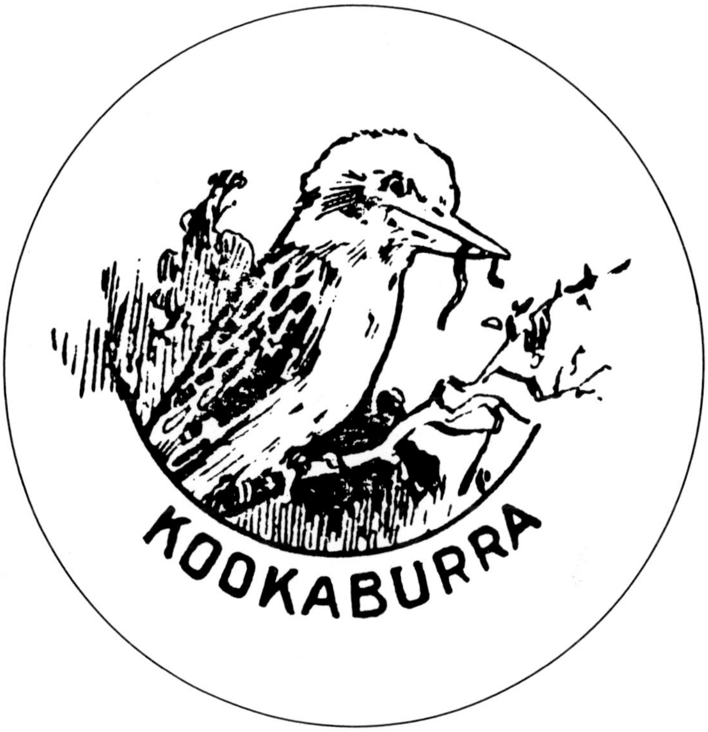

The Wallace Rubber Mills of Australia, 1907

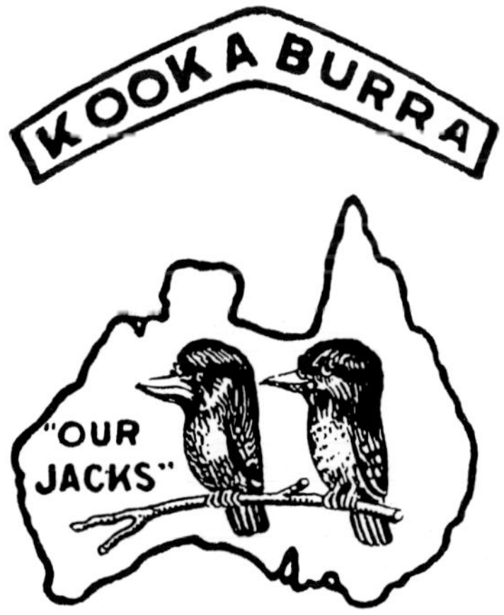

Hat trademark registered by D. W. Murray Ltd in 1930

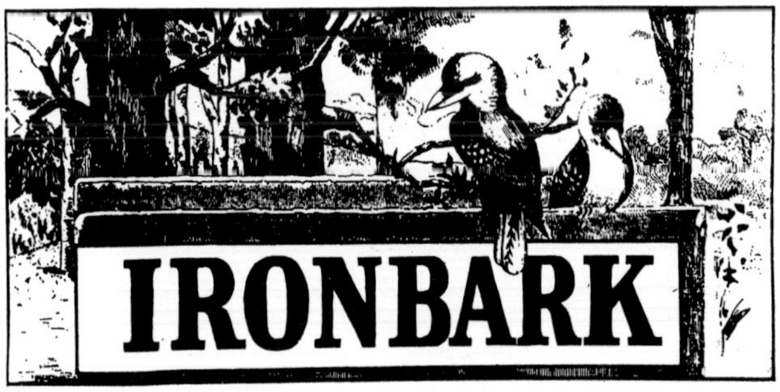

Ironbark brown wrapping paper trademark, registered by Sydney Paper Mills in 1912

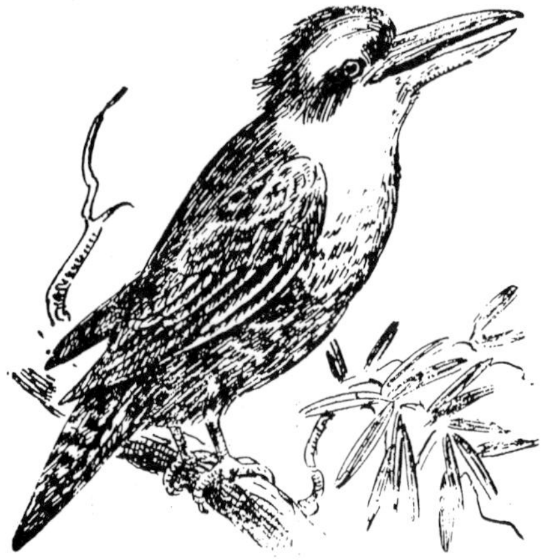

KOOKABURRA

Birt & Co. Ltd (frozen meat) registered this in 1907

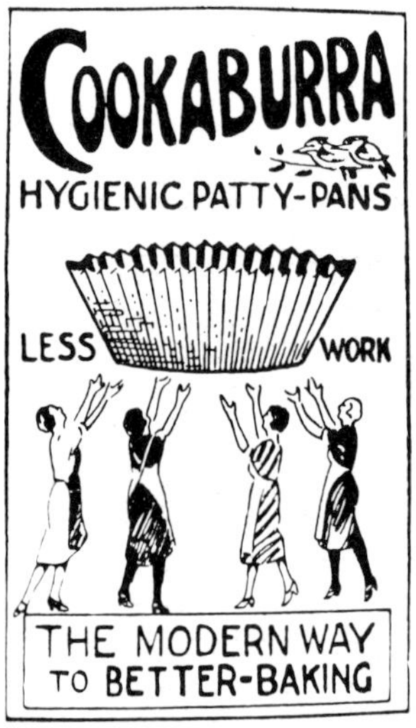

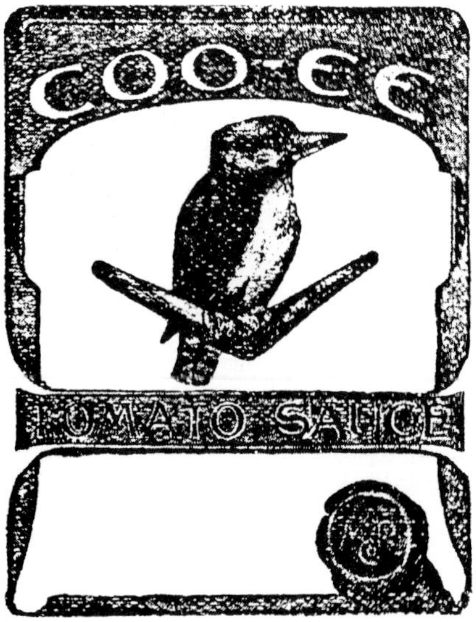

Coo-ee tomato sauce, registered by
N. Richards & Co., 1910

CULINARY COOKABURRAS

The kookaburra motif found its way into many an Australian kitchen. First there was that grand old stalwart, the Early Kooka stove, introduced by Metters in 1928. These were made in many splendid and functional designs in cast iron. Early Kookas are still going strong in many Australian homes although production ceased nearly thirty years ago.

There are kookaburra edibles still on the supermarket shelves – salt, biscuits and macaroni to mention a few! Kookaburra Macaroni was registered in 1928 by Hancock's Golden Crust Company. The company is now Rinoldi Hancock and the product range has expanded greatly to meet the sophistication of the times. Unfortunately no records of the old company exist. The only link with the past has been an elderly packet of macaroni on extended loan to the television series *The Sullivans*!

Cookaburra Hygienic Patty-pans featured another charming use of the kookaburra motif. Apart from kookaburra flour, kookaburra frozen meat and MacRobertson's chocolates in kookaburra tins, the kookaburra had strong associations with that grand old Australian beverage – tea. There was his own brand, Diggaburra, which honoured his involvement in the war. Jack Sundowner (pictured opposite page) swore by it. As well, kookaburra and three of his mates graced countless Bushells tea caddies.

Around 1920 E. W. Cole published *The Kookaburra Cookery Book of Culinary and Household Recipes and Hints*. The following verse appeared on the title page:

I'll tell thee, wife, we'll have our daughter bred
In bookerie, cookerie, needle, thimble, thread;
Let her be taught to shun all deluding,
To roast, to toast, to make a pudding.

– Anon

The helpful hints section contains useful advice on a variety of subjects like mending a leaking jug, treating sore gums or weak eyes, how to keep moths from a wardrobe – and even includes certain recipes for croup.

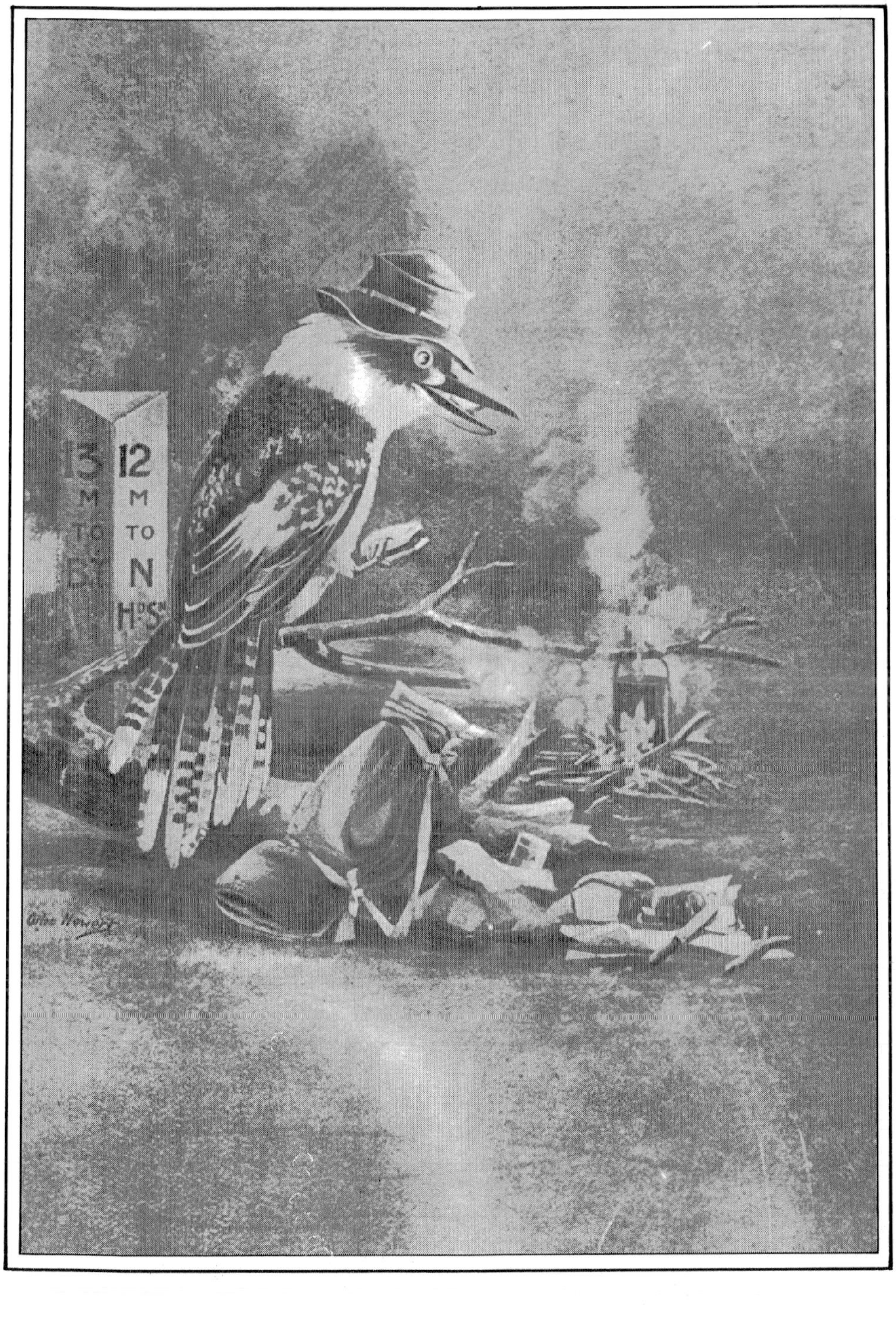

Jack Sundowner enjoying his Diggaburra Tea

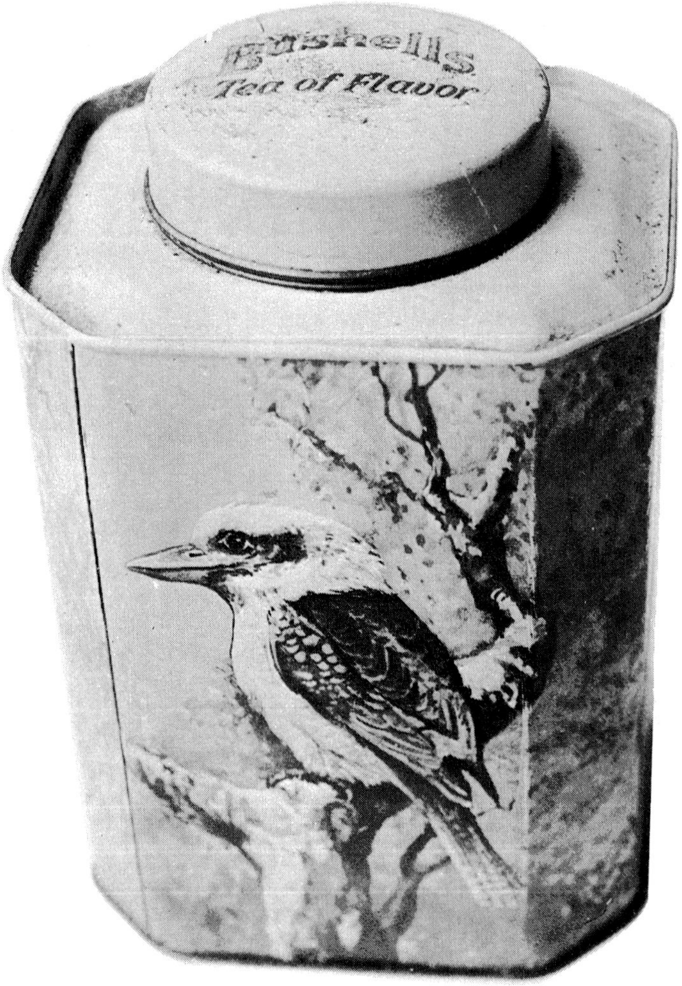

This Bushells tea caddy was in countless kitchens

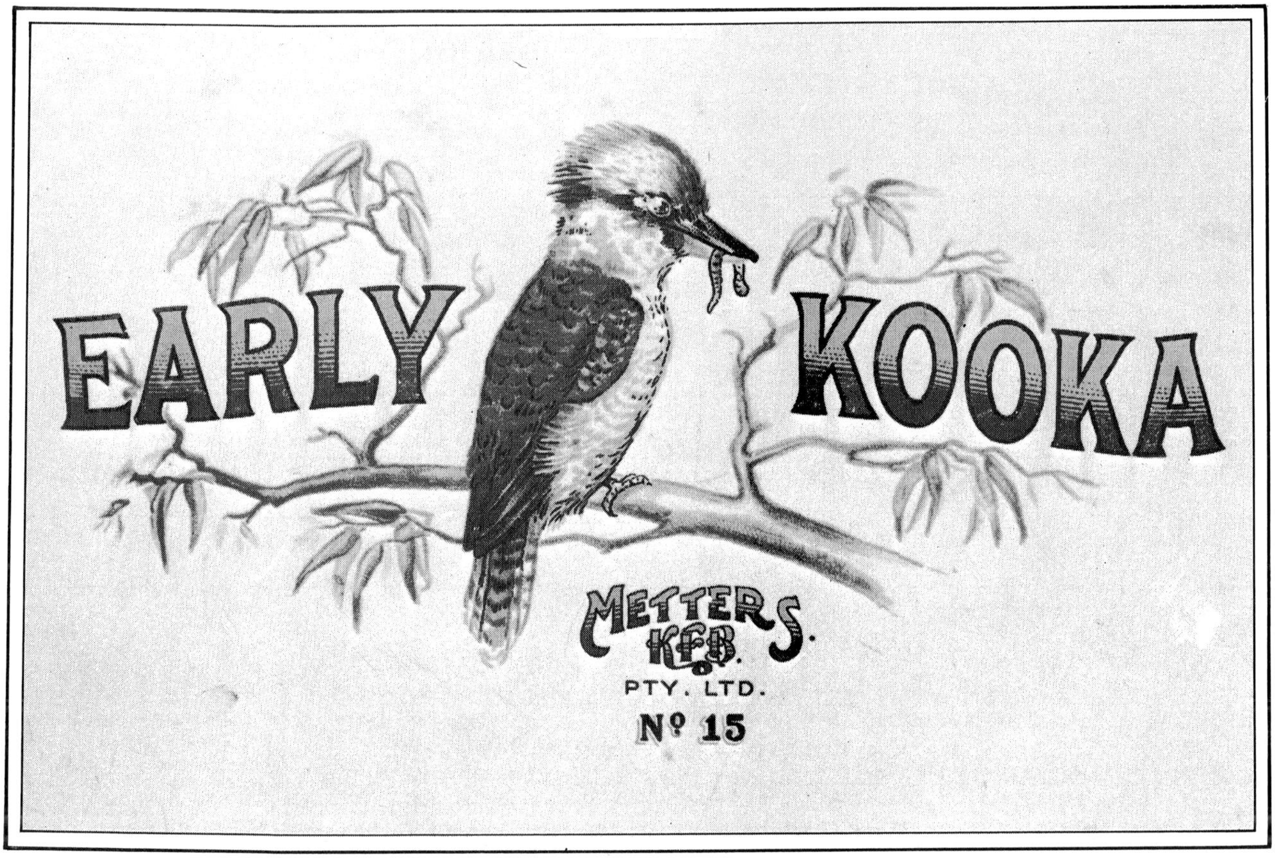

Early Kooka stove oven door by Metters is one of the best-known kookaburra symbols (above)

Kookaburra biscuits by Weston (right)

Kookaburra Brand Macaroni, registered 1928 (below)

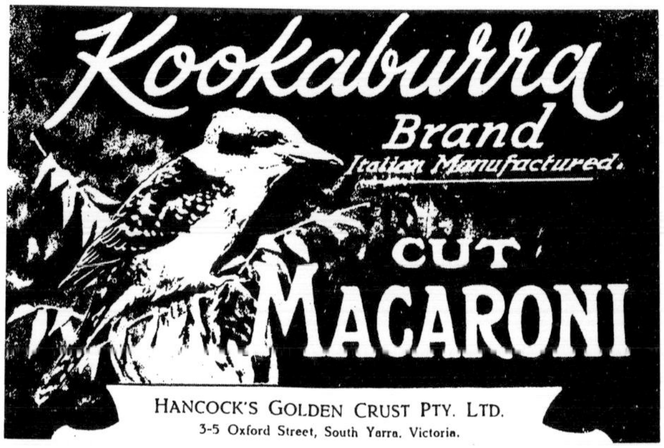

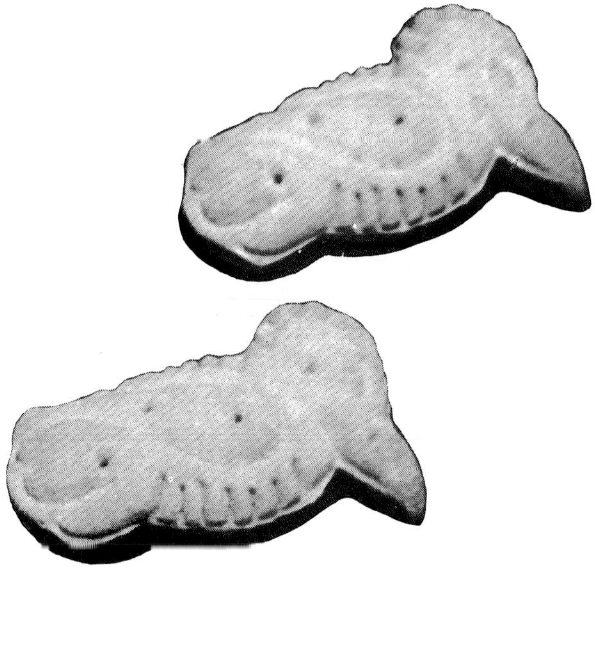

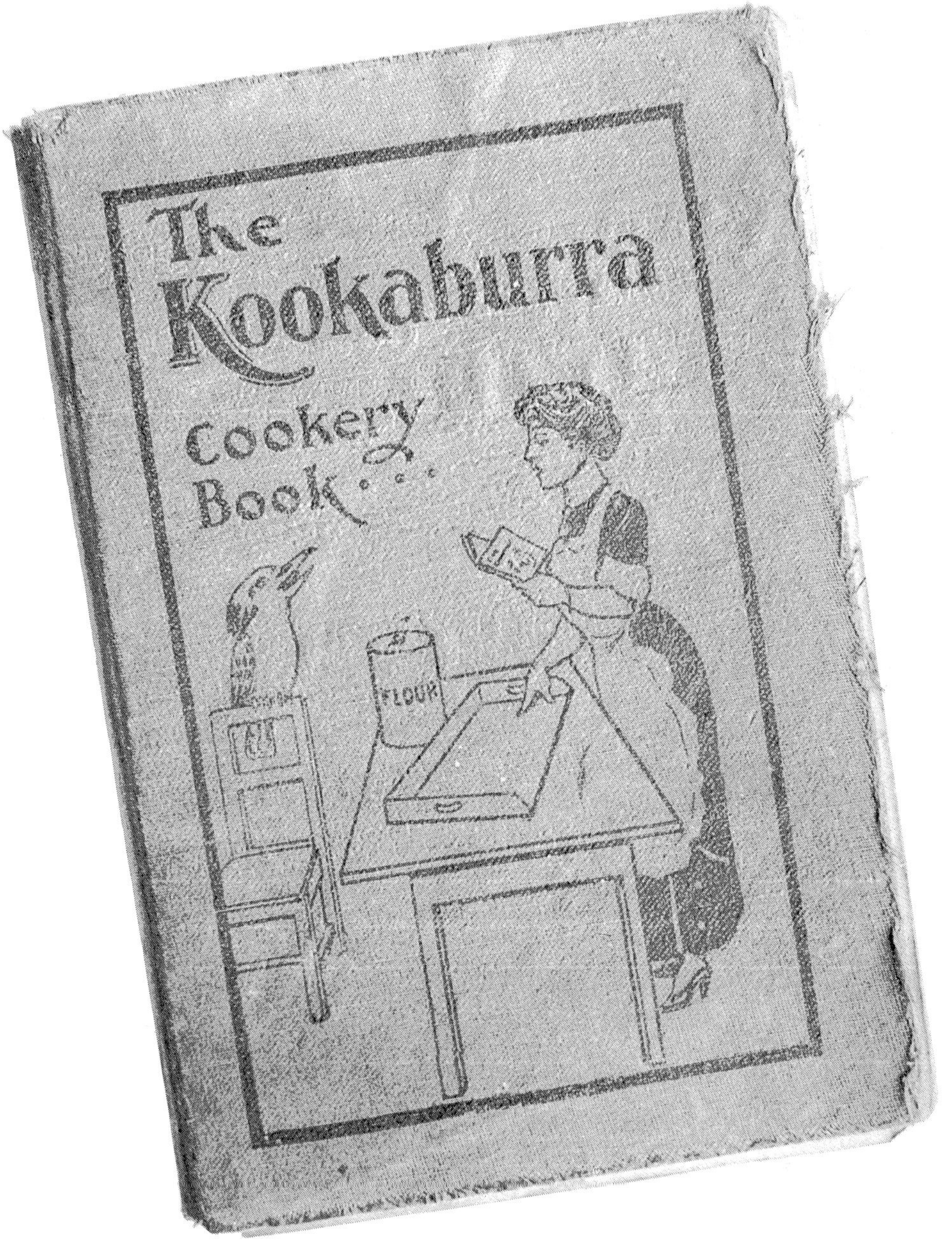

The Kookaburra Cookery Book of Culinary and Household Recipes and Hints was published *c.* 1920 by E. W. Cole

A kookaburra and a magpie share this marvellous beer advertisement for Carlton & United Breweries, published in *Australian Farm and Home* in September 1923 (opposite)

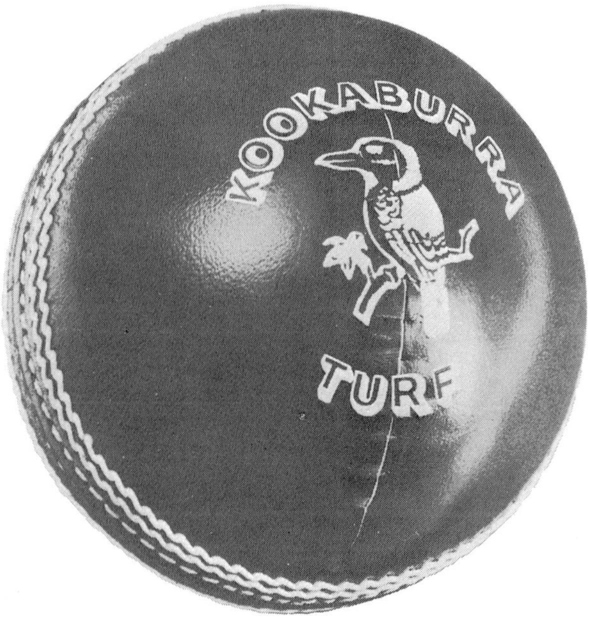

THE SPORTY KOOKABURRA

Because of his plucky, ockerish image, the kookaburra slotted easily into the sporting world, lending his name to a range of sporting gear. Kookaburra cricket balls have featured for decades in Test matches. The Kookaburra football is still a favourite among sportsmen. We thought we had unearthed another sporty association when we were told the Port Melbourne Football team was nicknamed the 'Burras'. Unexpectedly, this comes not from the Laughing Jackass but from the jackass or donkey. Meanwhile, Coca-Cola's sporting Kickaburra presents an image to appeal to all sportspersons: he's ready to take on all comers.

The sporty kookaburra has also advertised cigarettes, cigarette papers and our ubiquitous amber fluid.

This kookaburra cricket ball was manufactured by A. G. Thompson of Brighton (Victoria), as was the football below. A. G. Thompson's trademark (opposite page) was registered in 1913

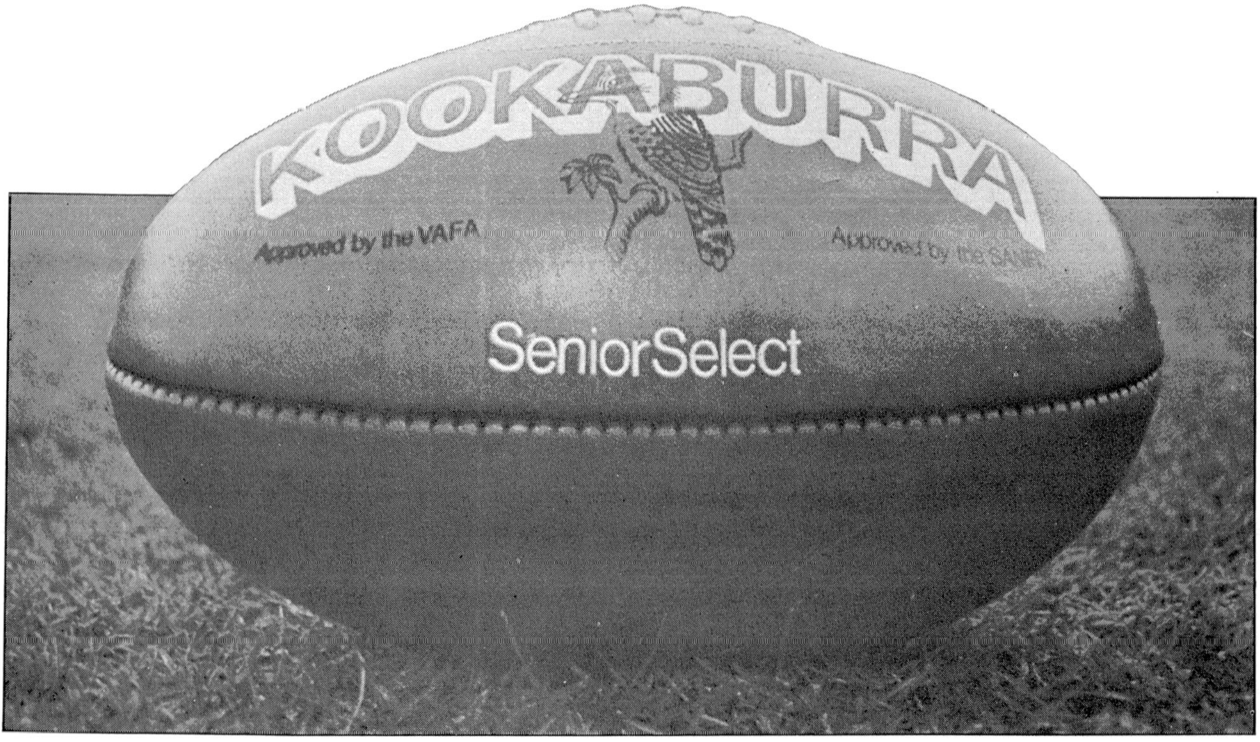

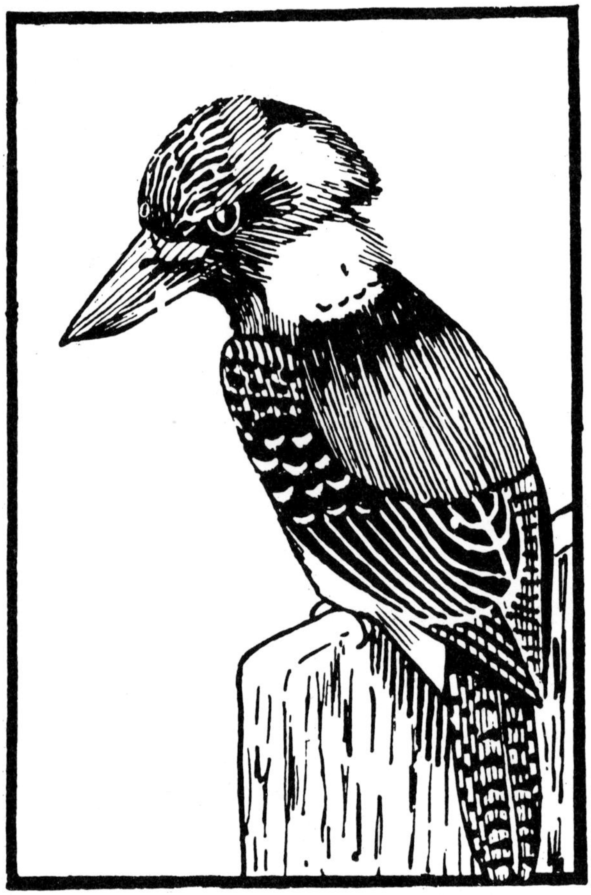

Commonwealth of Australia Hallmark Company, 1921

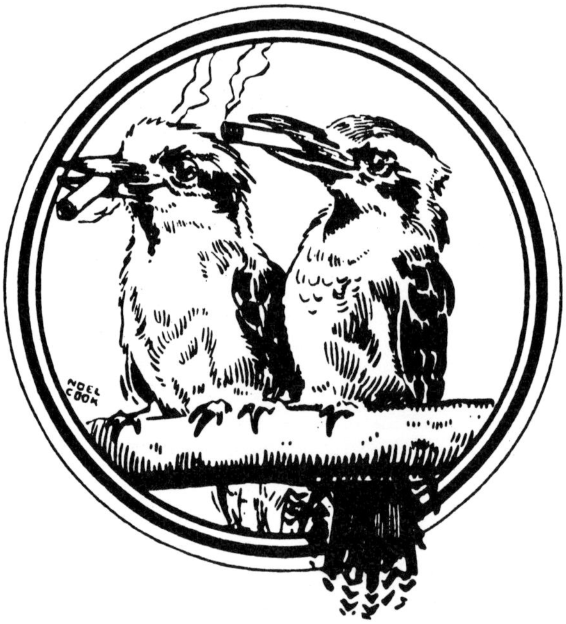

Kookaburra Cigarette Paper Tube Manufacturing Company, Sydney

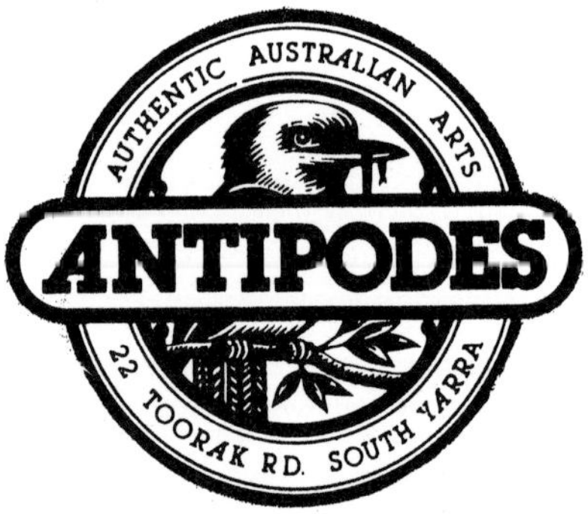

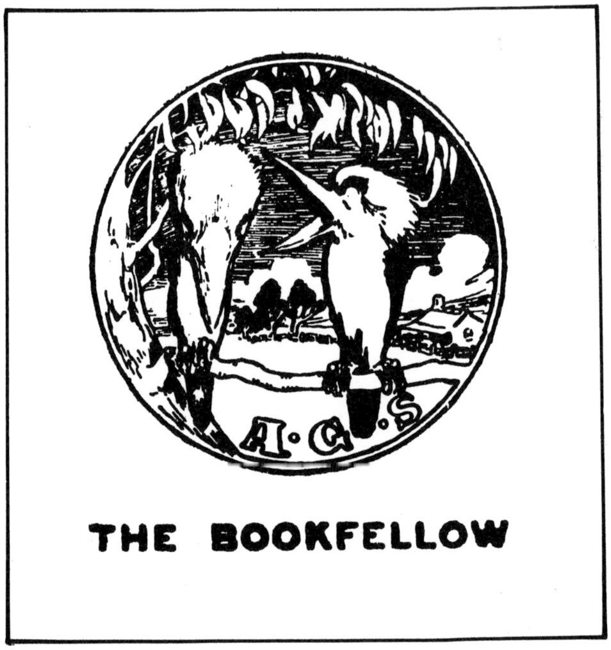

The Bookfellow, registered by journalist and publisher A. G. Stephens in 1911

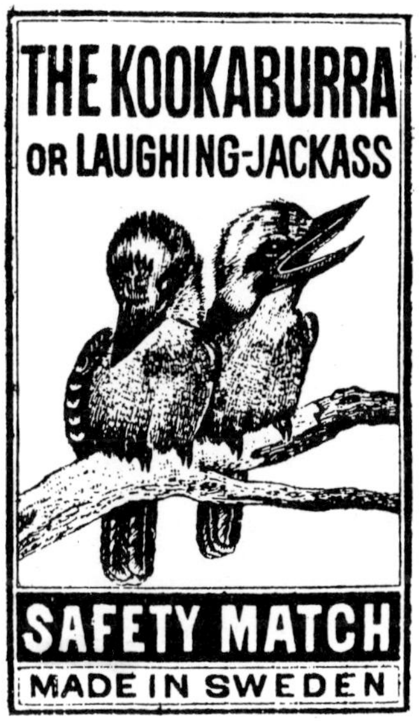

Claremont Kookaburra bulbs and seeds, registered in 1930 by Stinton & Son

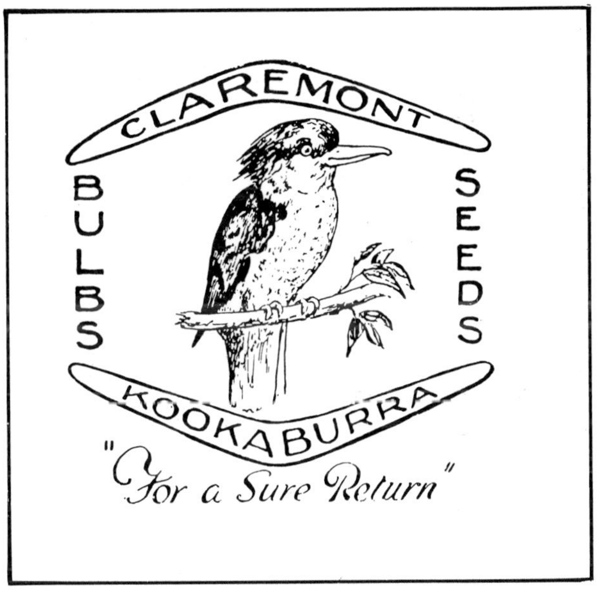

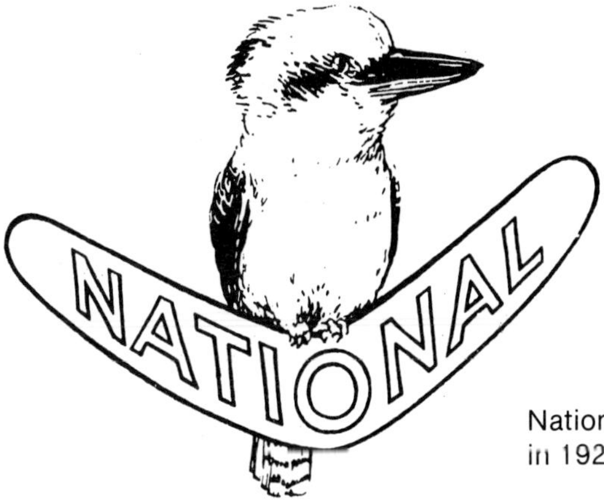

National Motor Company registered their trademark in 1926

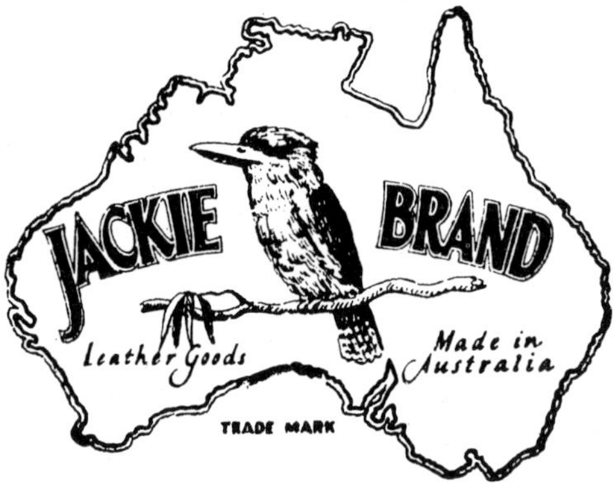

Jackie Brand leathergoods mark was registered by E. F. Martin in 1927

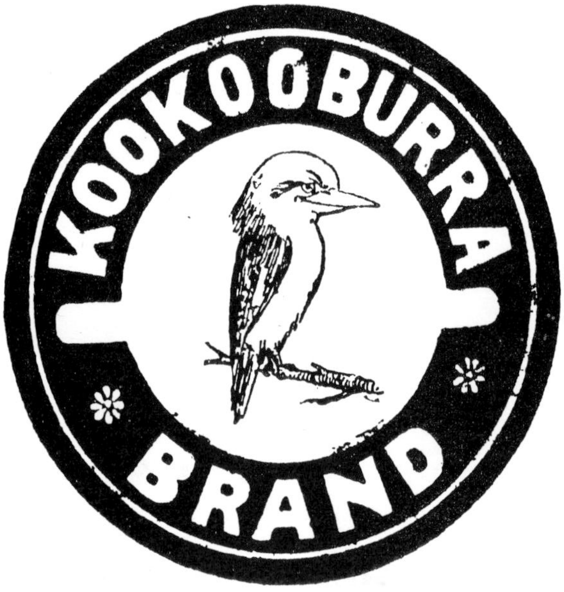

Lyon & Milling Ltd, porcelain and earthenware, 1912

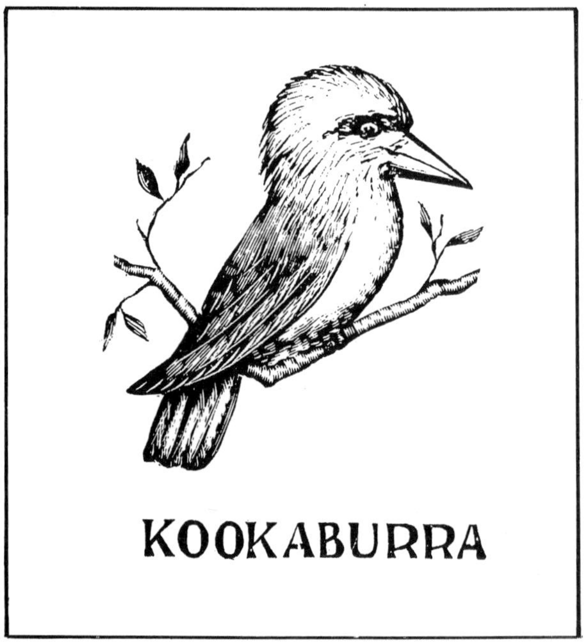

Orlo Smith & Co., books and albums, 1921

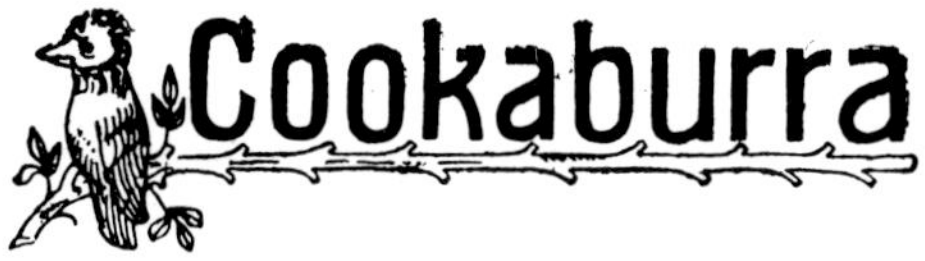

Cookaburra musical instruments, registered in 1911
by N. A. Rubens & Co.

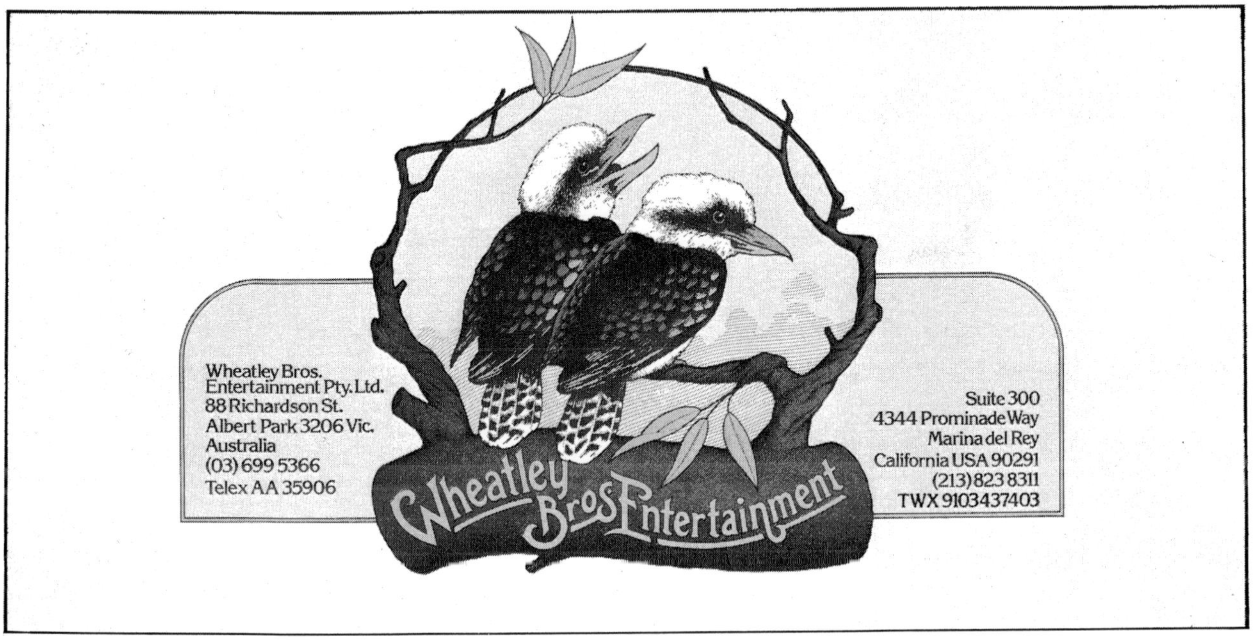

A modern letterhead

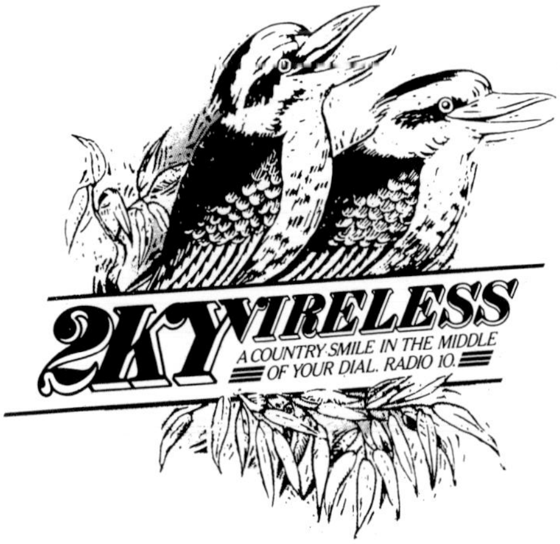

2KY Wireless, Sydney

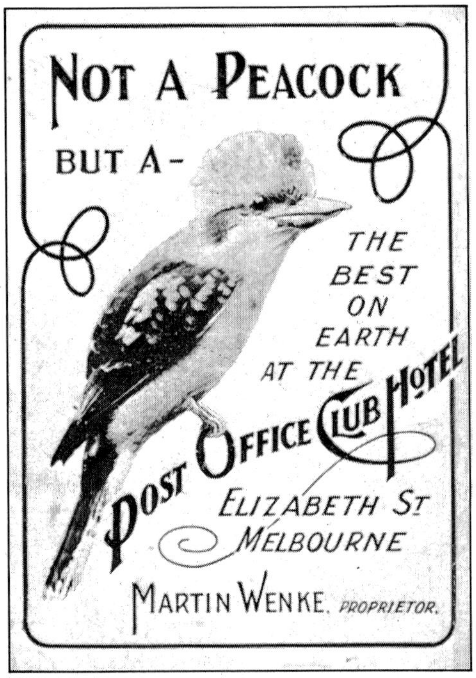

A puzzling trade card—can you work this out?

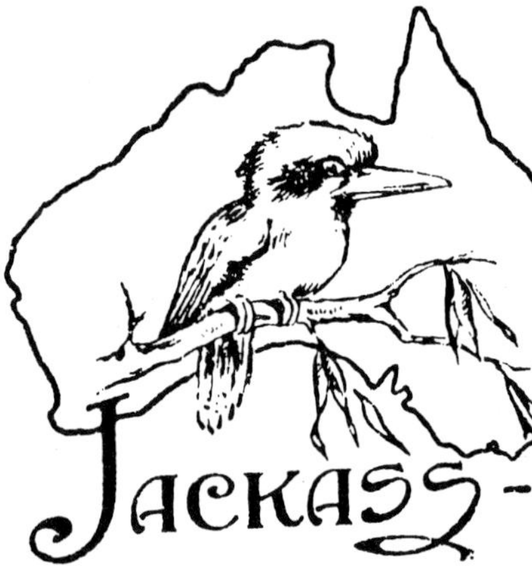

G. Gunnersen & Co., merchants, 1915

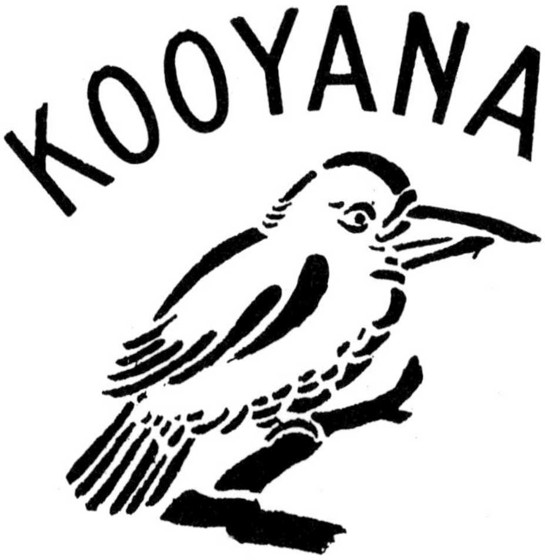

Steel & Baker, export flour, 1908

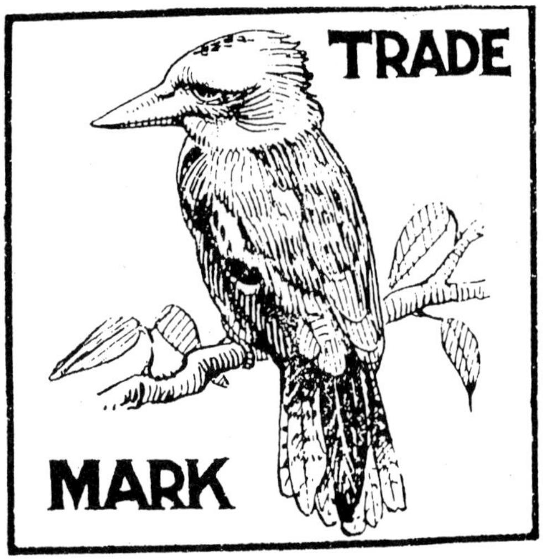

The Kookaburra Manufacturing Company, 1917

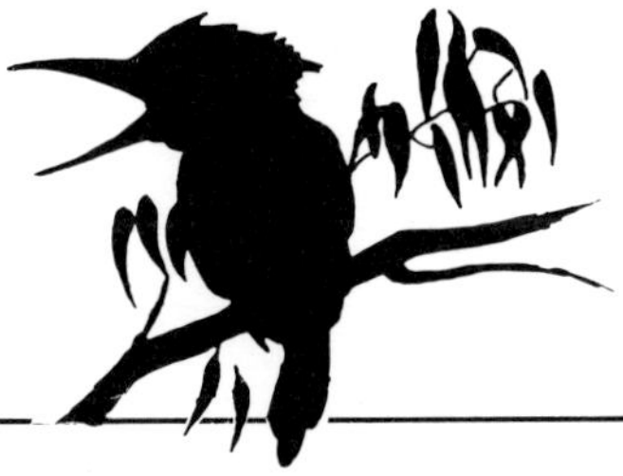

SOME AUSTRALIAN KOOKABURRA TRADEMARKS*

1893	COO-EE	Dixon & Sons, Sydney & Brisbane	Manufactured tobacco
1898	KOOKABURRA	Vodevalla Tandsticks, Sweden	Safety matches
1899	OUR JACK	A. M. Bickford & Sons, Adelaide	Various products
1907	KOOKABURRA	Wallace Rubber Mills, Melbourne	Rubber tyres
1907	KOOKABURRA	Birt & Co., Sydney	Frozen meat
1908	KOOYANA	Steel & Baker, Adelaide	Export flour
1910	COO-EE	N. Richards & Co.	Tomato sauce
1911	COOKABURRA	N. A. Rubens & Co.	Musical instruments
1911	THE BOOKFELLOW	A. G. Stephens	Journalist and publisher
1912	IRONBARK	The Sydney Paper Mills Ltd	Paper
1912	KOOKOOBURRA BRAND	Lyon & Milling Ltd, Sydney	Porcelain and earthenware
1913	THE KOOKABURRA	Vulcan Globe Match Co.	Safety matches
1913	KOOKABURRA	Aust. Knitting Mills Ltd, Melbourne	Hosiery
1913	KOOKABURRA	A. G. Thompson, Melbourne	Leather sporting goods
1915	JACKASS	G. Gunnersen & Co., Melbourne	Building products
1917	KOOKABURRA	The Kookaburra Manufacturing Co., Melbourne	Various products
1917	KOOKABURRA	W. S. Kimpton & Sons, Melbourne	Roller flour
1920	EARLY KOOKA	Metters Ltd, Sydney	Stoves
1920	'OUR JACKS'	D. & W. Murray Ltd, Adelaide	Hats
1921	KOOKABURRA	Orlo Smith & Co.	Books and albums
1922	DIGGABURRA	Digger Tea Supply Co., Queensland	Tea
1922	K'BURRA	Walther & Stevenson, Sydney	Whips
1925	KOOKOOBURRA	A. Forsyth & Co. Ltd, Sydney	Ropes
1926	NATIONAL	National Motor Car Manufacturing Co. Ltd, Sydney	Cars
1927	COOKABURRA	Briggs Bros. Pty Ltd, Melbourne	Patty-pans
1927	JACKIE BRAND	E. F. Martin, Victoria	Leathergoods
1928	KOOKABURRA	Hancock's Golden Crust	Cut macaroni
1930	KOOKABURRA	Stinton & Sons, Geelong	Bulbs and seeds
1930	JACKO	W. K. Burnside Pty Ltd, Melbourne	Shoe polish
1931	KOOKABURRA	Kookaburra Cigarette Paper Tube Manufacturing Co., Sydney	Cigarette paper tubes
1936	KOOKABURRA	Duval Trading Co., Sydney	Holland blinds
1956	KINGFISHER	R. Fisher Pty Ltd	Shelving racks, storage

* From *Symbols of Australia* by Mimmo Cozzolino, published by Penguin Books, Melbourne, 1980.

-7-
DECORATIVE KOOKAS

The kookaburra motif occurs widely in the Australian decorative arts tradition as a twentieth-century symbol. The kangaroo and the emu virtually reigned supreme as symbols in the nineteenth century. Kookaburra objects dating from before 1900 have emerged, but the heyday of the kookaburra is undoubtedly the twentieth century.

The kangaroo in particular inspired many objects that fell into the sphere of the fine arts. The kookaburra, in keeping with his larrikin folksy image, did not in the main inspire extremely fine objects, although many highly collectable items can be found. Most kookaburra objects were items of popular art; some bordered on the kitsch, of which the most obvious examples are the plaster kookaburras that occurred in an alarming variety of shapes and sizes and without which no Australian household was adequately furnished.

After Federation in 1901, a sense of nationalism was well established. Artists and craftspeople looked to Australia's unique fauna and flora for inspiration. Throughout this chapter, we investigate the kookaburras depicted in the various branches of the decorative arts such as watercolours, woodcarving, pottery, metalwork, jewellery, pokerwork, needlework and stained glass.

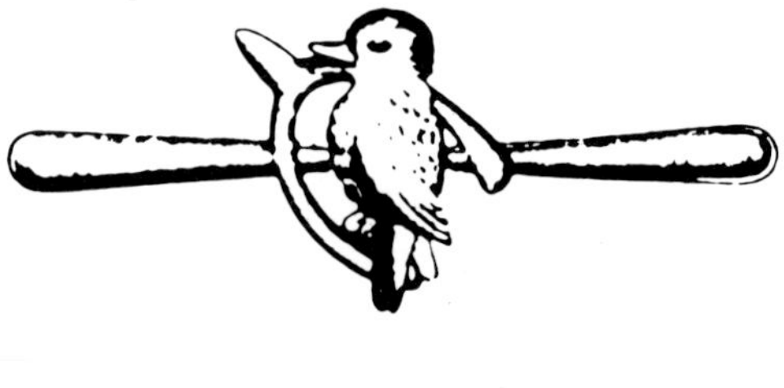

WATERCOLOURS

Some very effective public relations was performed for the kookaburra by popular watercolourists late last century and early this century. Of these, Neville Cayley senior was perhaps the most important. Neville Henry Peniston Cayley (1853–1903) was the father of the ornithologist, Neville W. Cayley of *What Bird is That?* fame. Cayley senior was a popular artist and painted many fine watercolours of magpies, blue wrens, game birds and, of course, kookaburras. The best of Cayley's kookaburras are among the finest depictions of the birds ever made. Cayley's work was popularised in a number of ways. Firstly, many of his kookaburra studies were used on postcards of the day. As well, he exhibited paintings at William Aldenhoven's gallery in Hunter Street, Sydney. Aldenhoven produced prints and Christmas cards of Cayley's works. In 1903 Cayley issued a small brochure containing eleven studies of birds.

Rumour has it that Caley paid for many a night's lodging in country pubs in New South Wales with his paintings of kookaburras. We can't confirm the rumour, but we do know of a lot of Cayley kookaburras in the country, and the quality of Cayley's work does vary.

Two other bird painters of the day whose work was popularised on postcards and Christmas cards in the first decade of this century were Oscar Stahl and John Mitchell Cantle.

Another popular early twentieth-century painter of birds was H. H. Calvert whose kookaburra (illustrated) is a fierce larrikin indeed. One of the charming conceits of the period was the painting of English and Australian 'cricket elevens' with native birds comprising each team. The kookaburra invariably got his cap. H. H. Calvert painted many Australian Elevens, and some charming amateur versions were done as well. Harry Bright's Elevens were issued as a pair of prints.

Although watercolour was the most popular medium in which the kookaburra was depicted, there are other famous works, like Sir Lionel Lindsay's woodcut of the kookaburra.

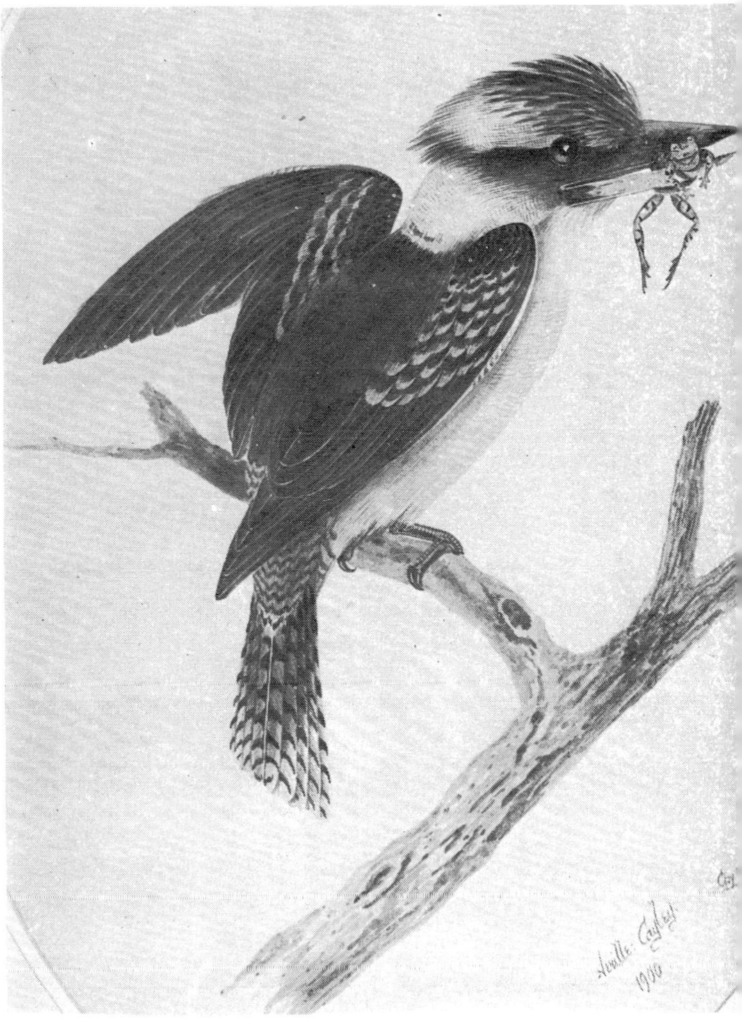

The Laughing Frog, a watercolour by Neville Cayley senior, 1900 (above) and a decorative poster (below)

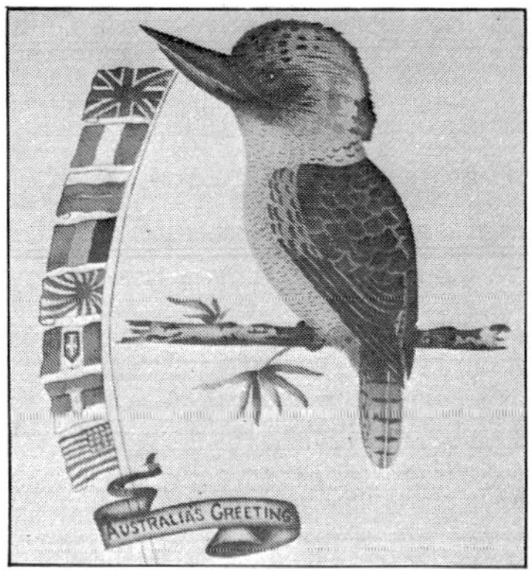

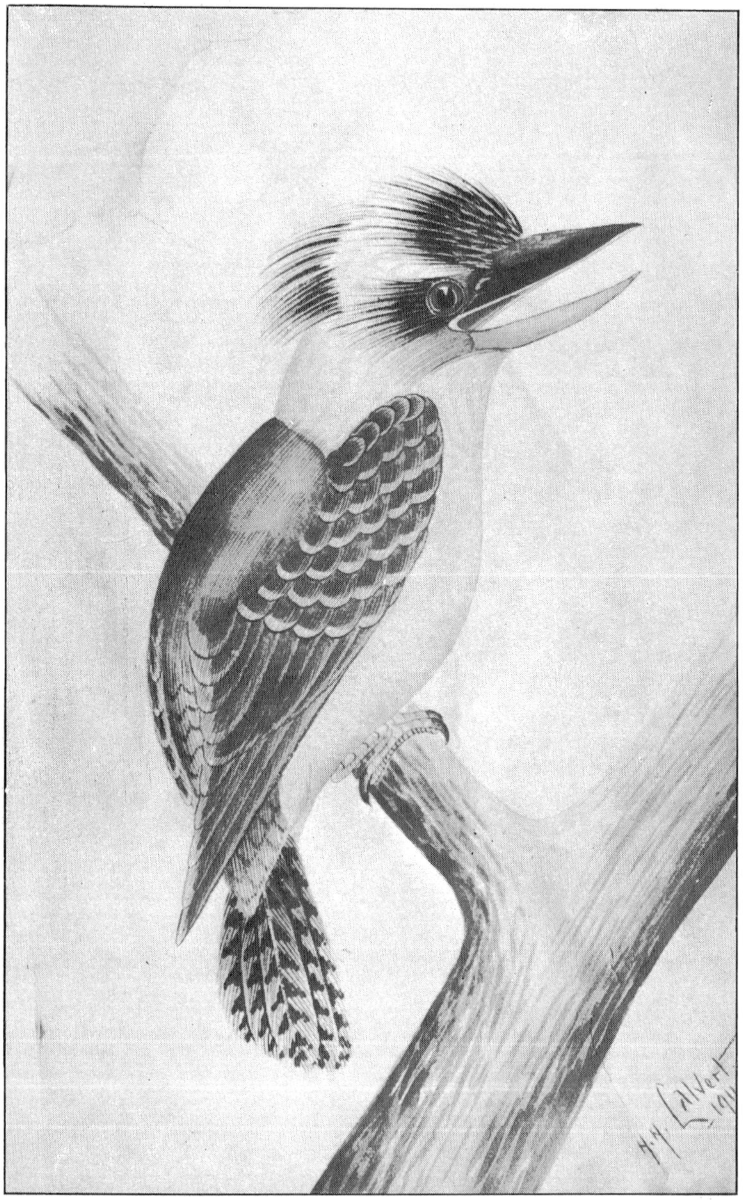

A Fierce Larrikin: watercolour by H. H. Calvert, 1911

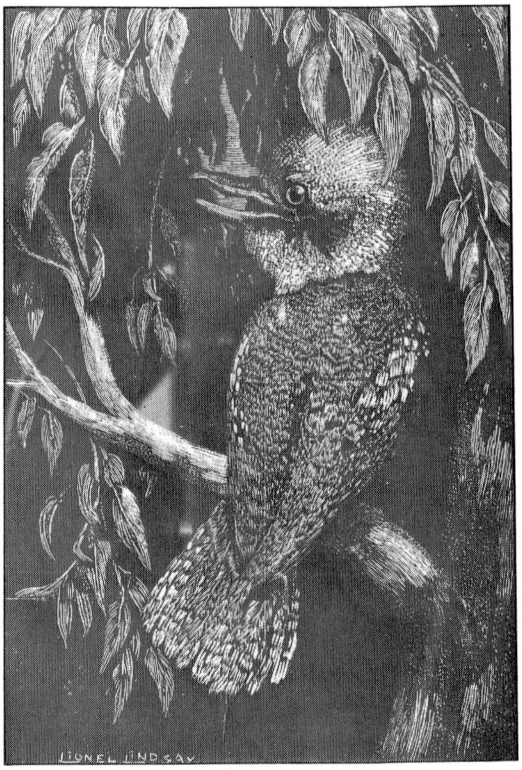

Woodcut by Lionel Lindsay

Primitive oil painting, *c.* 1900

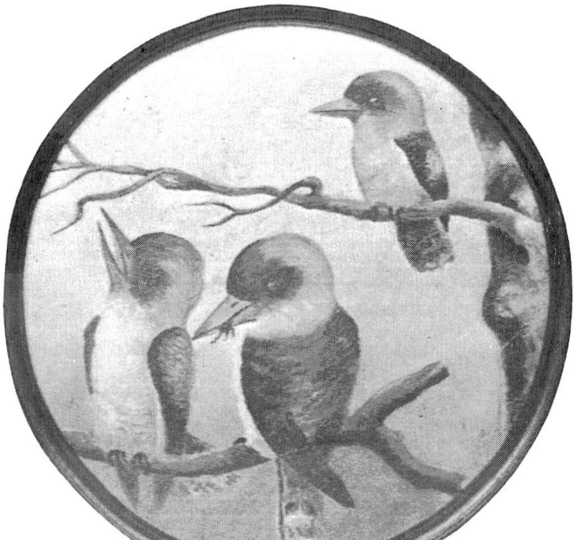

WOODCARVING

One branch of the decorative arts to flourish in the post-Federation period was woodcarving, and many interesting pieces featured the kookaburra. The range of items and quality is wide, from the unsigned, naïve, folk-art kookaburras (possibly the work of hobbyists) through to the masterful kookaburra carvings of Robert Prenzel, who was born in Prussia in 1866 and settled in Melbourne in 1888.

Originally, Prenzel worked in the elaborate traditional German style. But post-Federation, the influence of his adopted land appeared in his work, as well as that of the European movement that later became known as art nouveau.

In some of his finest work the blending of European art nouveau with depictions of Australian flora and fauna produced very fine examples of what has been called 'gumnut nouveau'. The most famous example of this is the Mathias Suite in the National Gallery of Victoria. The suite was commissioned in 1906 and originally comprised a bed, a large wardrobe, a gentleman's wardrobe and a washstand. A number of other pieces were added to the suite in 1908. Made from black bean – which was a highly innovative timber to use at the time – the Mathias Suite is decorated with Australia's best known and loved animals and birds, usually placed in appropriate botanical backgrounds. Naturally, we find the kookaburra revelling in such company, in this case providing a striking decorative element in the headboard of the bed.

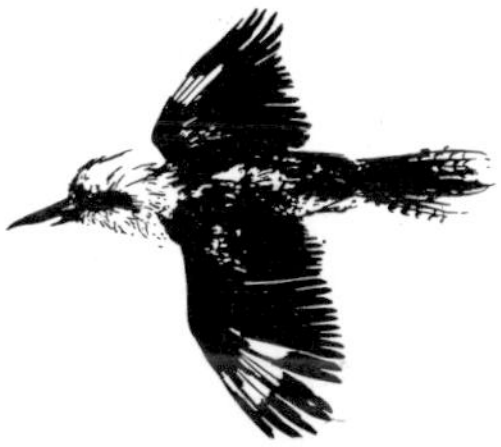

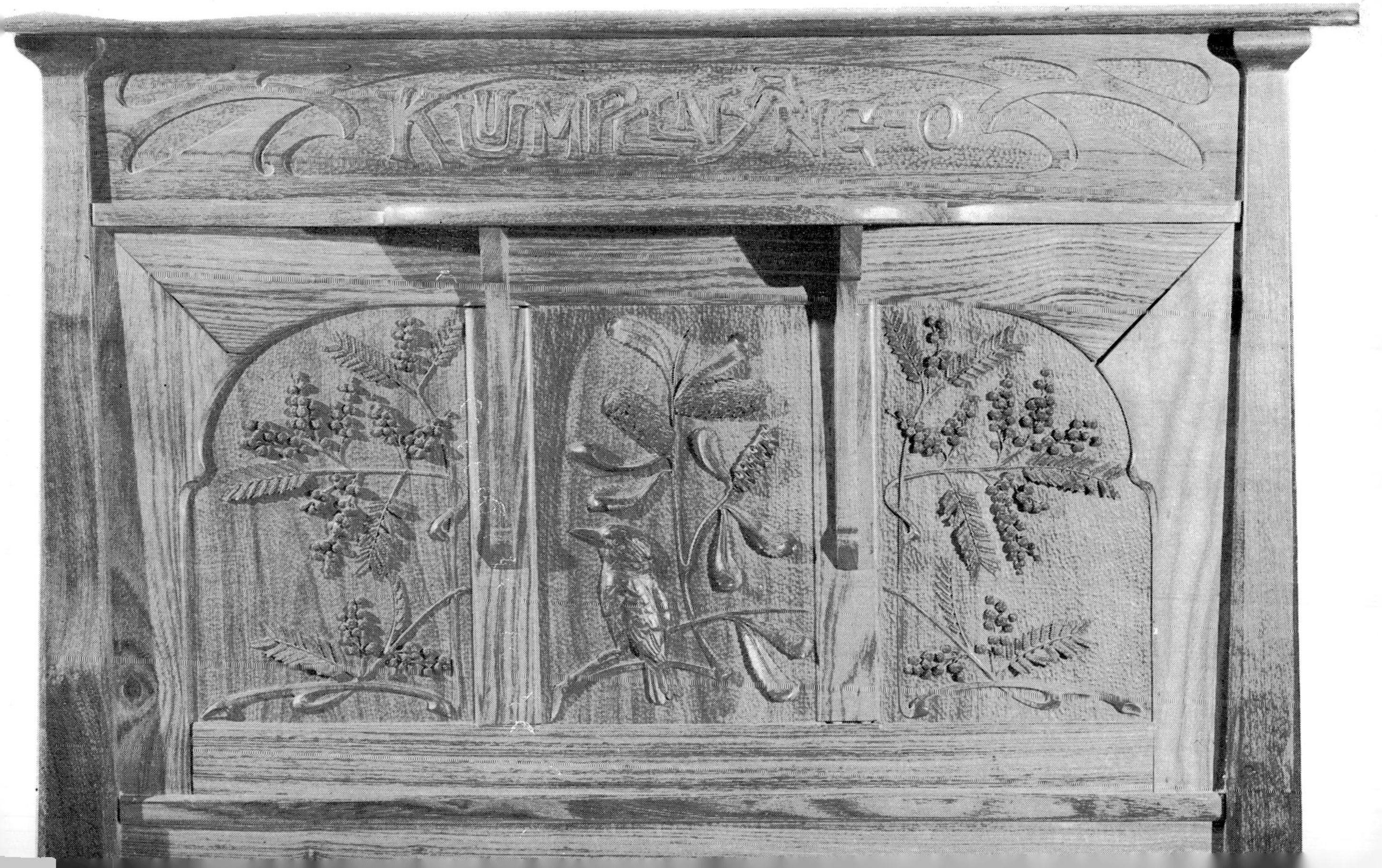

Bed headboard carved in Queensland black bean by Robert Prenzel in 1906. 'Kuumpeenyang-o' means 'Goodnight' in the language of the Chaap Wuurong Aboriginal tribe of south-western Victoria

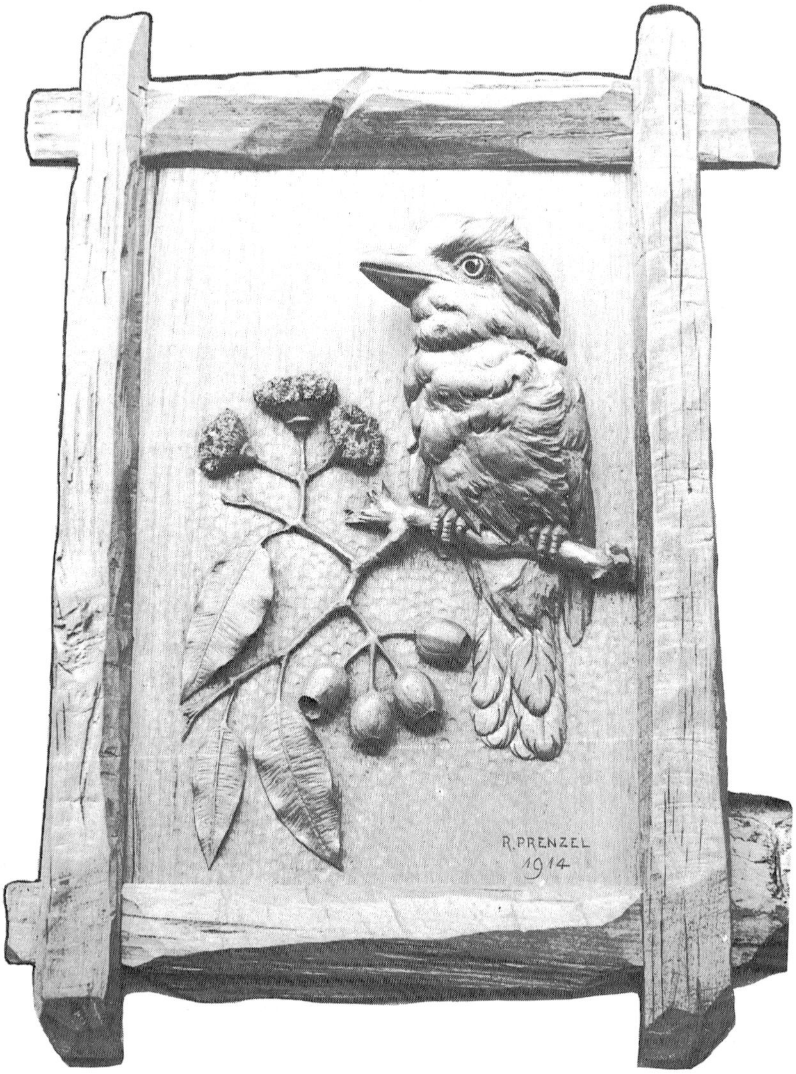

Kookaburra carved in relief with gumnuts in this post-and-rail frame by Robert Prenzel, 1914 (left).
Gumnut nouveau picture frame by Robert Prenzel, containing a small watercolour by Alice Cayley (below)

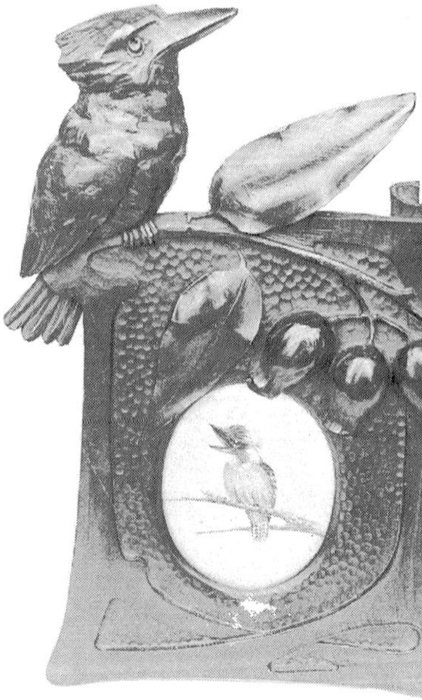

Prenzel appears to have had special feeling for kookaburras, and superb artifacts featuring them have turned up in recent years. The carved kookaburra picture frame (illustrated in colour between pages 88 and 89) is a small masterpiece of gumnut nouveau where typical art nouveau form blends with the kookaburra, gum leaves and gumnuts.

A number of superb carved studies by Prenzel of kookaburras enclosed in their own carved post-and-rail frames are known to exist. In our illustration the three-dimensional kookaburra is so life-like he looks as if he could fly from his frame at any minute.

POTTERY AND PLASTER

Years ago many ceramic and plaster kookaburras were made, and the latter were all the rage as souvenirs, mantlepiece ornaments and fairground prizes. British and European ceramic manufacturers exported myriad moulded kookaburras and domestic and decorative items featuring the kookaburra motif. Australian art and commercial potters also used the motif extensively.

Traditionally, most of our domestic crockery was imported from Britain, while Australian potteries in the nineteenth and early twentieth centuries largely concentrated on a range of functional and utilitarian items including agricultural pipes and bricks. As a result, bread plates, cheese dishes, tobacco jars and money boxes that were made here are keenly collected today.

Some very handsome pottery workmen's pieces, dating from the late nineteenth and early twentieth centuries, like vases, jars, garden ornaments and umbrella stands, have survived, and many feature kookaburras. These pieces were not part of scheduled production but were made by pottery workers in their spare time.

In the 1920s British ceramic manufacturers like Royal Doulton, Royal Worcestershire, Royal Staffordshire and other exporters, cognisant of the kookaburra's popularity here, sought to cash in on the wave of Australian nationalism. There had been English jug and basin sets with transfer decoration featuring kookaburras early this century, but the 1920s saw a rash of kookaburras decorating imported cups, saucers, plates, jugs and ashtrays. There was a range of kookaburra china from Czechoslovakia made by IBC Royal Scenic China, and one from Bavaria. Royal Staffordshire pieces hand-painted by H. Crisp are among the most decorative of the foreign kookaburras. The Dutch Gouda Art Pottery also produced some fine kookaburra-decorated pieces in this period.

Australian potters took up the theme in the late 1920s and 1930s when Australian art pottery began to flourish. Vases, pots and jugs were made by small potteries and individual potters around the country. Australiana motifs

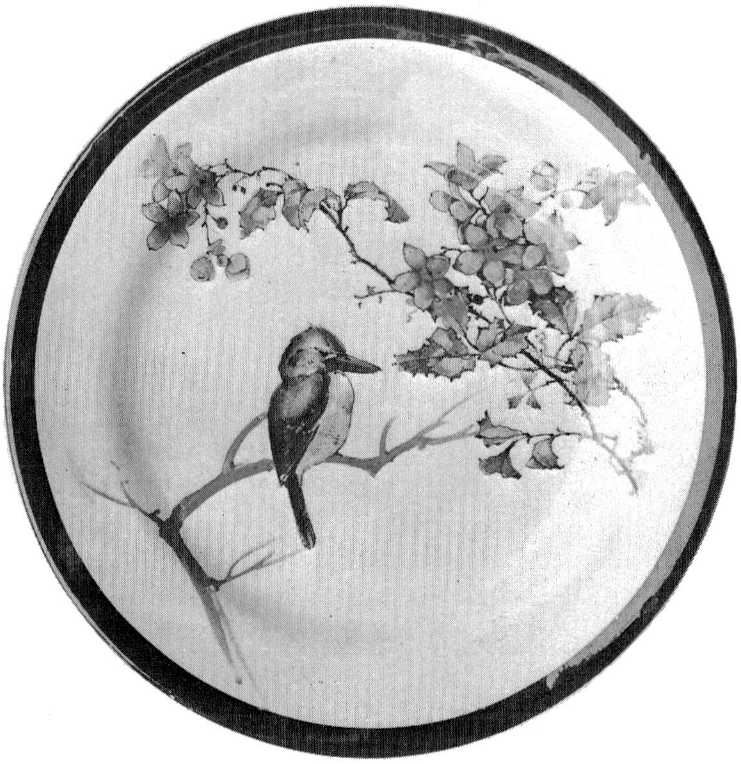

Royal Doulton plate, *c.* 1920, with impressed and transfer marks (above). Below is a similar dish

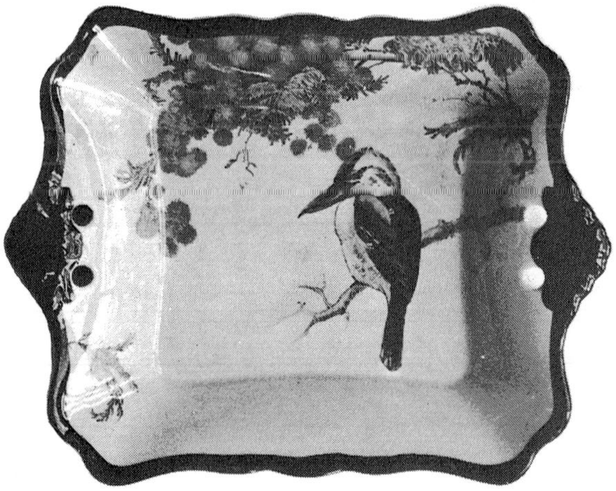

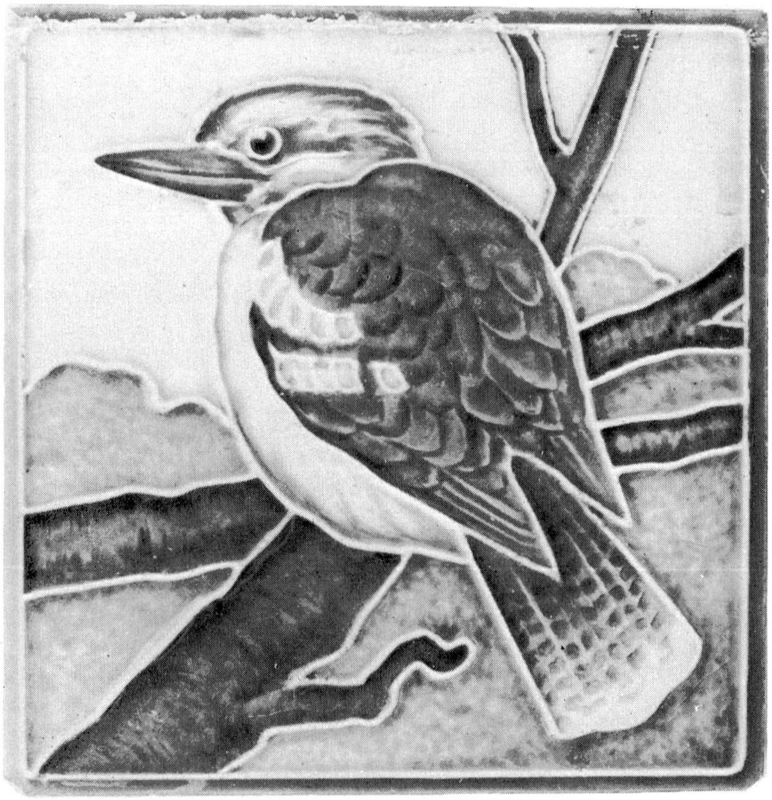

This ceramic wall tile was made in England

Pottery kookaburra by Hatton Beck (below). Hatton Beck started the famous Murrumbeena pottery with Merric Boyd

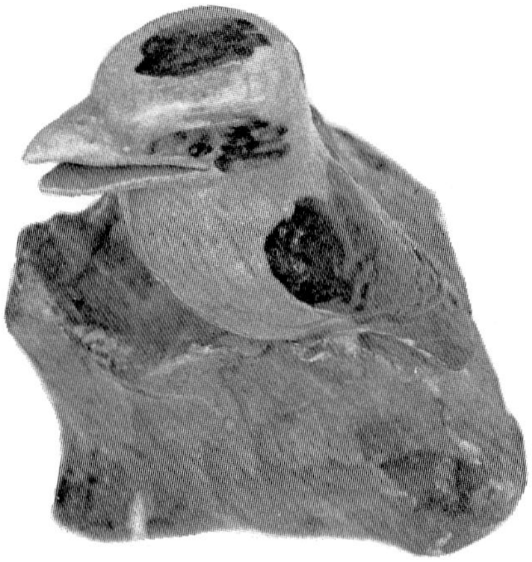

were very popular. Many of the pieces were decorated with drip glazes, gum leaves, possums and of course kookaburras. Many leading potters featured the kookaburra motif, including Merric Boyd, Hatton Beck and Castle Harris in Victoria, Gladys Reynell in South Australia, John Campbell in Launceston and Grace Seacombe in Sydney. The last-named artist in particular is noted for the many charming groups of kookaburras she made. Commercial potteries such as Bennetts, as well as other Adelaide potteries, produced moulded kookaburras.

Ceramic pin trays, dishes and ashtrays were imported from Japan to be sold in the local gift shops. British manufacturers also exported a profusion of unmarked kookaburra wares to Australian gift shops.

Plaster kookaburras came in a variety of forms. Depictions of 'Happy Jack', 'A Story of Love' and many others were decorated in pastel colours. Often, they were coveted prizes on hoopla stalls. A friend tells of being heart-broken as a child when she tripped and smashed her newly won 'Happy Jack'. Her only consolation was that the broken bits kept her in hopscotch chalk for years. Many of these gift-shop plaster kookaburras and cheap ashtrays are regarded today as true kitsch, rather like the flying ducks of the later era. Some are of very poor quality, some are most collectable; the astonishing thing is the popularity of the kookaburra in those years. So many Australians related to the bird and were ready to purchase a reminder of its bush merriment.

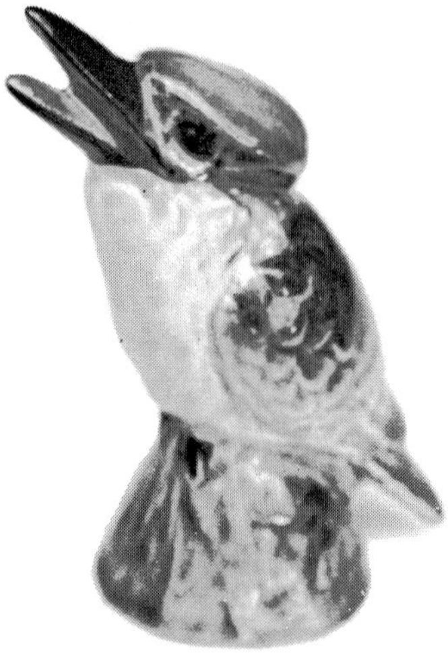

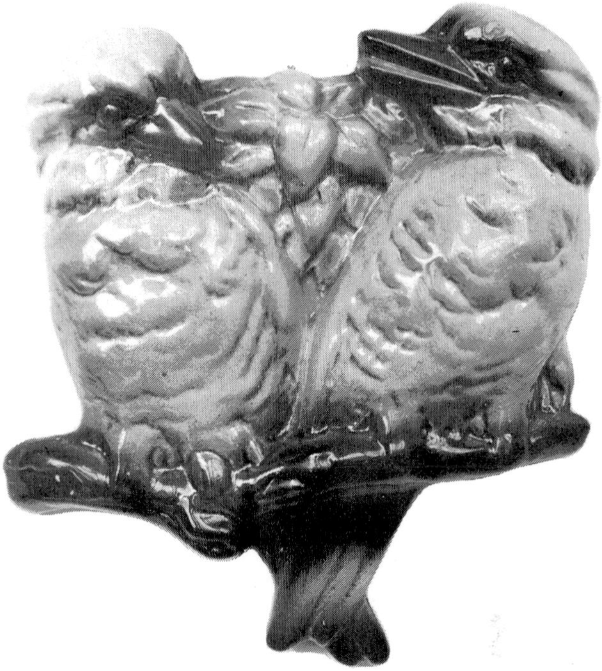

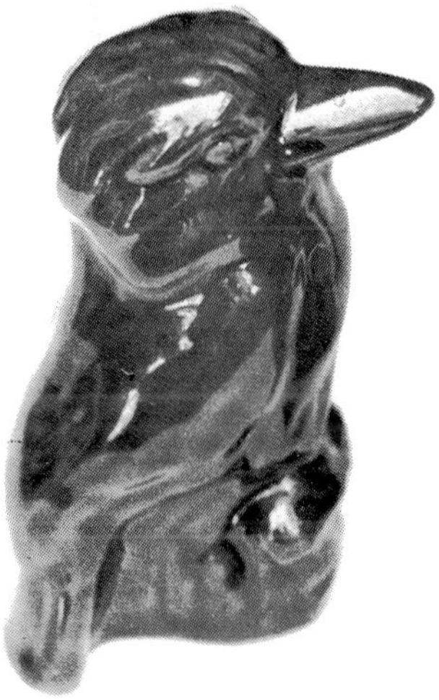

Two more pottery kookaburras (left and above left). The wall vase (above) was made by Pates Pottery in Sydney in the 1930s. Below are seven little Australians by Grace Seacombe

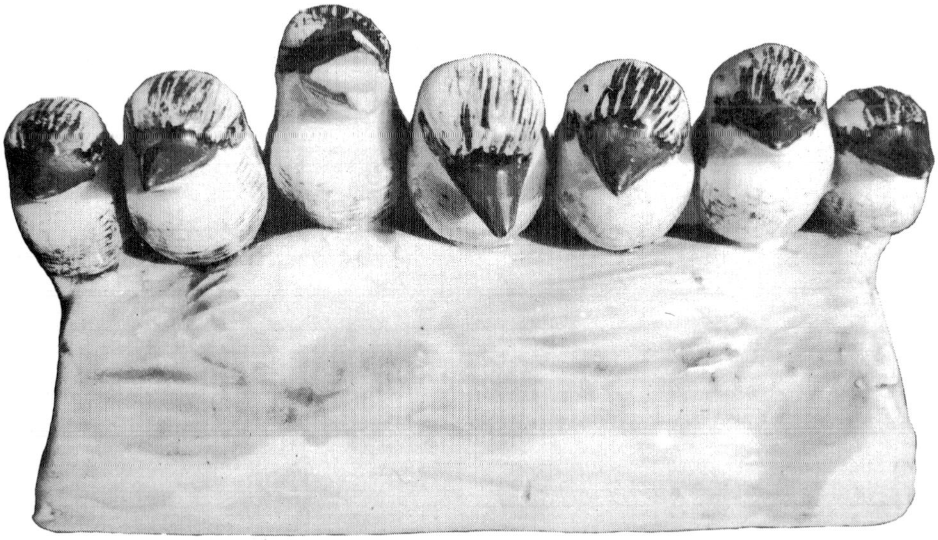

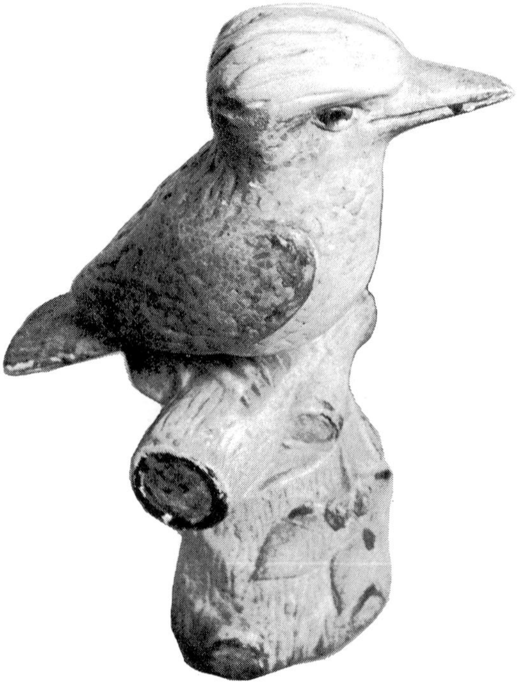

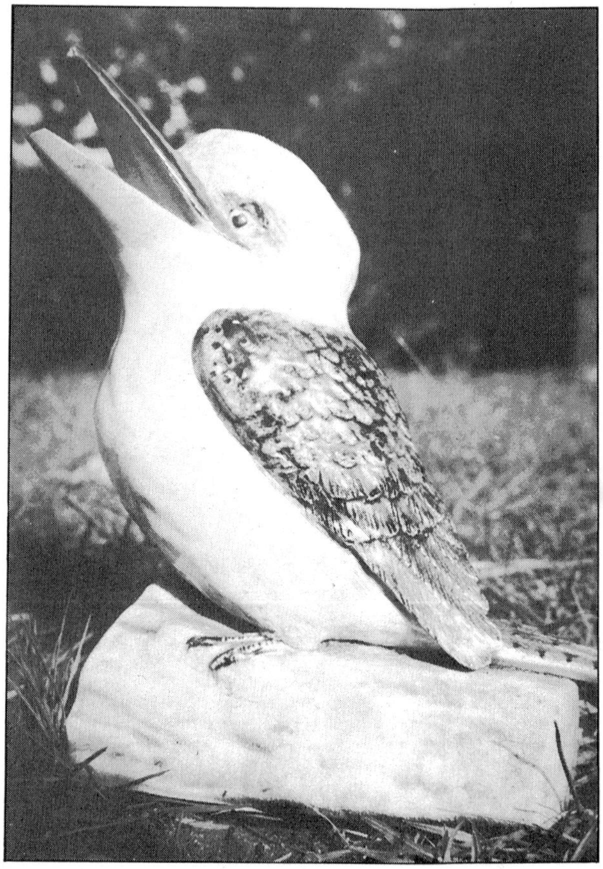

1930s plaster kookaburra, of the type commonly presented as prizes on hoopla stalls (above). At right is another of Grace Seacombe's pottery kookaburras

METAL KOOKABURRAS

Many decorative kookaburra objects were made in metal. Moulded or cast kookaburras abound in bronze, silver, brass and cast iron. A wide range of decorative and souvenir items was made, such as inkwells, paperweights, plaques, paperknives and shoe horns. Few of these rank as works of art but all are items of great charm to the unrepentant kookaburra addict.

Brassy kookaburras appear as cast door-knockers, firescreens, bookends and bottle openers. The kookaburra bottle opener brings to mind the story of a picnic in the Dandenongs when a cheeky kookaburra took the sausage from a guest's fork 'twixt the table and his mouth.

An interesting range of metal kookaburras is illustrated, including a primitive iron weather-vane and the familiar old kookaburra bronze plaque; some of these were realistically overpainted.

Few solid or sterling silver kookaburras were made, although we have seen one by the Queensland silversmith, Frederick James Mole. Numerous minor items were made in sterling silver, for example buttonhooks, spoons and savoury picks. The buttonhook illustrated has the Birmingham date mark for 1911. Most of the silver kookaburra items were not solid silver but electro-plated, like the toast rack and sugar bowl illustrated. Souvenir items include paperknives, shoe horns and napkin rings.

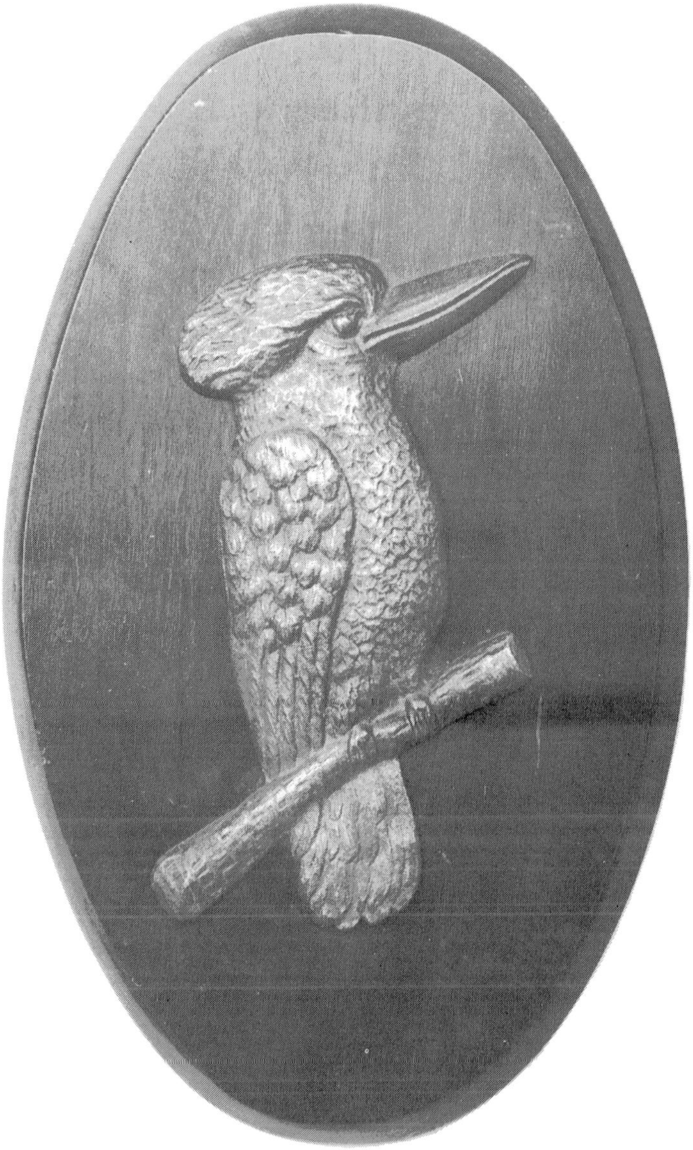

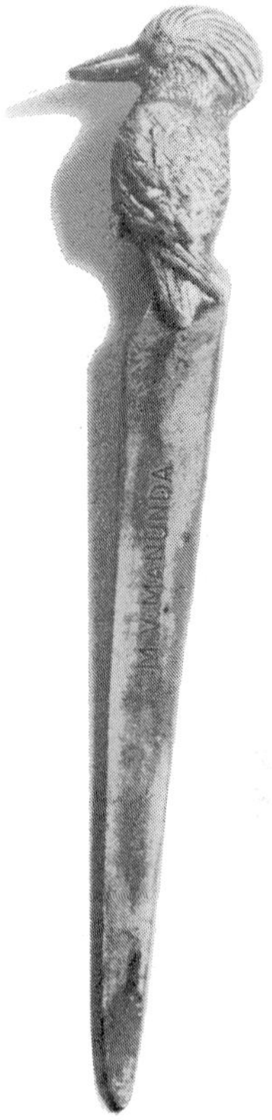

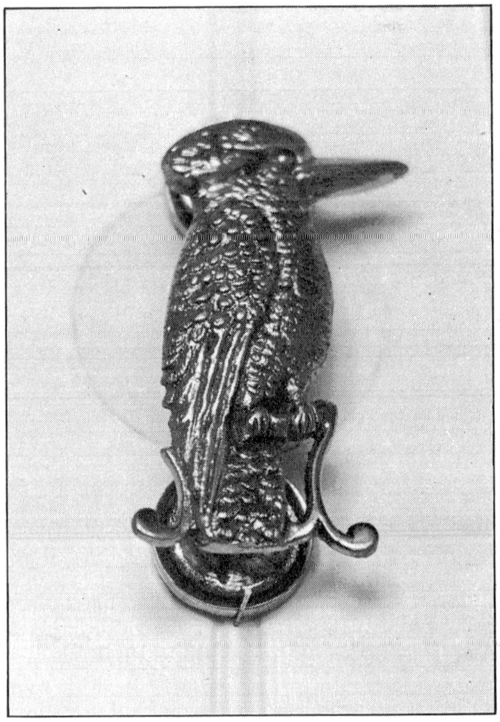

Bronze kookaburra plaque (above), souvenir paperknife from the M.V. *Manunda* (above right) and brass door knocker (right)

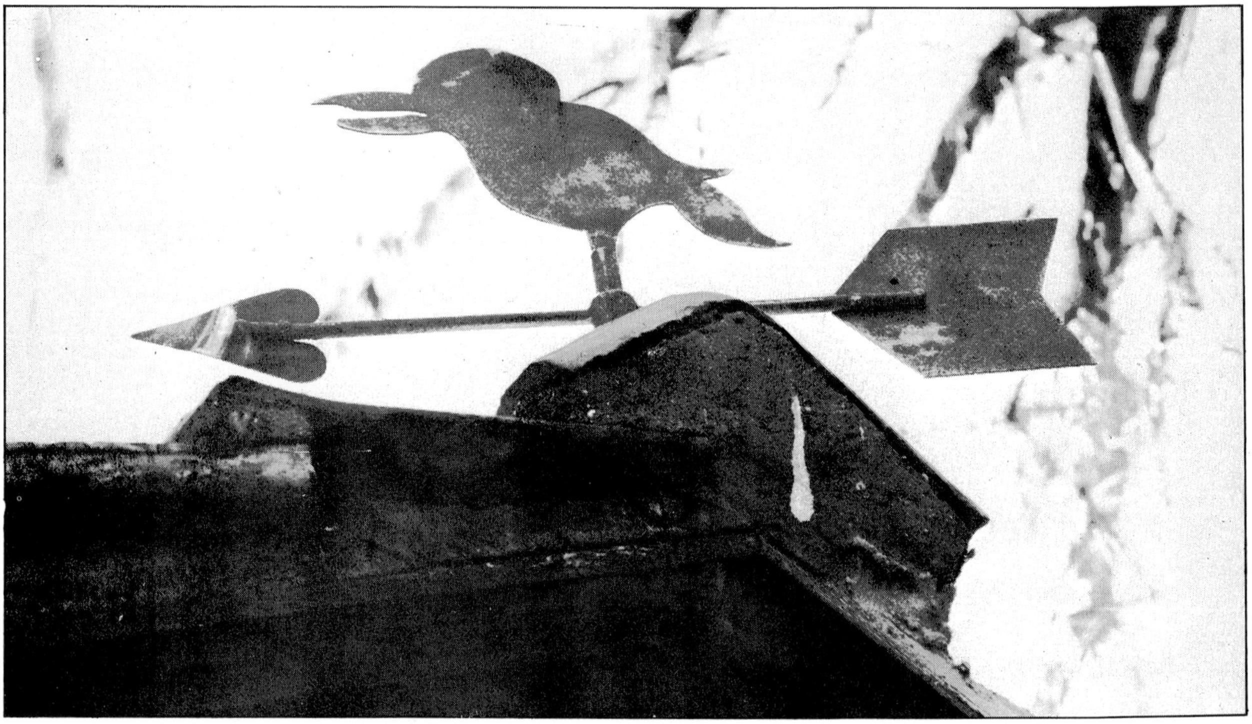

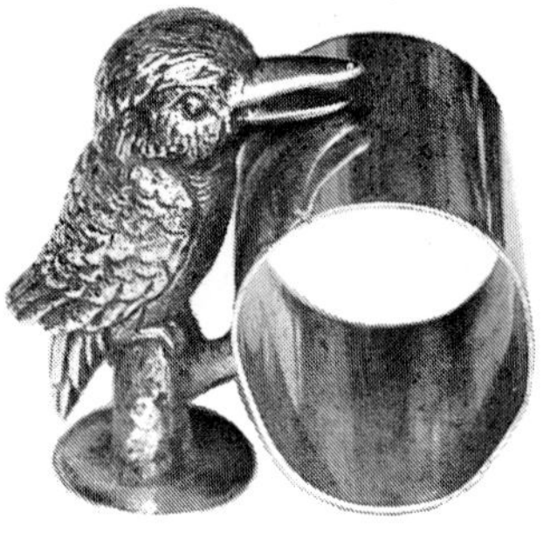

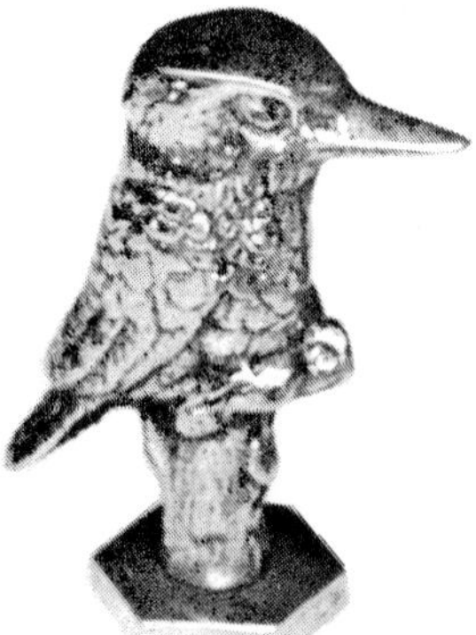

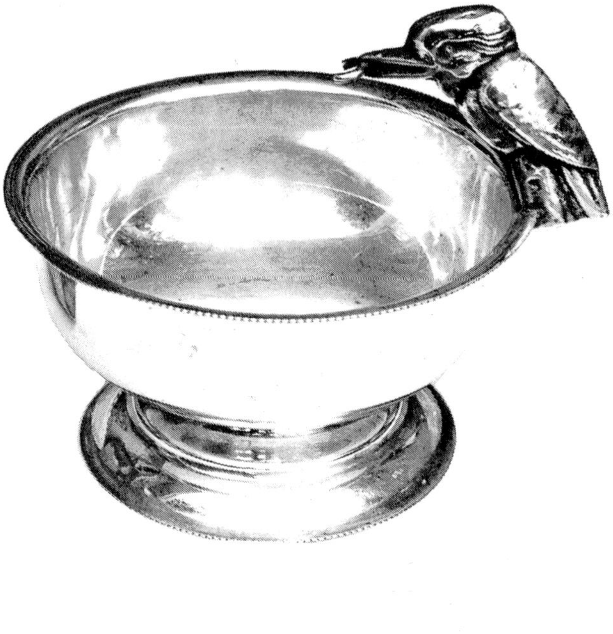

Primitive iron weathervane (opposite page, top). Below it are some silver-plated kookaburras. From left to right: car mascot, napkin ring and sugar bowl

Below from left to right: an English buttonhook in sterling silver, marked Birmingham, 1911; an enamelled kookaburra savoury pick; an Australian silver savoury pick. The silver-plated kookaburra souvenir shoe horn engraved with Sydney Harbour Bridge (right) and the brass kookaburra bottle opener (below right) are both very collectable items

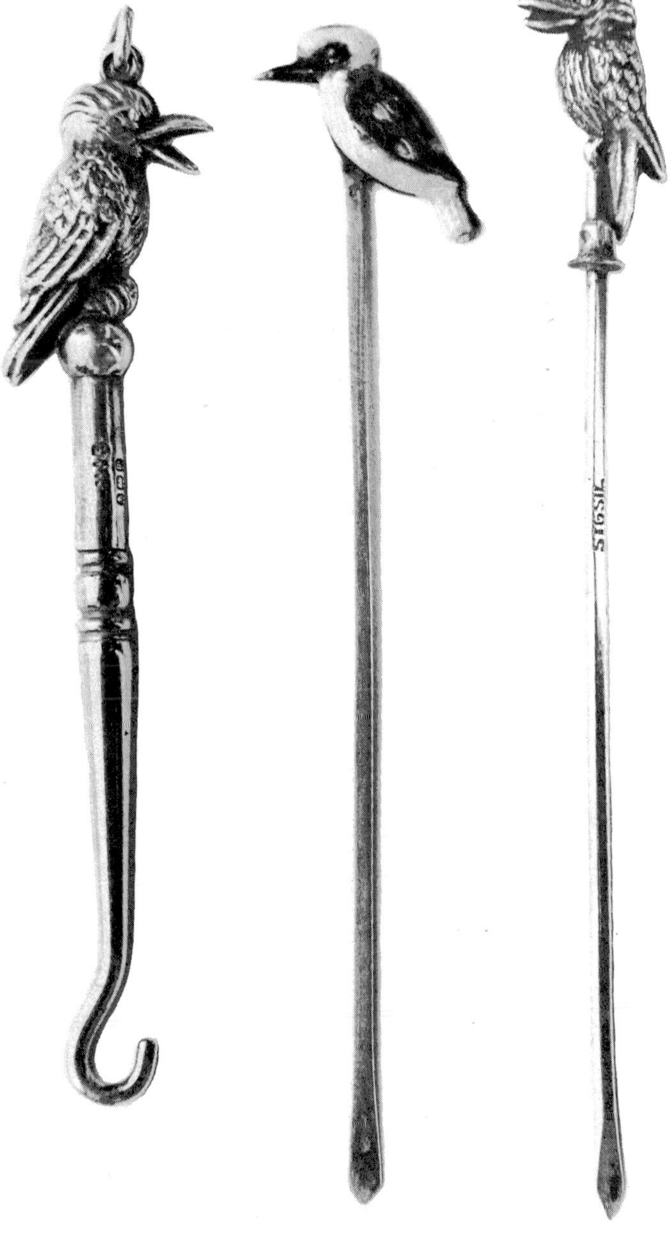

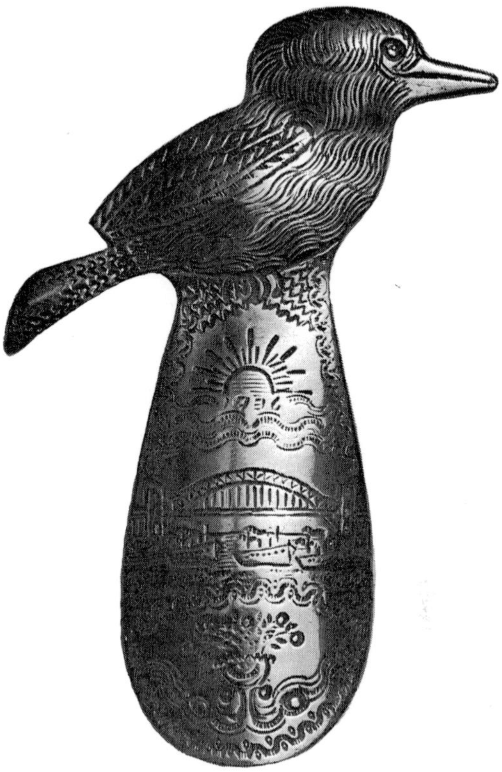

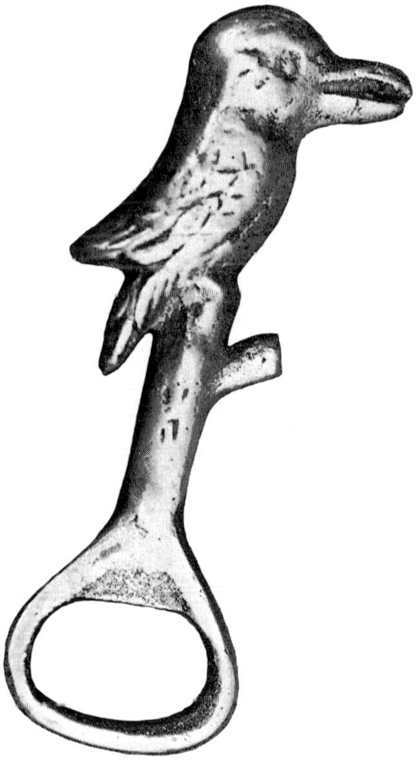

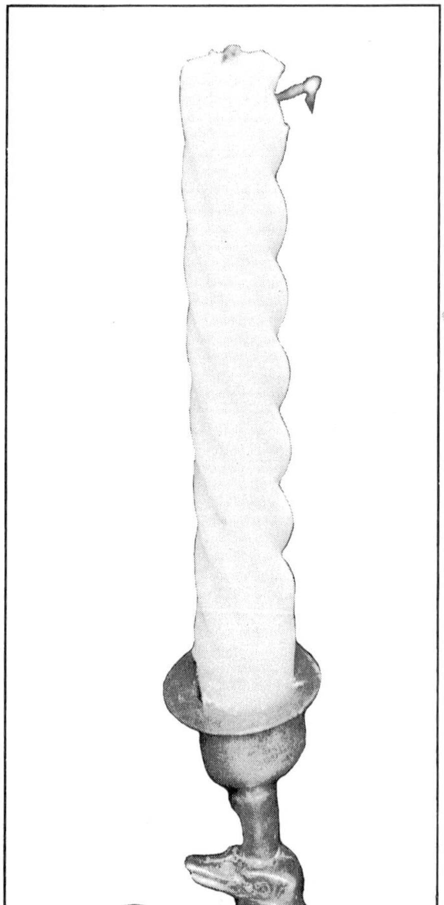

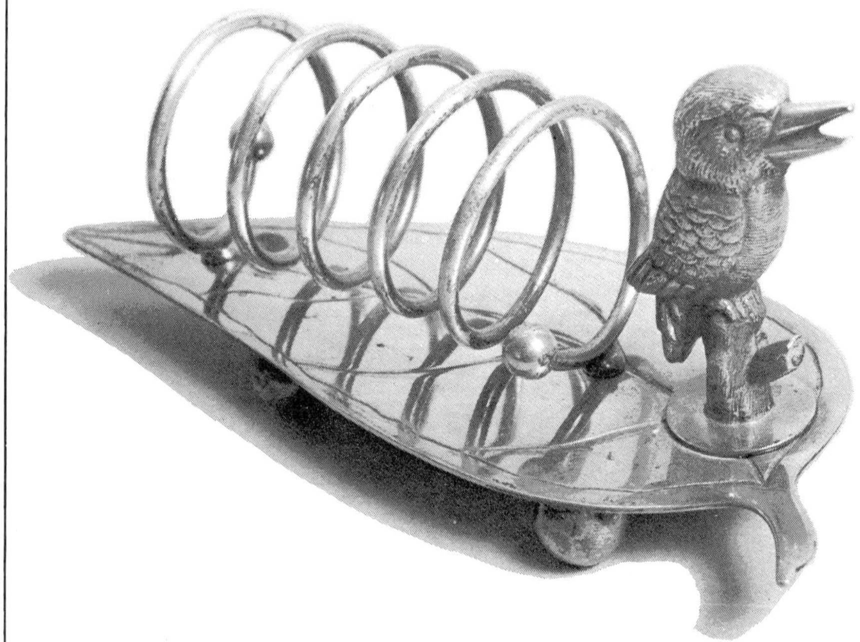

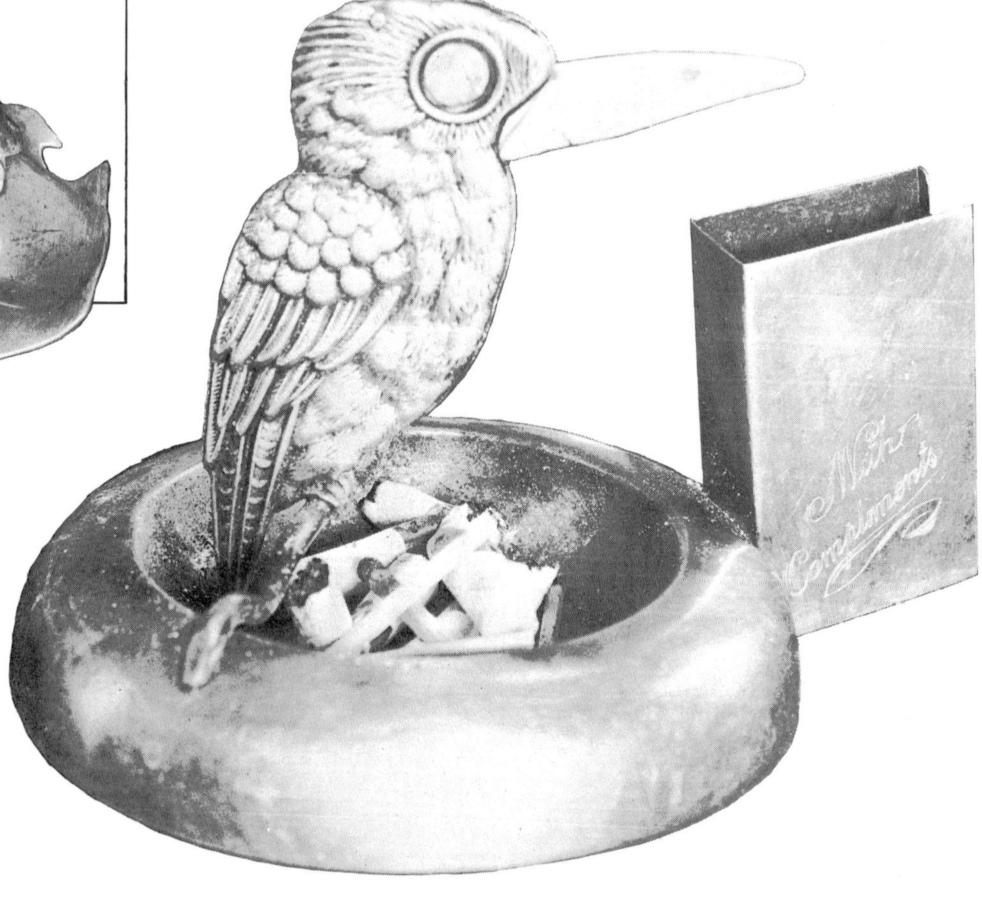
With Compliments

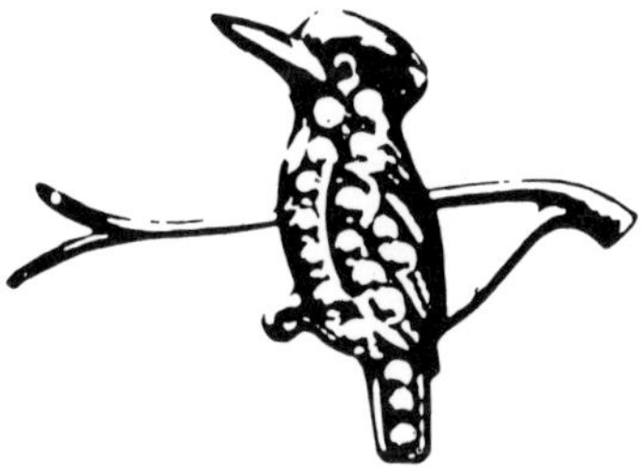

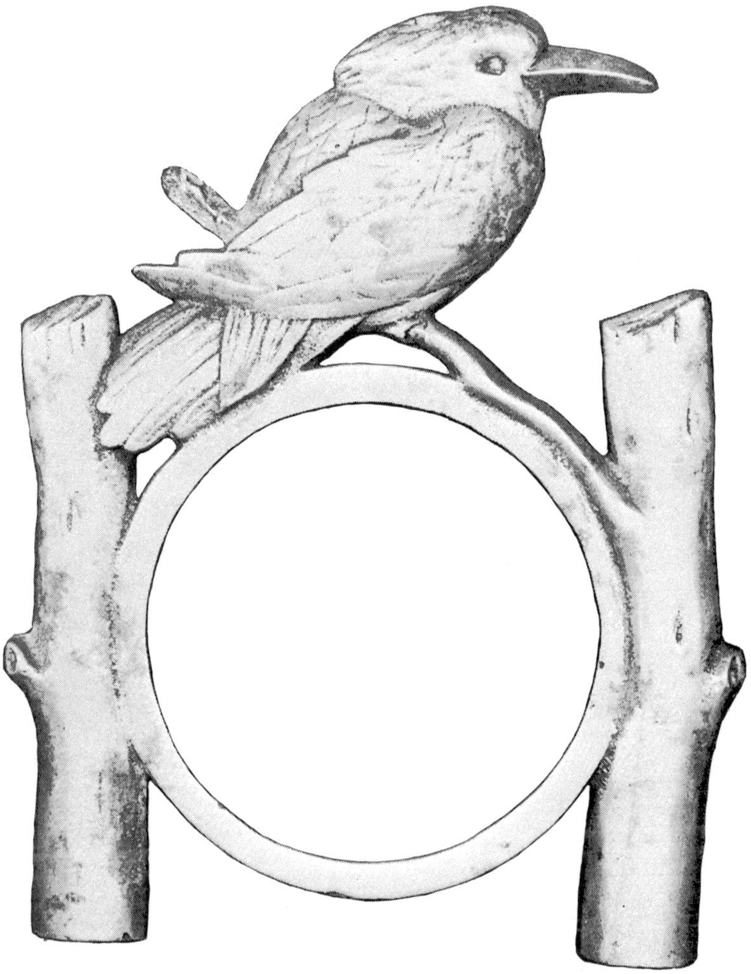

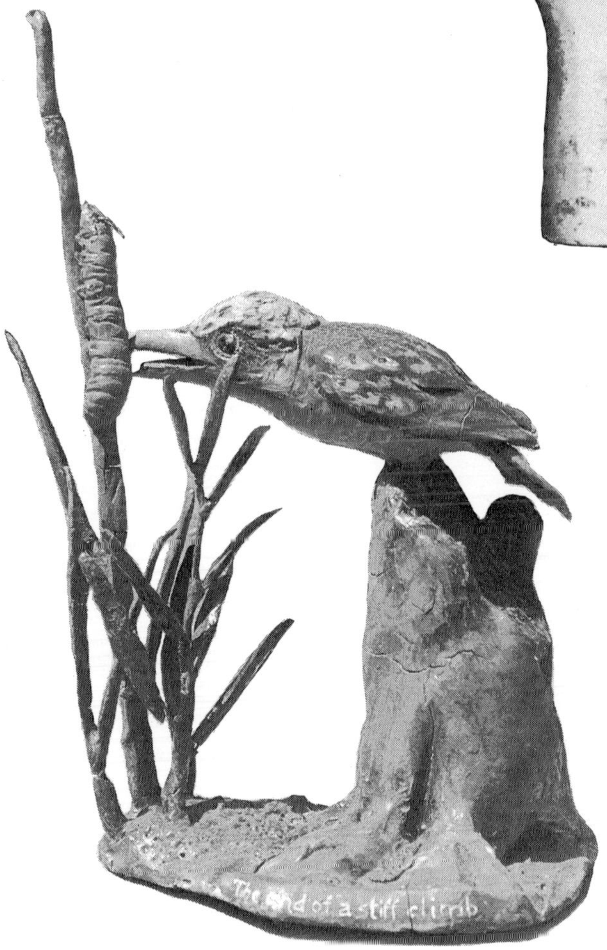

On opposite page: brass candlestick and ashtray, a silver-plated, gum-leaf-shaped toast rack with a kookaburra sitting on a stump, and a metal ashtray with matchbox holder and cigar cutter. On this page are a silver-plated napkin ring (above) and a composition ornamental kookaburra (left)

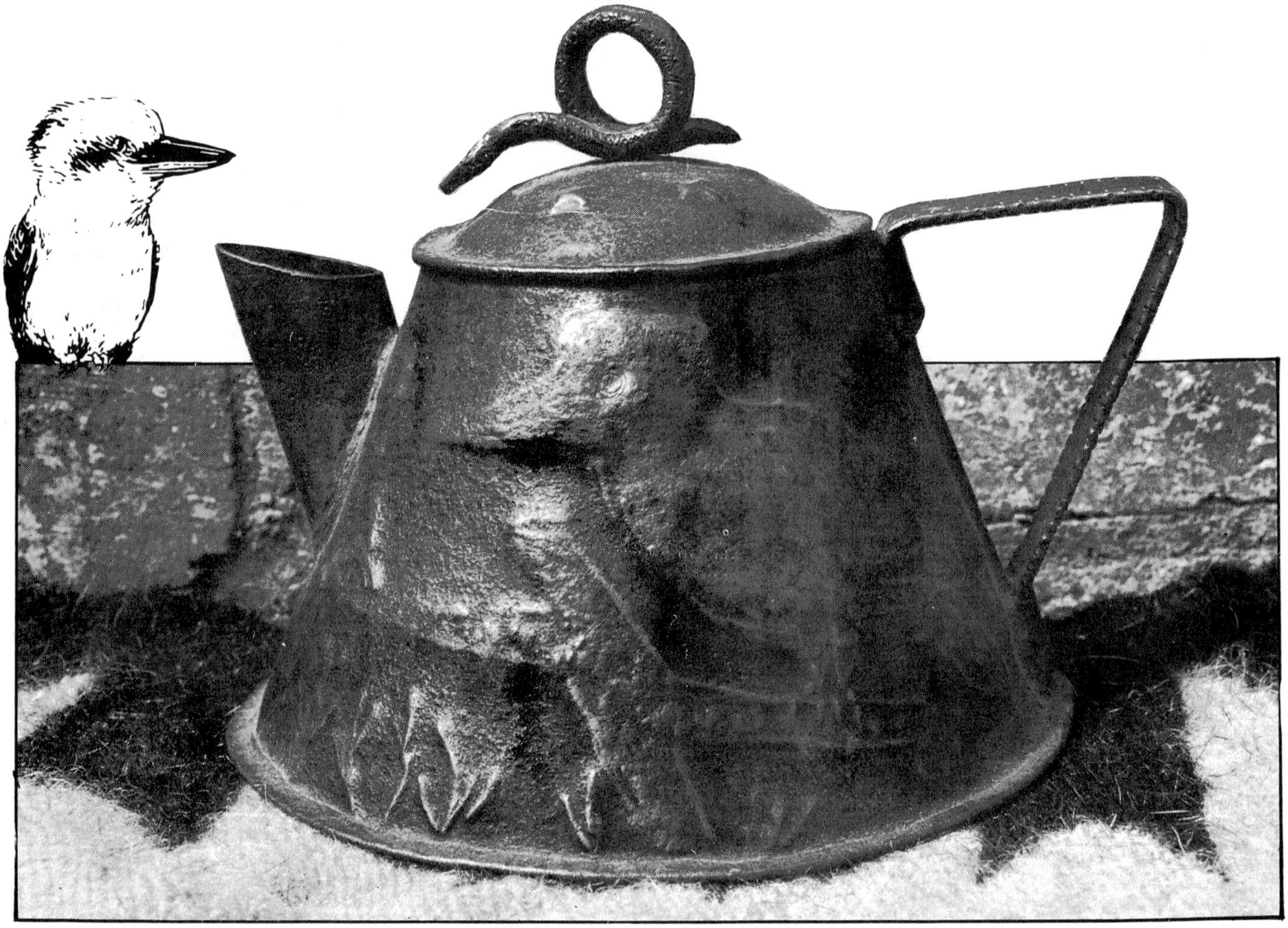

Jacko hunting for his snake on a metal teapot

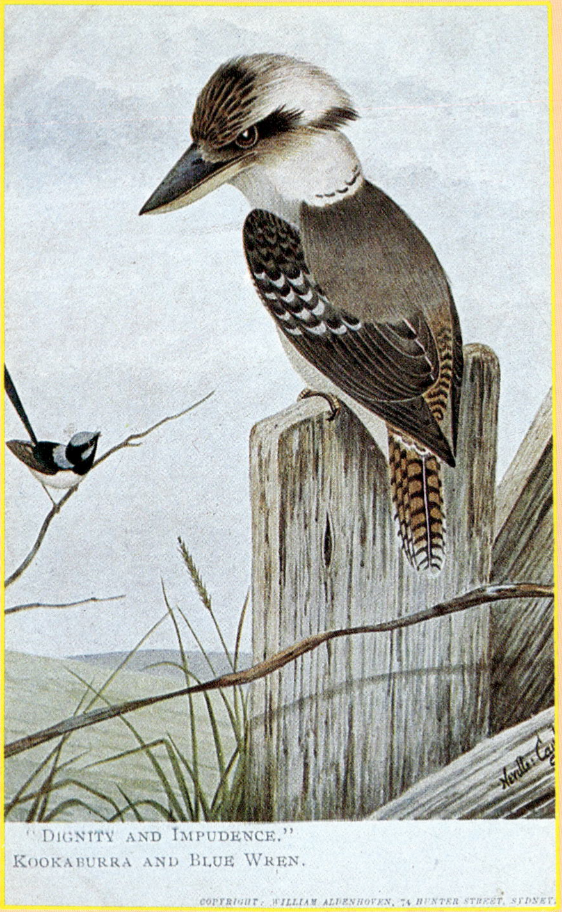

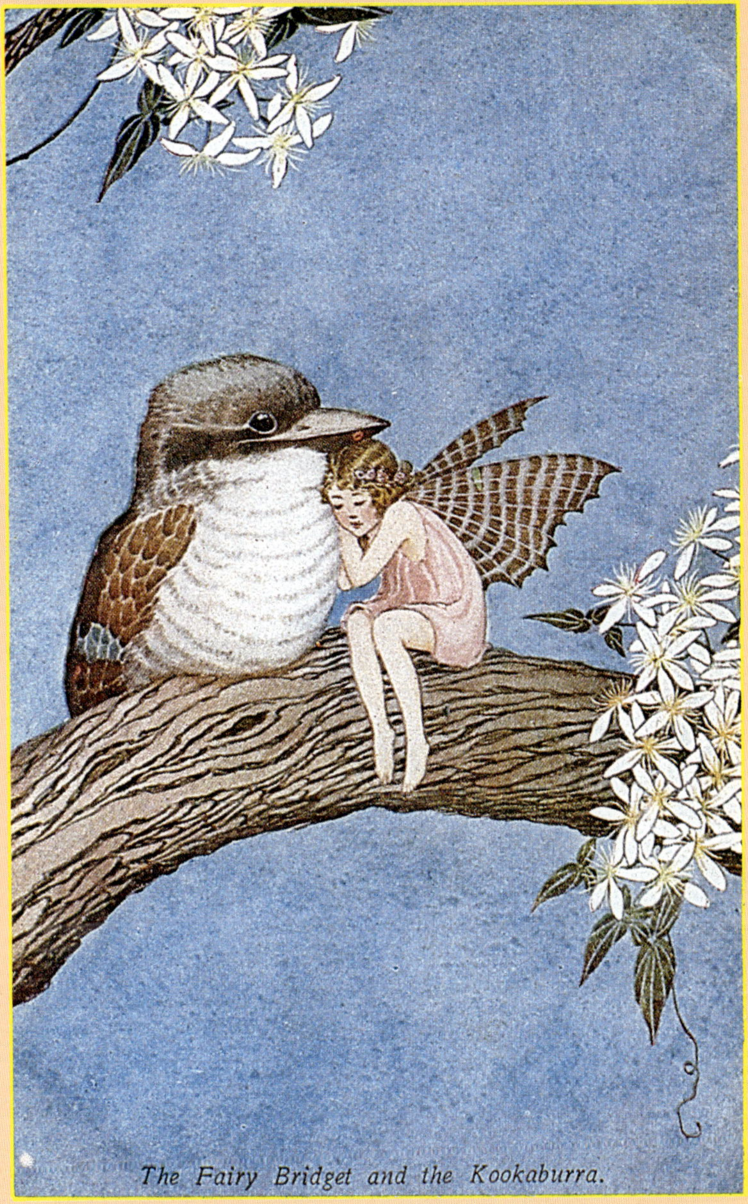

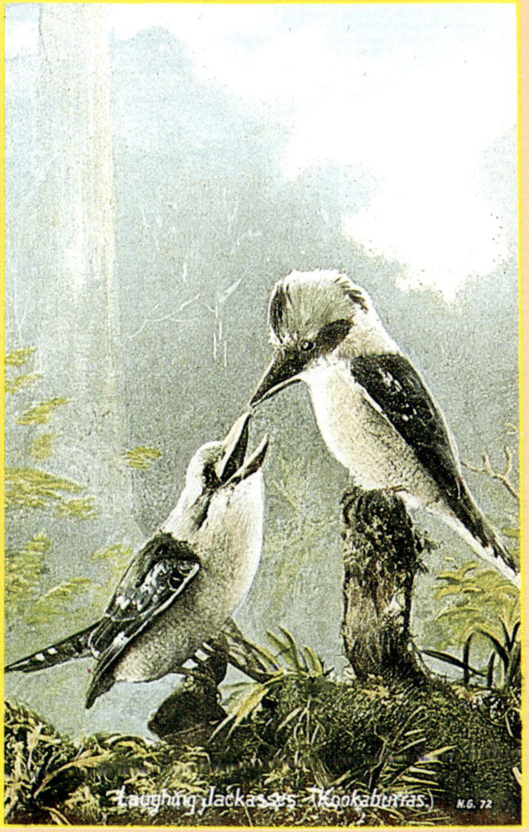

'Dignity and Impudence.' *Kookaburra and Blue Wren*: postcard from a painting by Neville Cayley senior (above left)

The Fairy Bridget and the Kookaburra: postcard illustration by Ida Rentoul Outhwaite (above)

Laughing Jackasses: postcard (left)

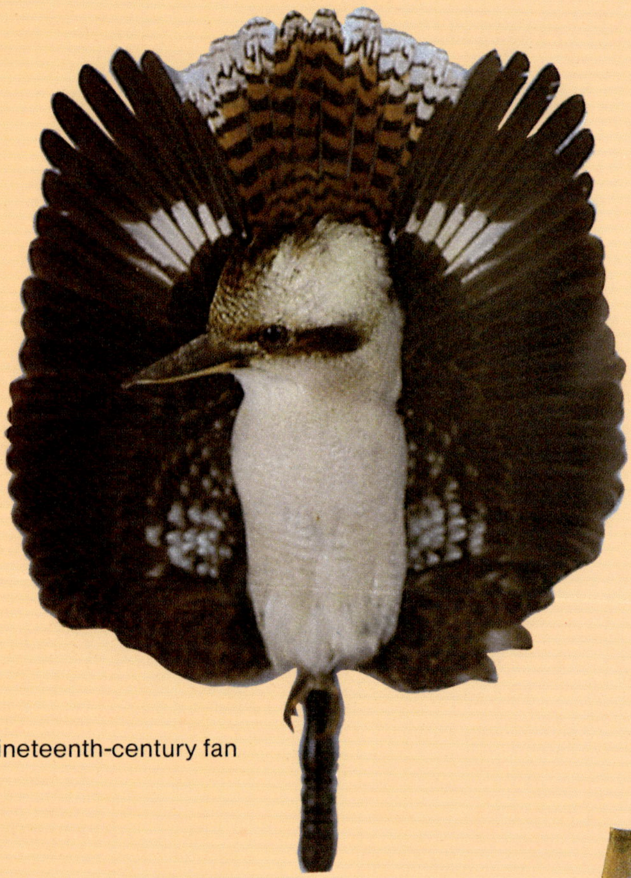

Nineteenth-century fan

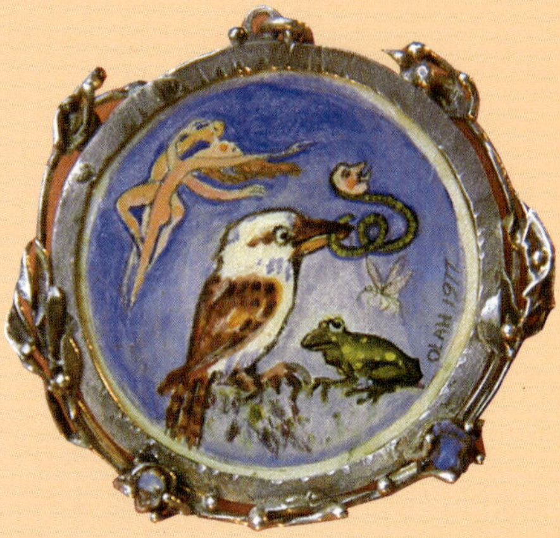

Enamelled silver brooch by
Elizabeth Olah, 1978

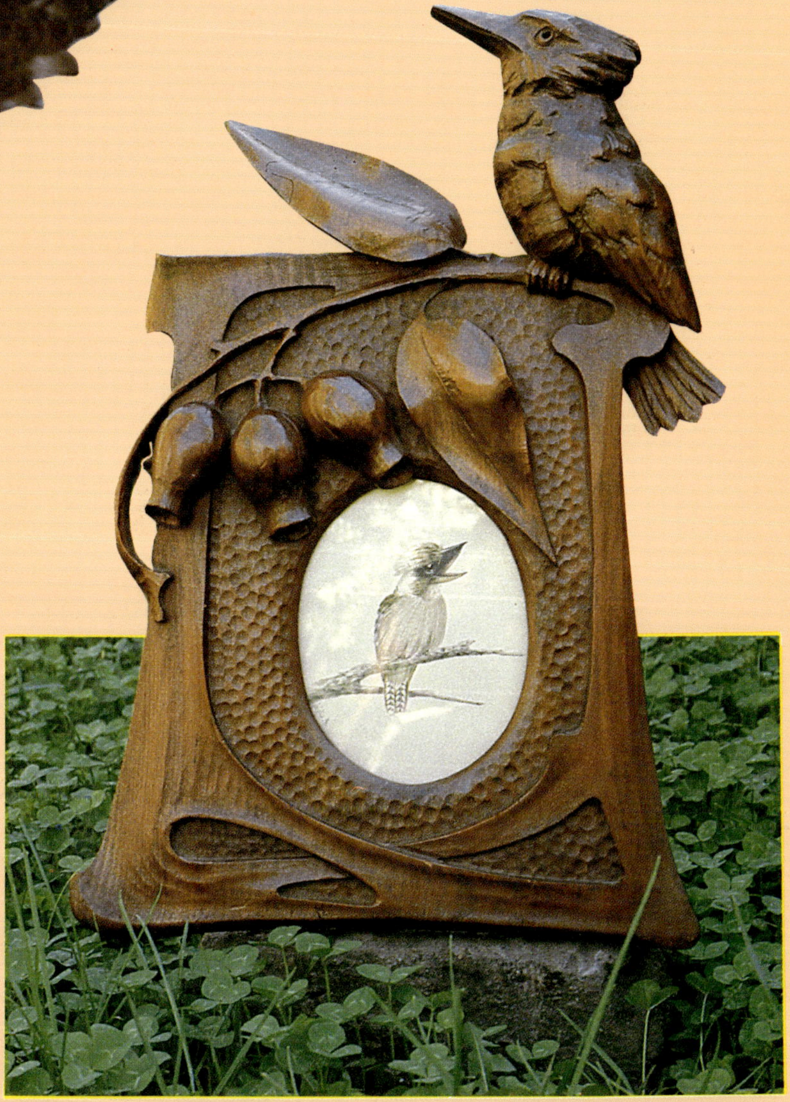

Gumnut nouveau picture frame by
Robert Prenzel

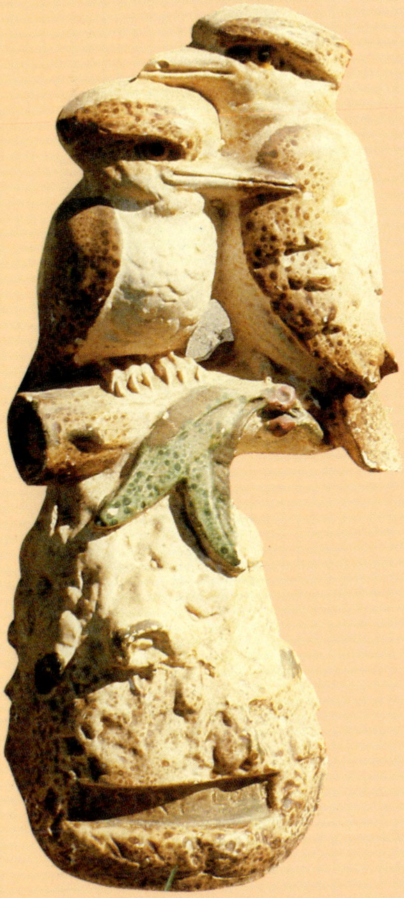

'A Story of Love' in plaster

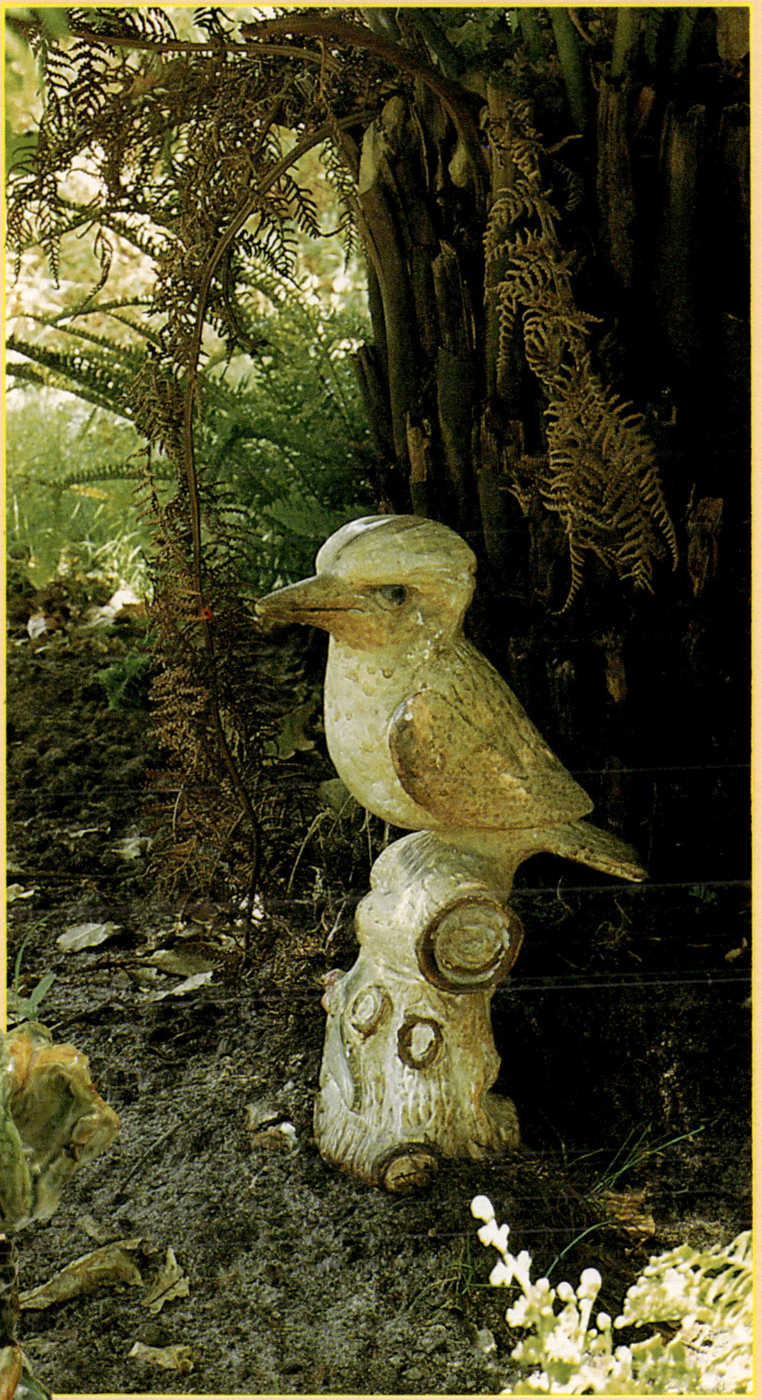

A common variety of the plaster kooka

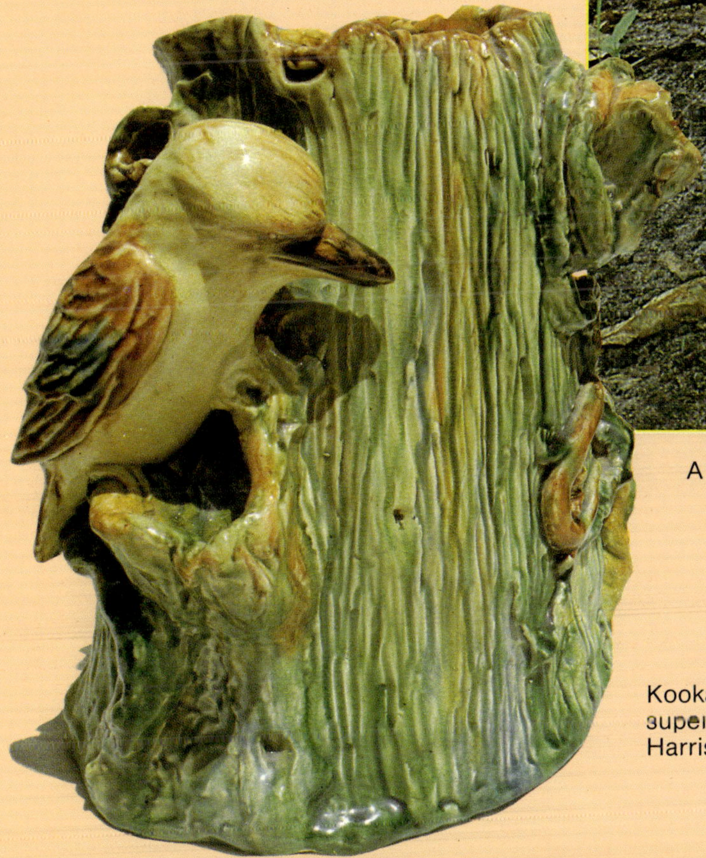

Kookaburra forever seeks his lizard on this superb pottery vase of the 1930s by Castle Harris

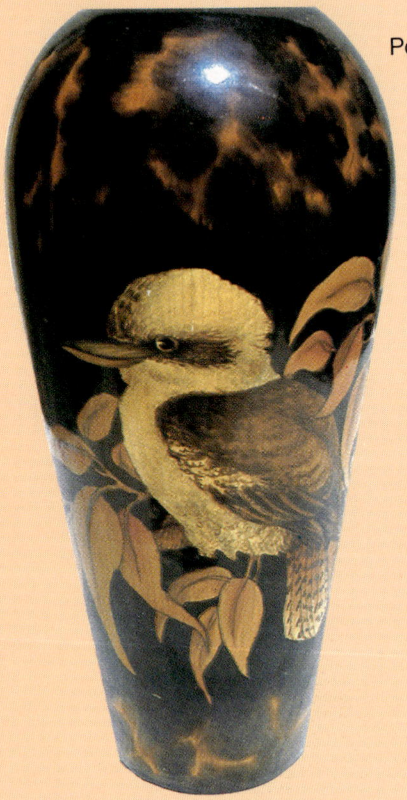

Pokerwork vase

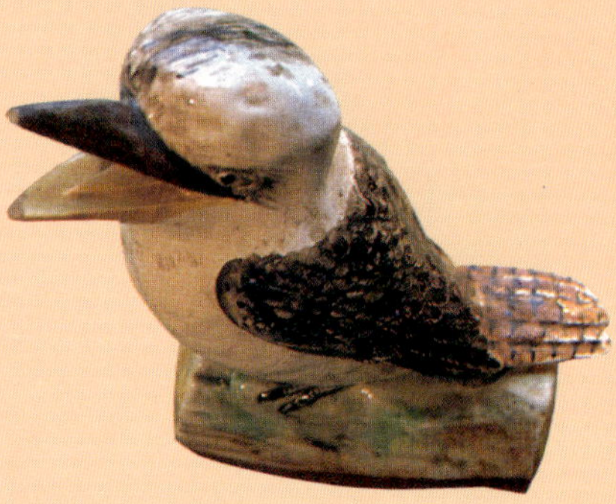

A fine pottery kookaburra of the 1930s (above) by Grace Seacombe of Sydney

Collection of pokerwork kookaburras (below)

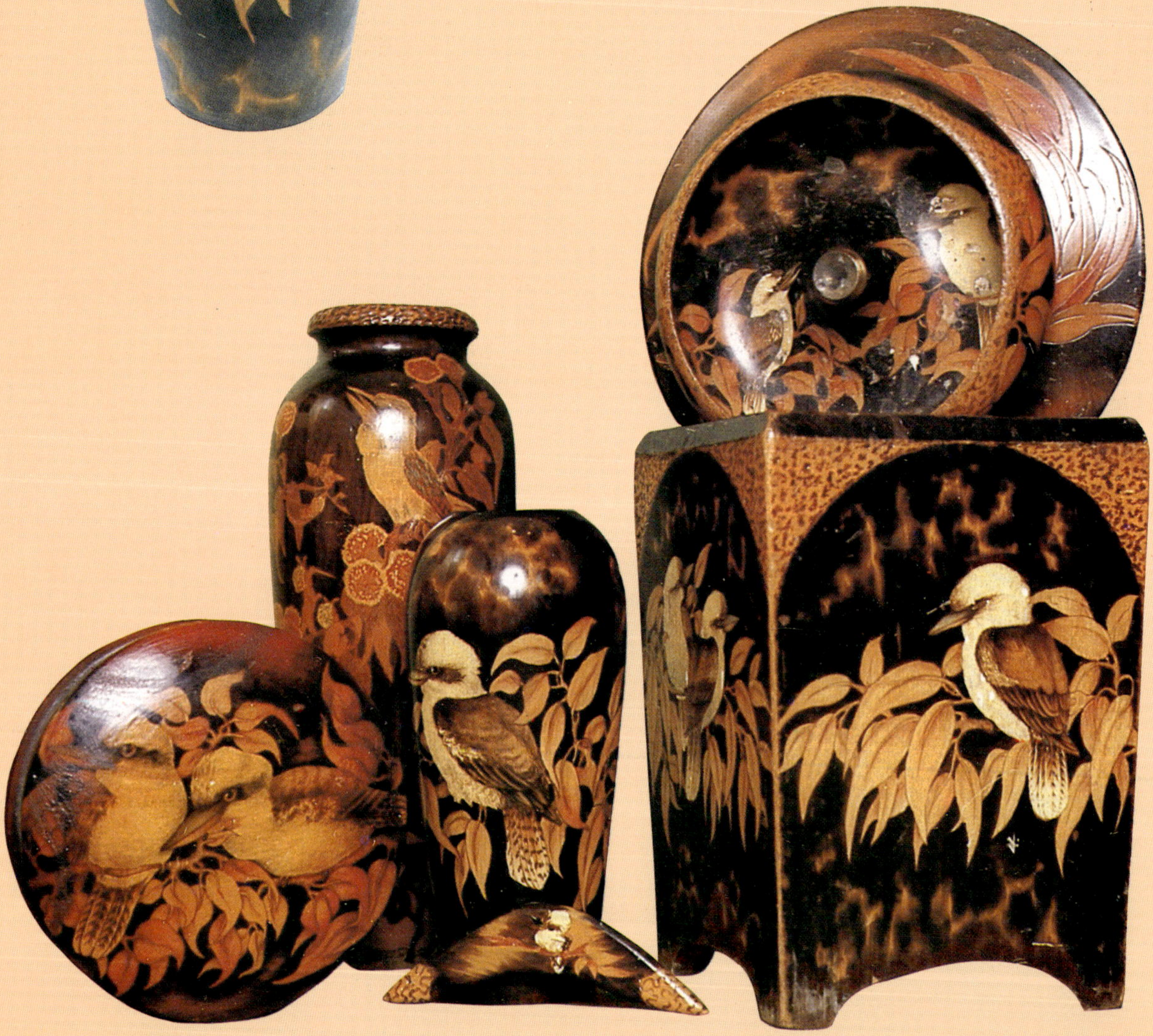

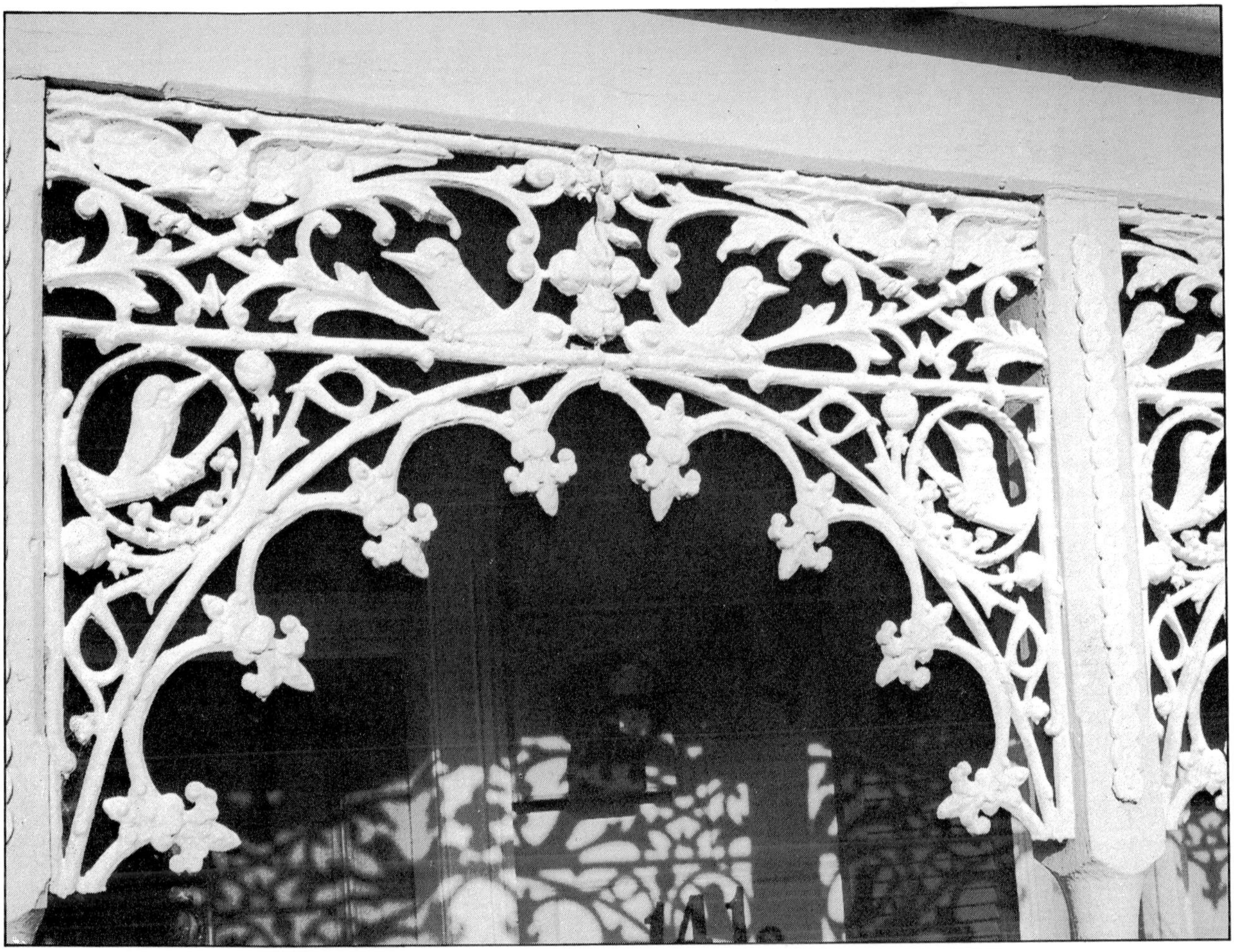

Kookaburra cast-iron frieze on a Melbourne house

CAST-IRON KOOKAS

The last decades of the nineteenth century saw the absolute heyday of ornamental cast iron in Australia. Australia's climate lent itself ideally to verandahs, so Victorian buildings in many Australian cities were lavishly provided with verandahs decorated with ornamental cast iron. On the authority of the late Dr E. Graeme Robertson, who did so much to arouse interest in this important part of our heritage, we have the assertion that Melbourne has more architectural cast-iron work than any other city in the world! Ironically (pardon the pun), Australians travel to New Orleans just to see the lace-decorated buildings.

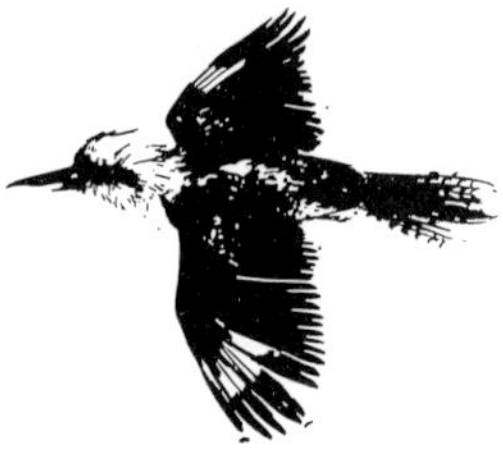

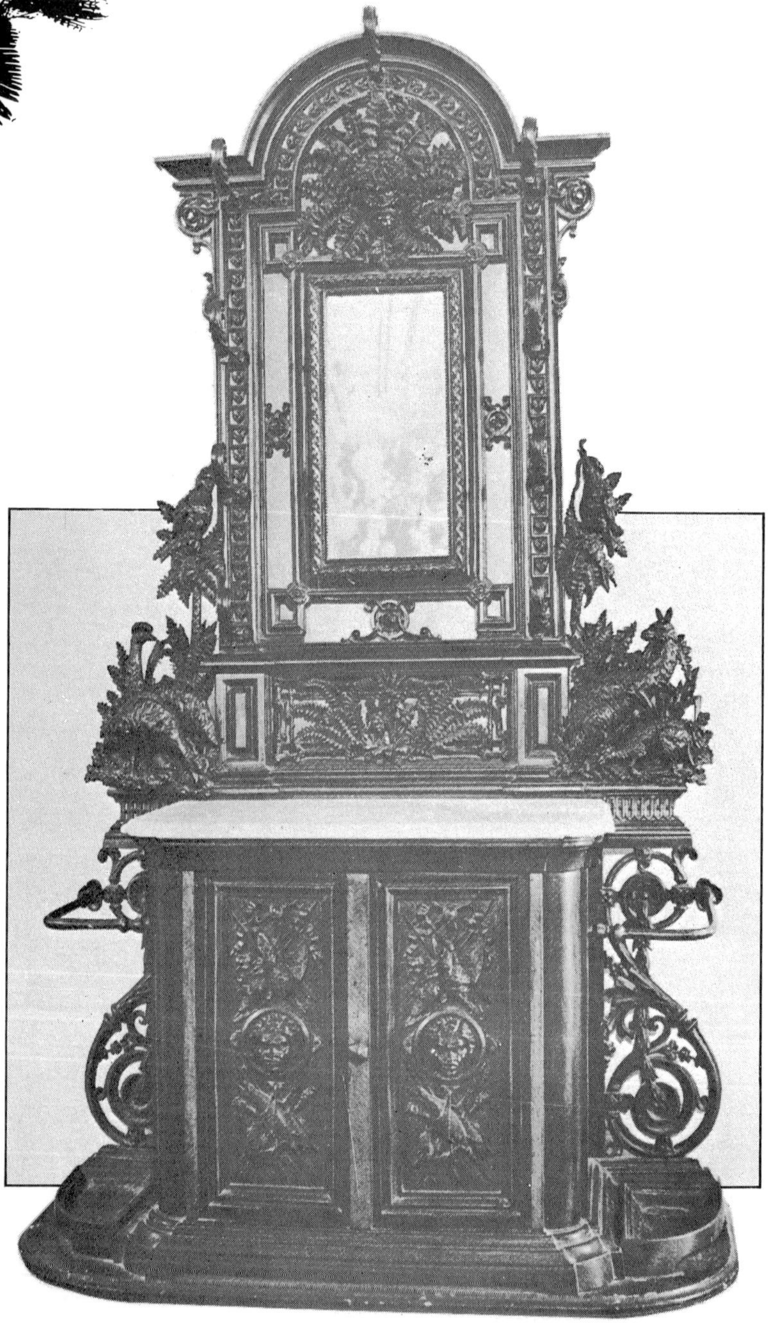

Cast-iron and marble hallstand in the collection of the National Trust (Victoria) at Ripponlea. Note the kookaburra with his snake on the right-hand side of the mirror

Foundries flourished in Australian cities and many original lace designs were registered for copyright purposes. Dr Robertson records that in New South Wales 23 foundries registered 161 designs between 1870 and 1900. In South Australia 29 designs were registered in the period 1880–85 and in Queensland 8 foundries registered 74 patterns between 1885 and 1902.

Although most of the motifs used in this period were of universal significance, some memorable Australian motifs included the kangaroo, the emu, the sulphur-crested cockatoo and various honeyeaters. One wonderful frieze and bracket featured a kookaburra depicted side on, with wings outstretched. Some years ago there were a number of houses in Melbourne fortunate enough to have this unusual design. But again, progress strikes; now, we do not know of any kookaburra lace remaining intact.

Another important cast-iron kooka lives on a rather grand hallstand (see illustration on page 90). An Aboriginal mask backed with fern fronds decorates the top; on one side cassowaries nestle into tree ferns upon which perches a cockatoo, and on the other side there are kangaroos. Triumphantly flanking the mirror is our hero in typical pose, brandishing a snake. Further Aboriginal masks and implements decorate the two lower doors.

The hallstand, a small number of which are known to exist, bears English registration marks from 1864. However, the Australian-motif brackets were registered on 20 January 1886 by W. K. Thomson and S. Renwick (trading as J. McEwan & Co.). The original carved timber moulds were collected at Bendigo, so the castings for this ornate piece may have been done there.

JEWELLERY

One decorative application of the kookaburra motif was in the manufacture of jewellery, usually the popular variety rather than grand pieces, although the odd diamond-set kooka does exist. Because the kookaburra was a folk symbol, the majority of decorative kookaburra items were homely and within most people's reach, not made for connoisseurs or the wealthy.

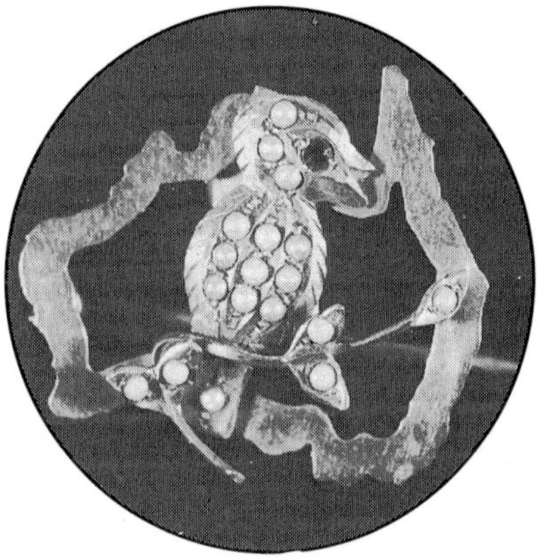

Pearl-studded kookaburra brooch framed in a map of Australia

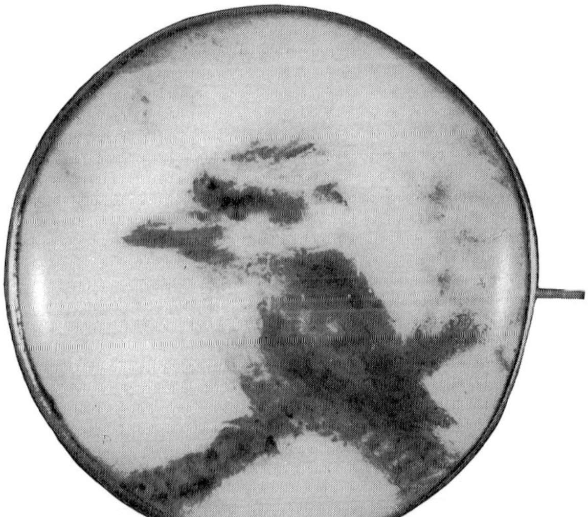

Painted porcelain brooch

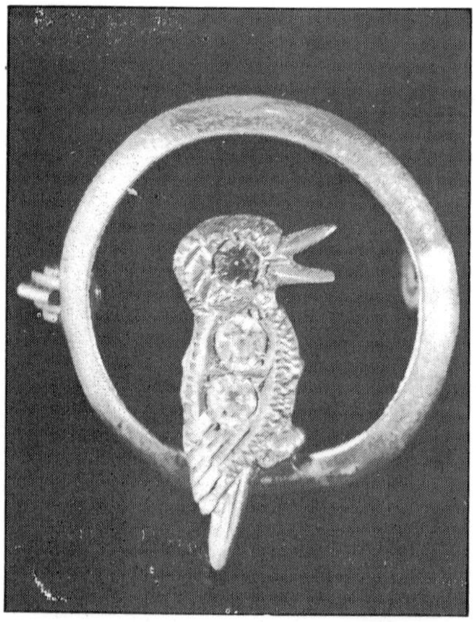

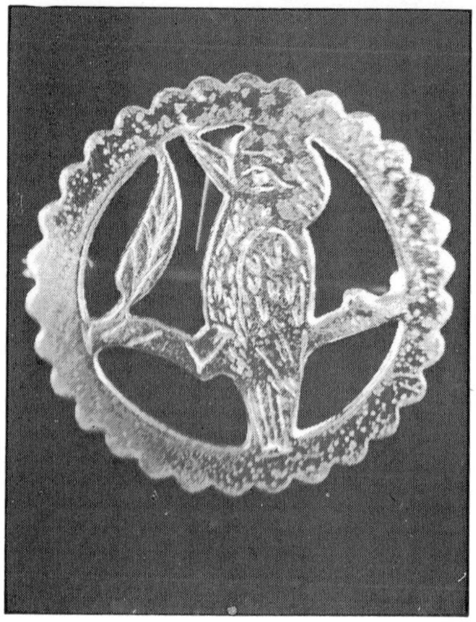

Two decorative metal brooches

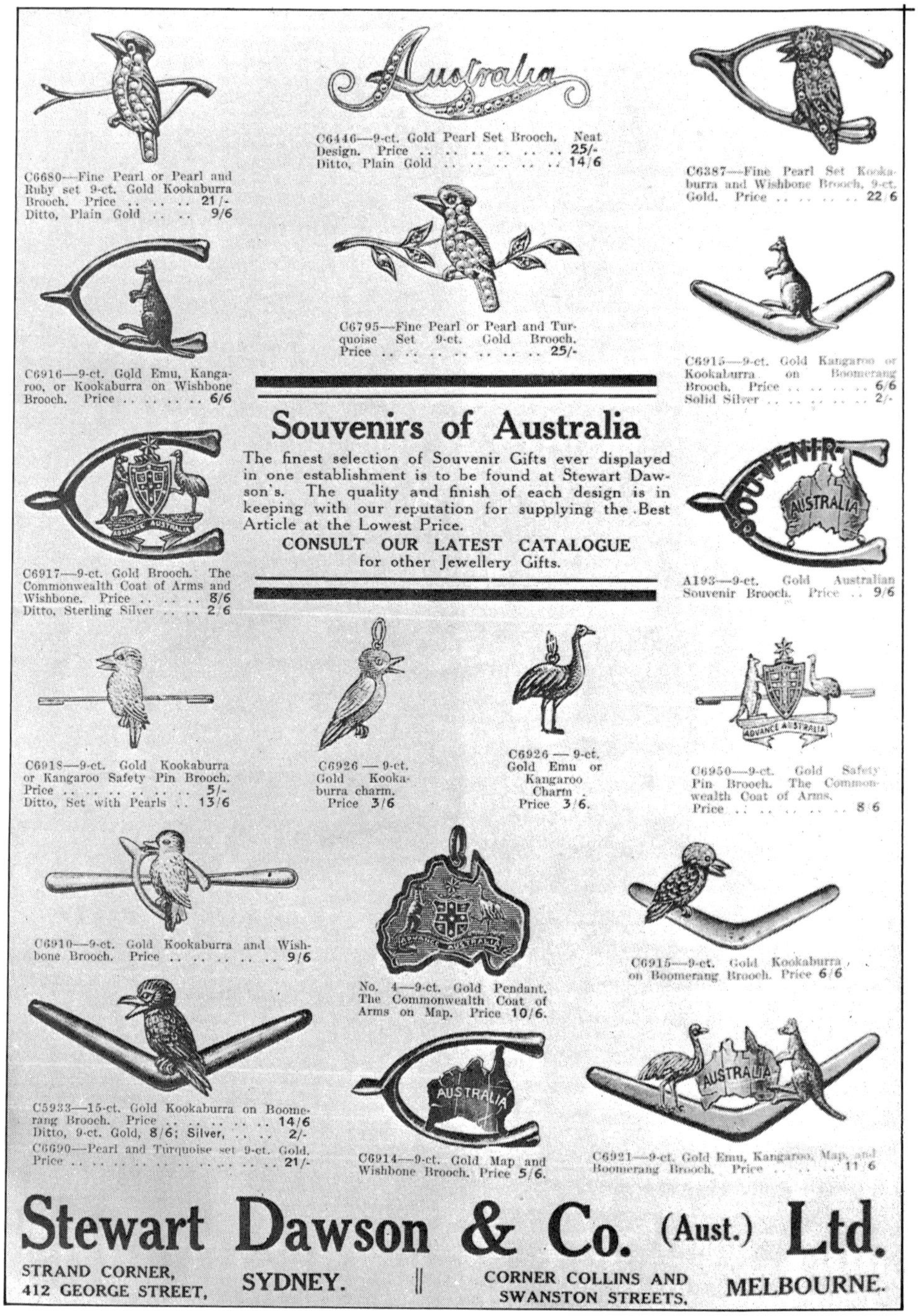

Full-page advertisement by Stewart Dawson & Company, 1917. Jewellery illustrated here can be found in antique or second-hand shops today

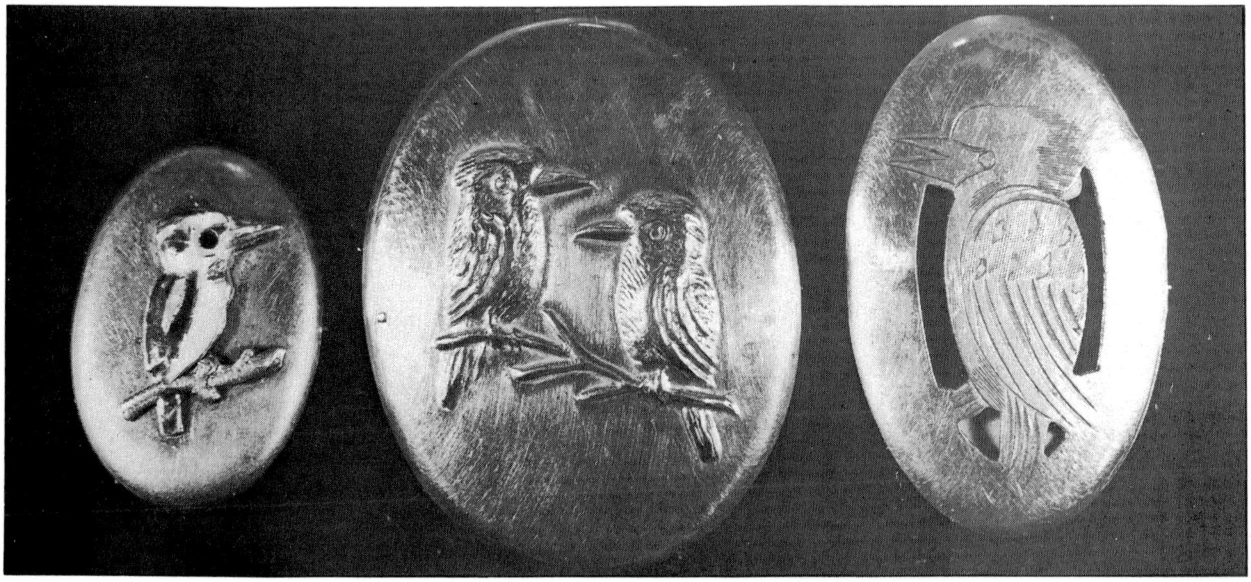

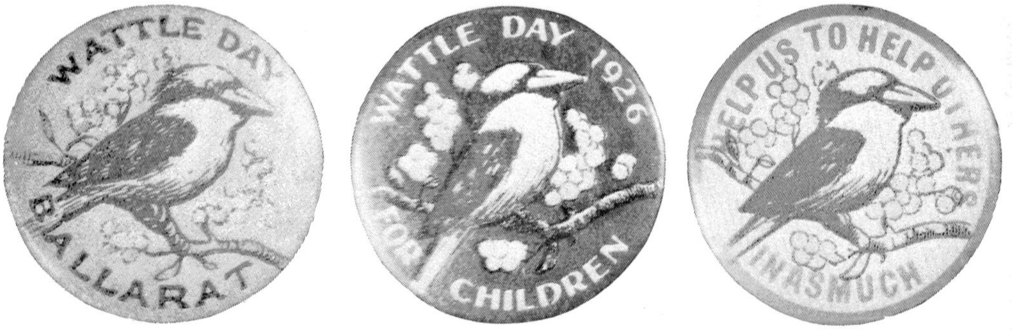

Pressed brass kookaburra brooches and Wattle Day badges (above). Painted ceramic brooch right)

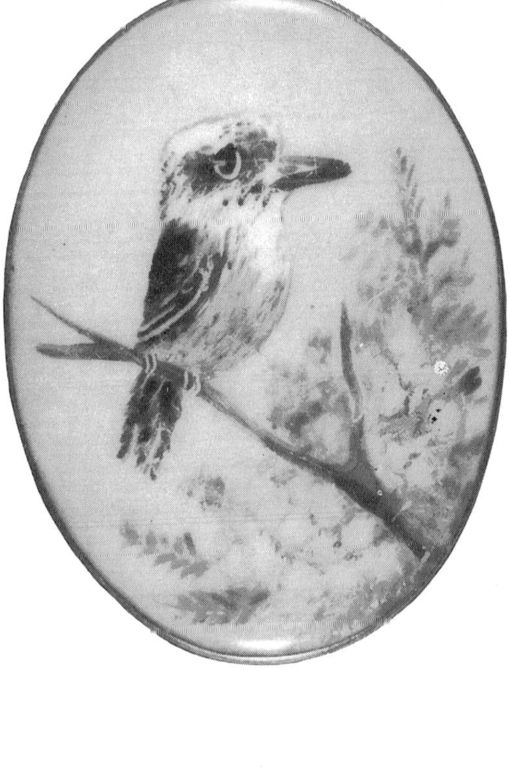

Many kookaburra brooches were moulded or stamped in brass or base-metal and plated with silver or gold. Some were roughly engraved. Charming painted ceramic versions and kookaburras set with semi-precious stones also occur.

At the time, brooches were made with kangaroos, emus, maps of Australia and Southern Crosses as well. In a 1917 jewellery advertisement (illustrated on opposite page), typical items are displayed. Popular demand continued into the 1920s and 1930s.

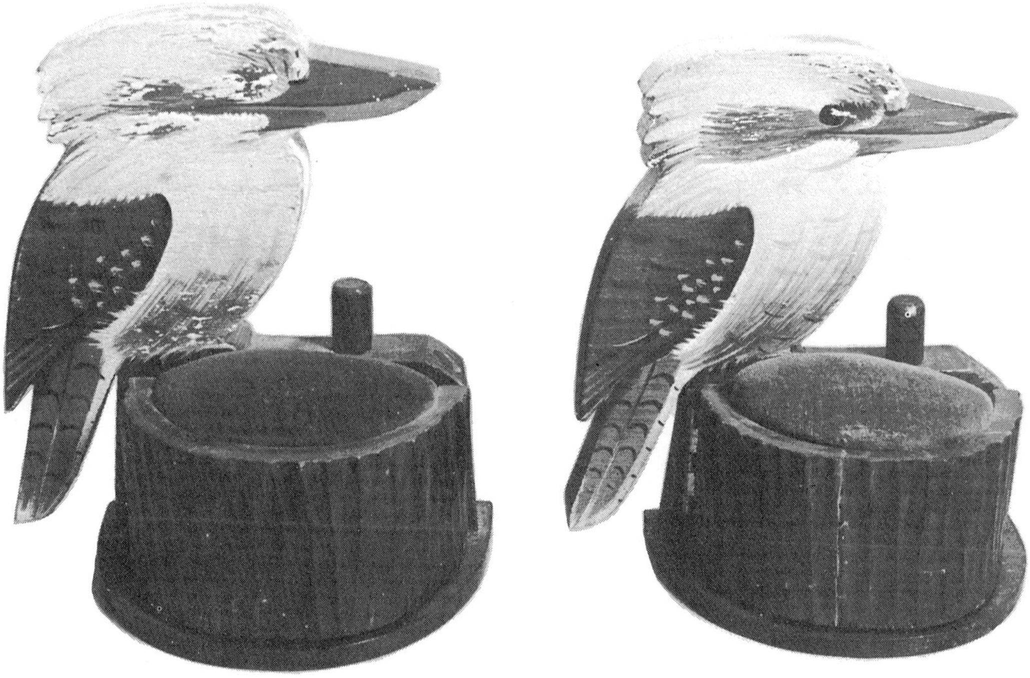

Painted wooden kookaburras adorn cottonreel holders and pincushions

POKERWORK AND PAINTED WOOD

The kookaburra was a favourite subject in Australian pokerwork and painted wooden items. Pokerwork (or pyrography) is done by rubbing the tip of a hot pokerwork tool over the surface of the wooden object being decorated. Tones from light brown to black can be produced. Pokerwork had been a folk art for centuries in places like Madagascar, Africa, Central Europe and South America. Dürer, the famous sixteenth-century German artist, is known to have worked in this medium. In nineteenth-century England, pokerwork was a favourite hobby. Australian hobbyists took to this ancient craft in the early twentieth century and used it to depict their favourite symbols. Often Australian pokerwork items were painted in bright colours. Other items in this genre were simply painted and did not feature any actual pokerwork.

The kookaburra, often used in conjunction with gum leaves, was the favourite motif. A wide range of items like vases, doily holders, smokers' stands, pedestals, boxes, jardinières, bookends, breadboards and other small gift items were made, especially in the 1920s and 1930s. The craze became so popular that commercial factories in Australia produced machine-made pokerwork items for the souvenir market.

Many interesting little painted, cut-out kookaburra items were also made in the form of matchholders, needleholders, cottonreel holders and good luck tokens.

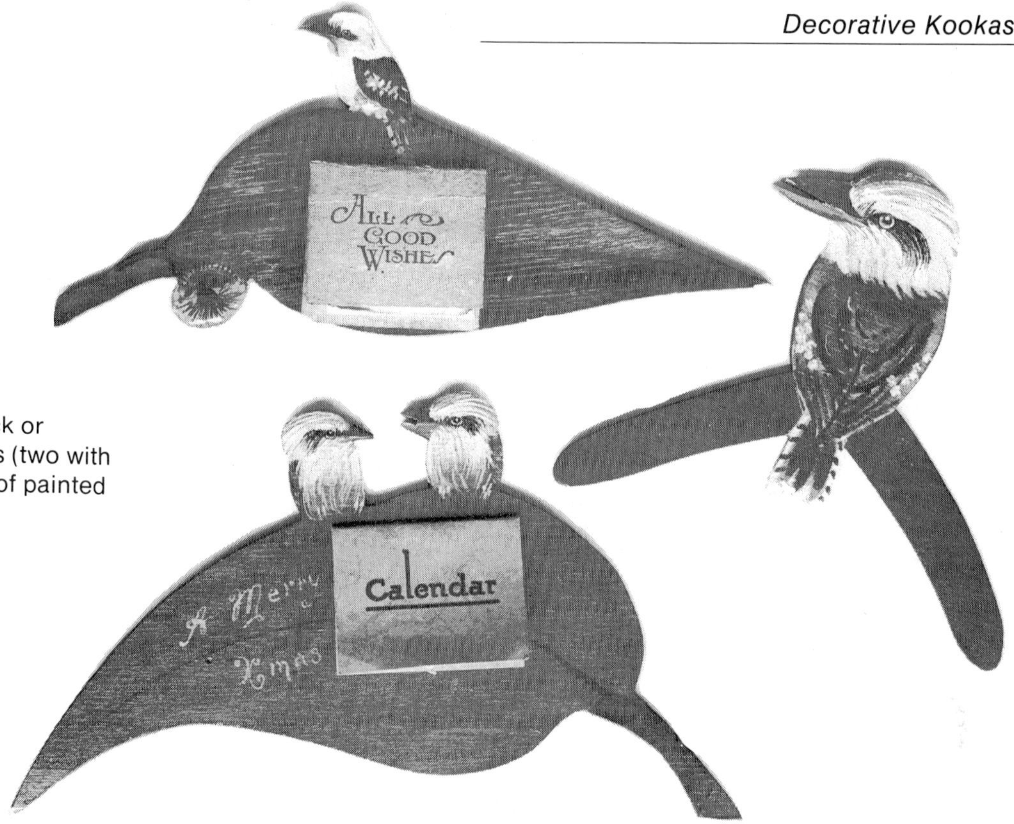

These good luck or greeting tokens (two with calendars) are of painted wood

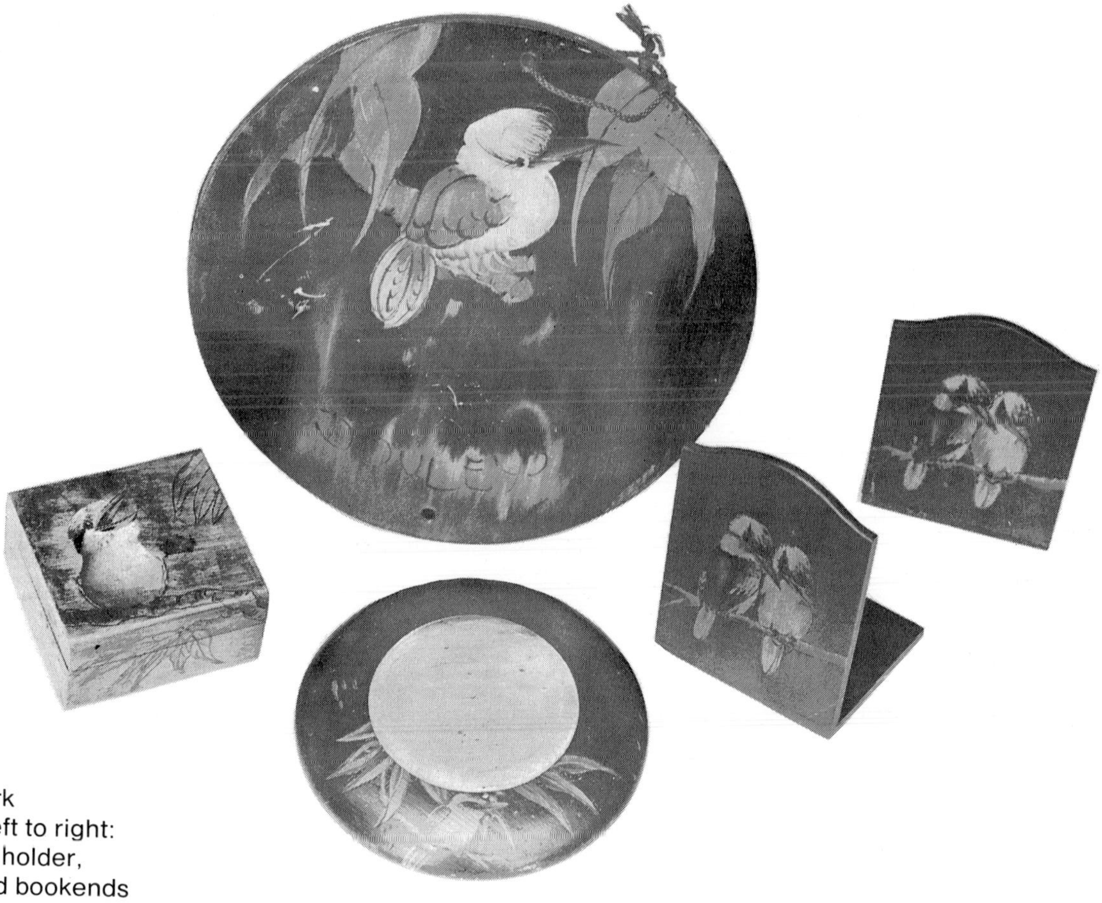

Some pokerwork kookaburras. Left to right: small box, doily holder, teapot stand and bookends

NEEDLEWORK

Another medium in which one finds many decorative kookaburras is needlework, produced in the days when long winter evenings had to be filled with activities other than watching television. Legions of keen needlewomen devoured the information and ideas that came to them through the women's pages of the popular newspapers, like *The Weekly Times* in Victoria, and through the women's magazines of the day like *New Idea*, *Australian Home Journal* and the *Australian Woman's Mirror*. Prominent needlewomen supplied patterns to these magazines for crochet, lace and embroidery. Additionally, manufacturers produced printed designs. A number of examples using the kookaburra motif are illustrated.

An embroidered teacosy

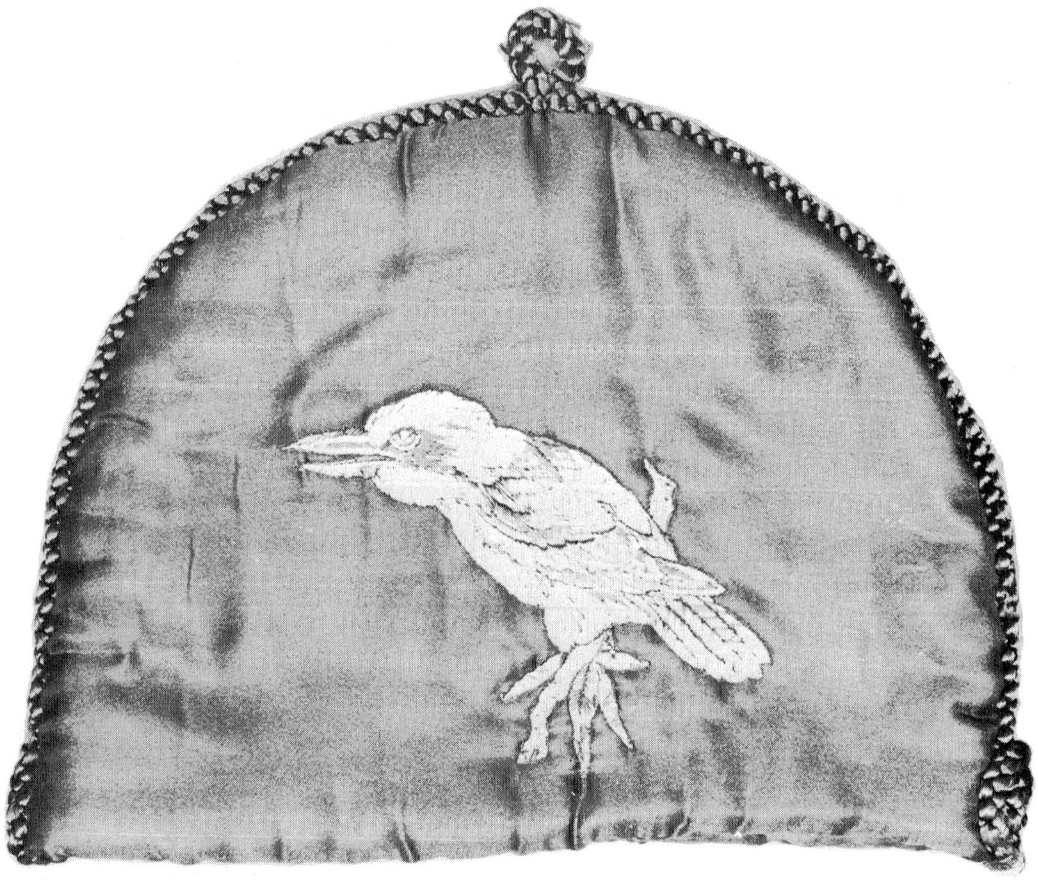

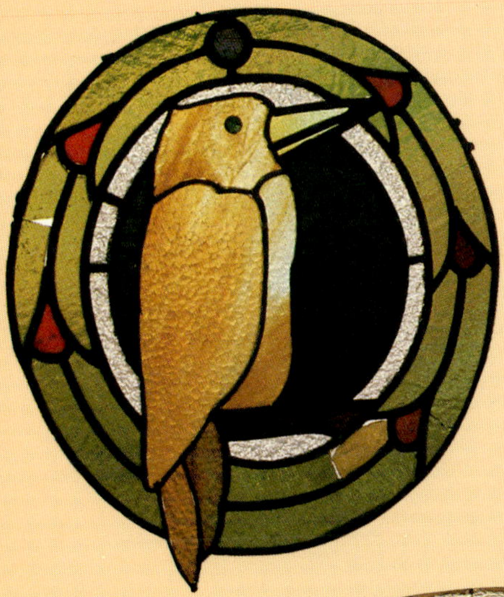

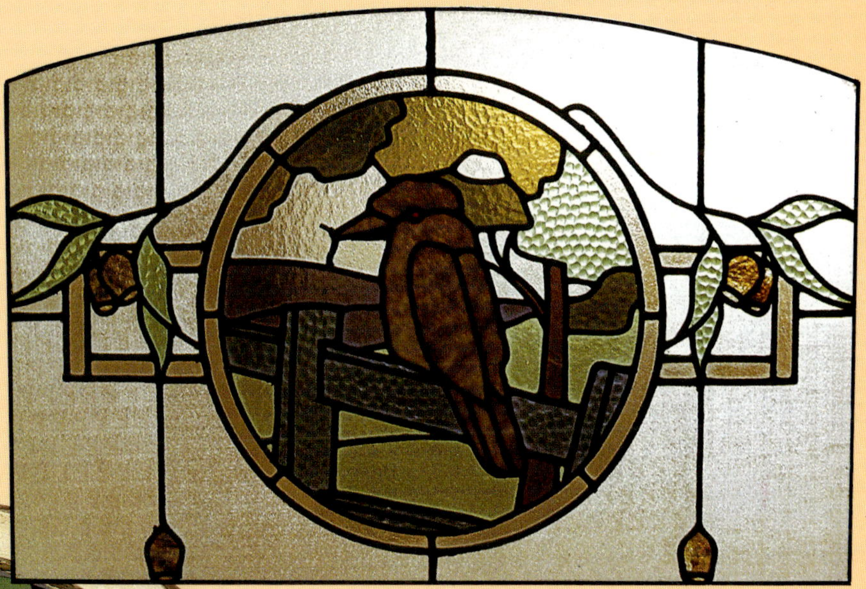

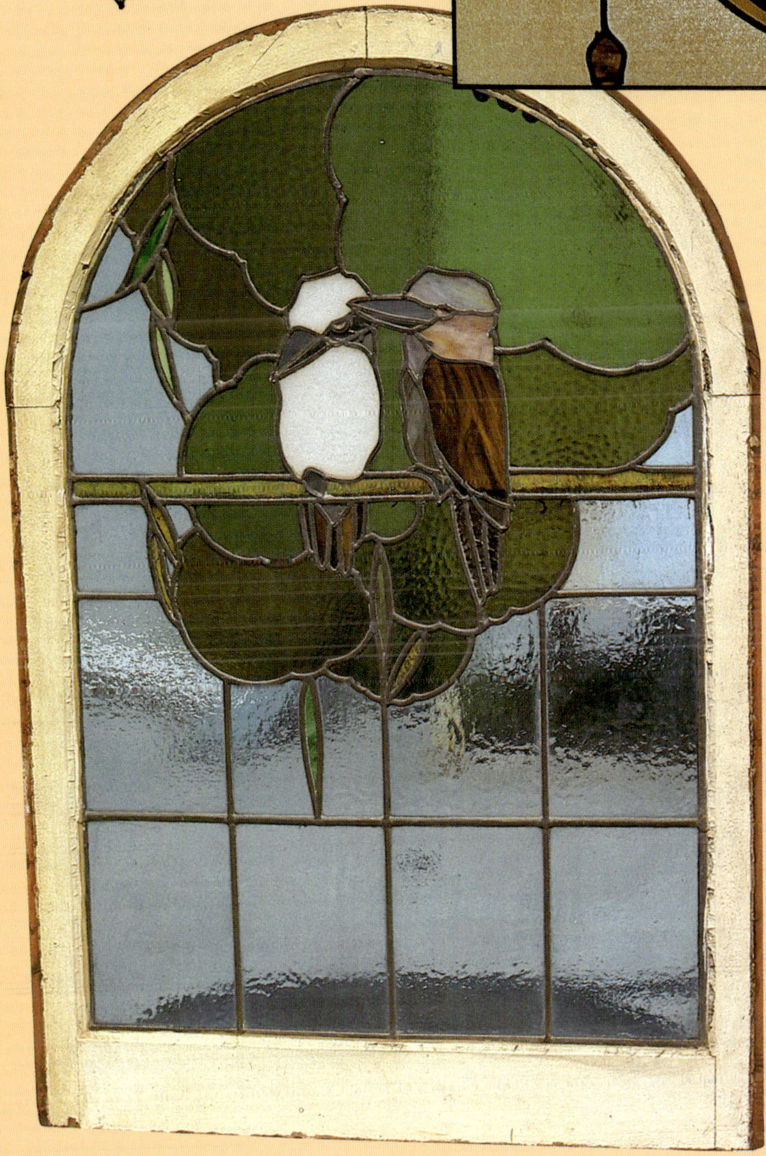

Four pieces of twentieth-century stained glass that feature Laughing Jack

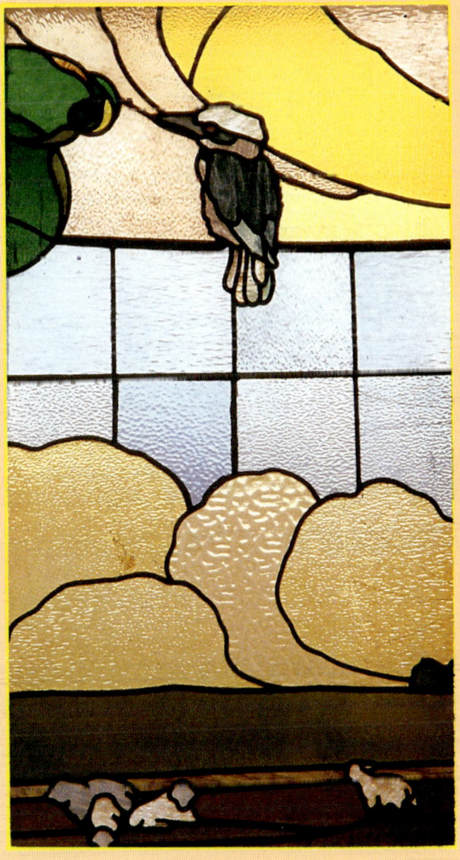

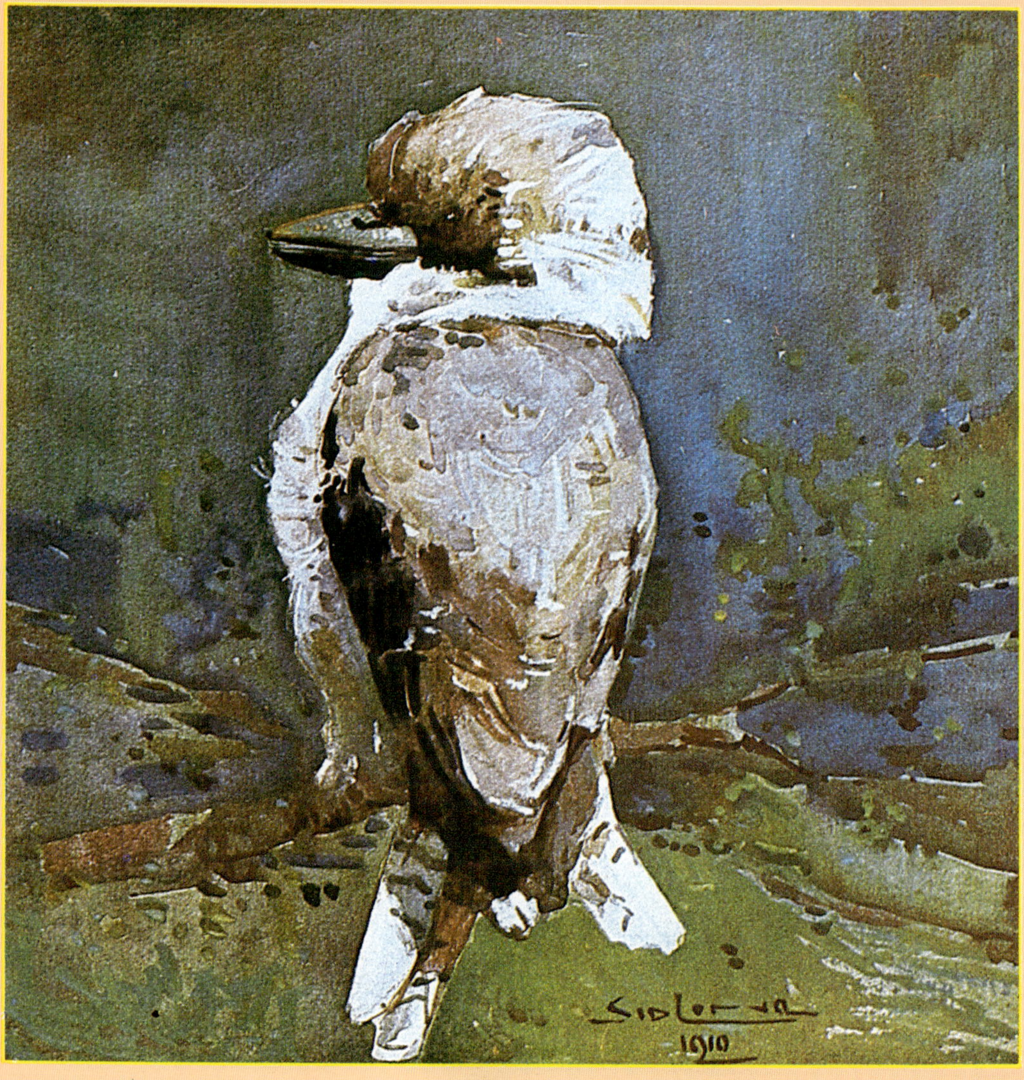

Oil painting by Sid Long
1910

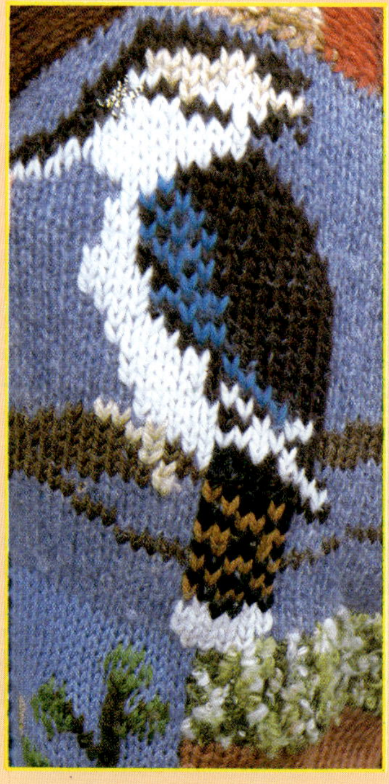

Art knitwear by Rachelle
King of Melbourne

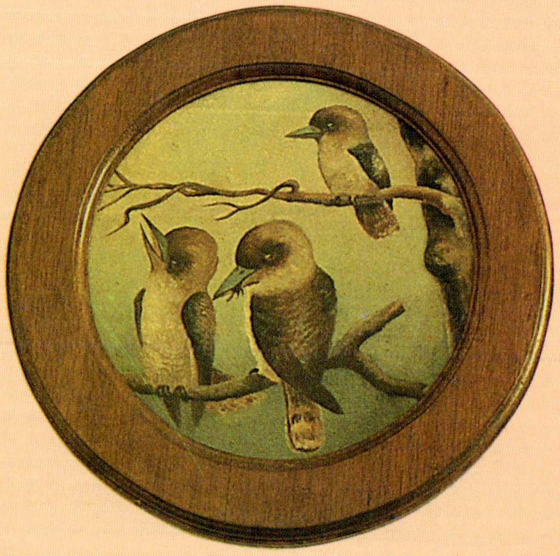

Primitive oil painting on wood

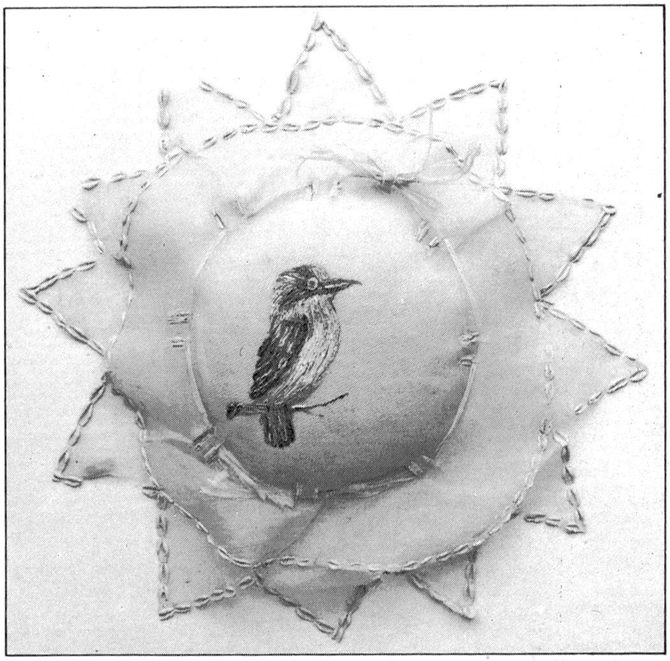

Embroidered and beaded pincushion (right) and a machine-made crochet milk jug cover (below)

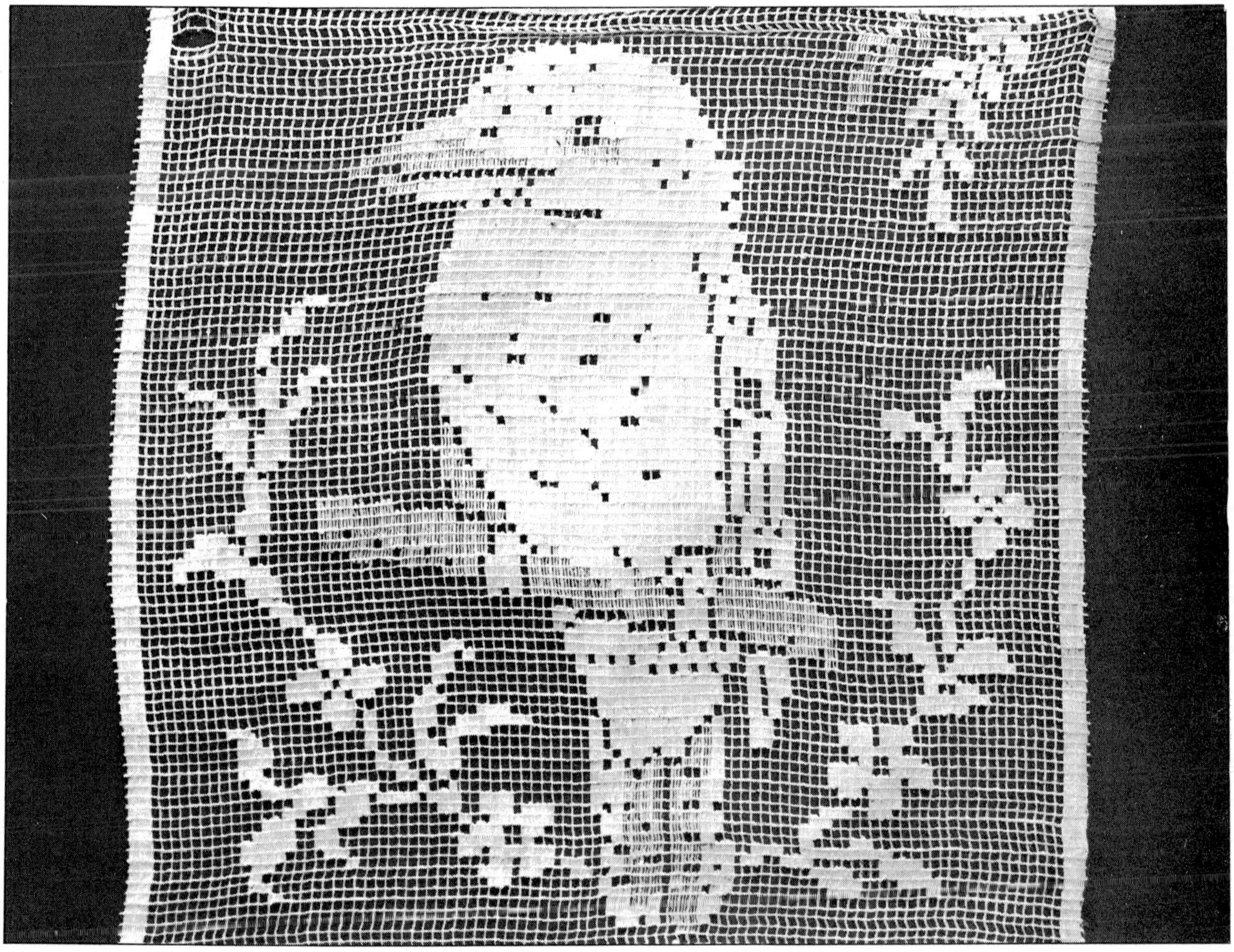

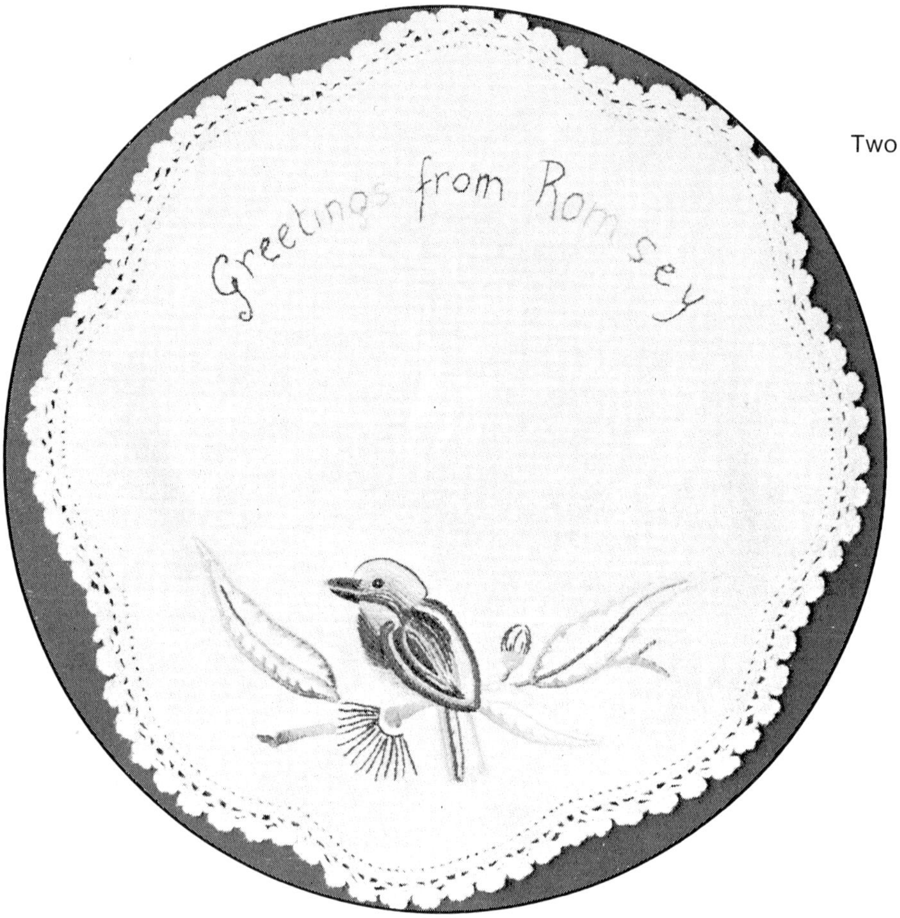

Two embroidered kookaburras

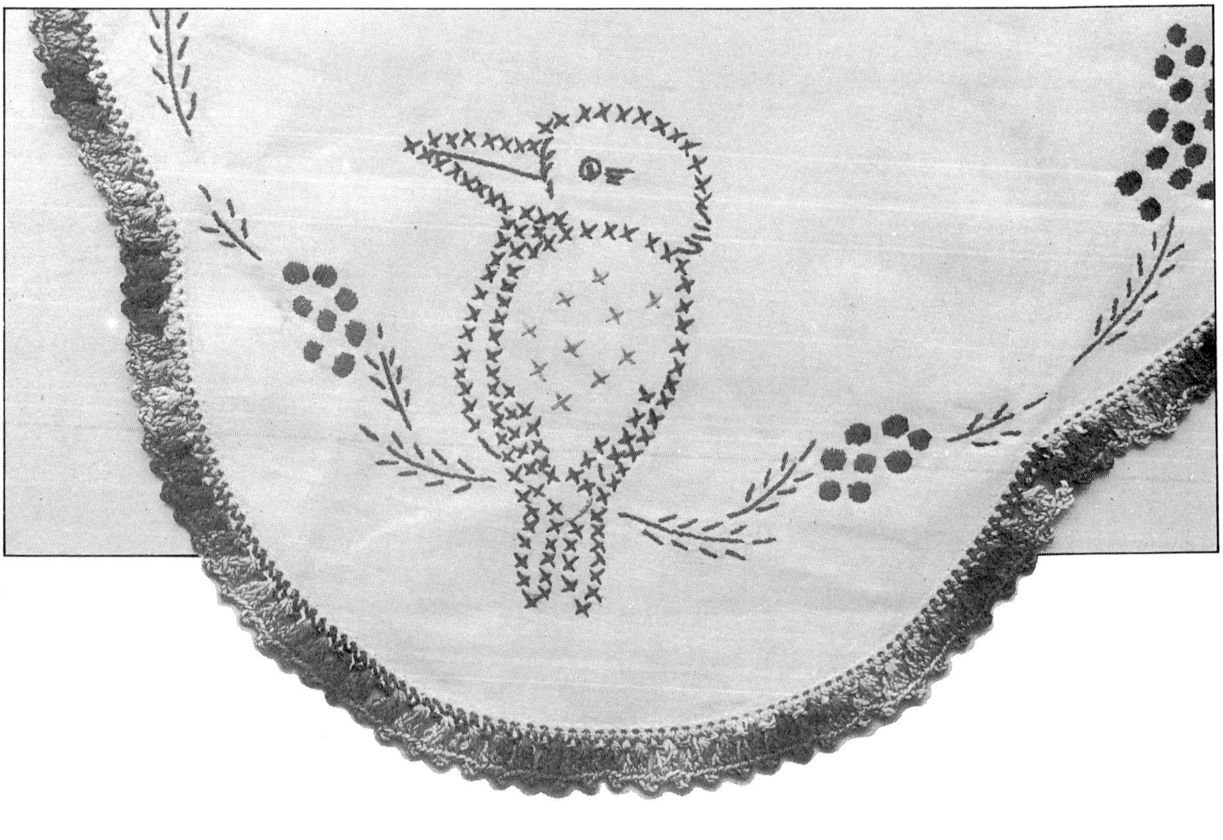

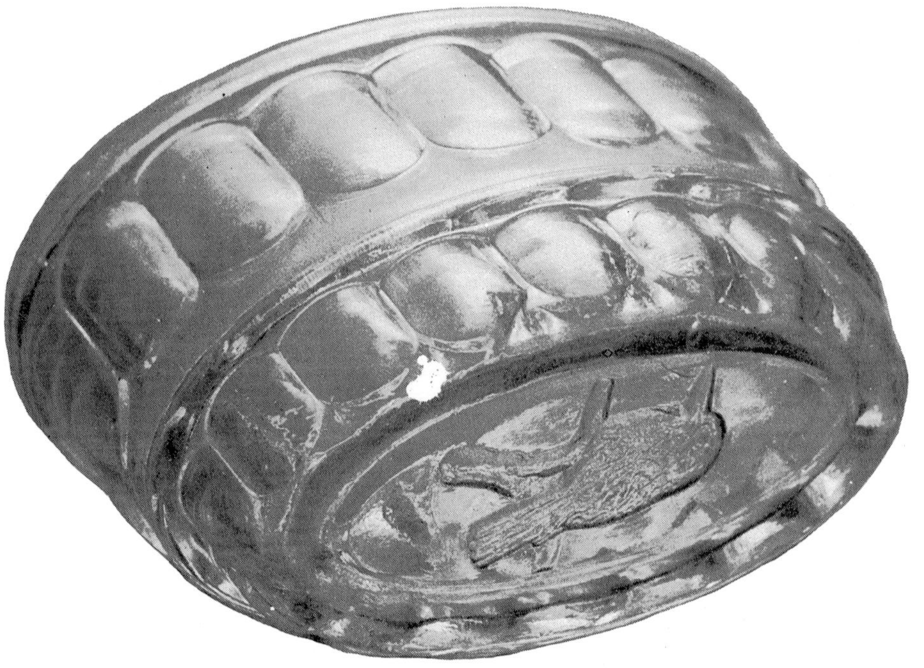

Glass jelly mould (above) and a carnival-glass bowl (below)

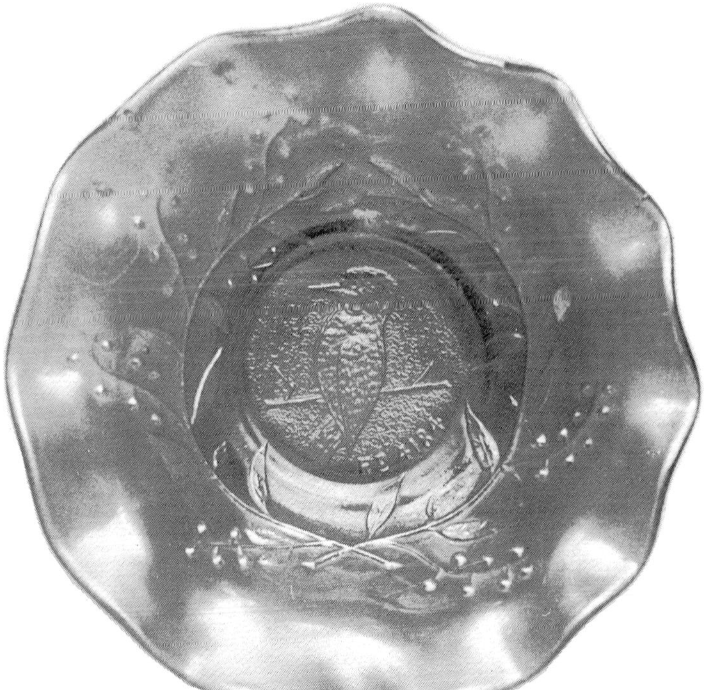

GLASS KOOKABURRAS

The kookaburra managed to have himself immortalised in glass. He was a favourite subject in leadlight windows, and leadlight glass kookaburras still adorn our suburbs. Most date from the 1920s and 1930s and are to be found in the red brick or stucco villas of that period. Many round windows featuring kookas are to be seen, and often the kookaburra is juxtaposed with the magpie in these applications. Very few earlier stained-glass kookaburras of the late nineteenth century are known to exist, although one fine example is pictured opposite page 96.

One kookaburra is forever embedded in a jelly mould. Other glass kookaburra objects include a number of carnival-glass bowls, made by Crystal Glass Ltd, in Sydney. A range of drinking glasses, carafes, and souvenir items decorated with etched kookaburras were also made by Flavel & Sons in Adelaide.

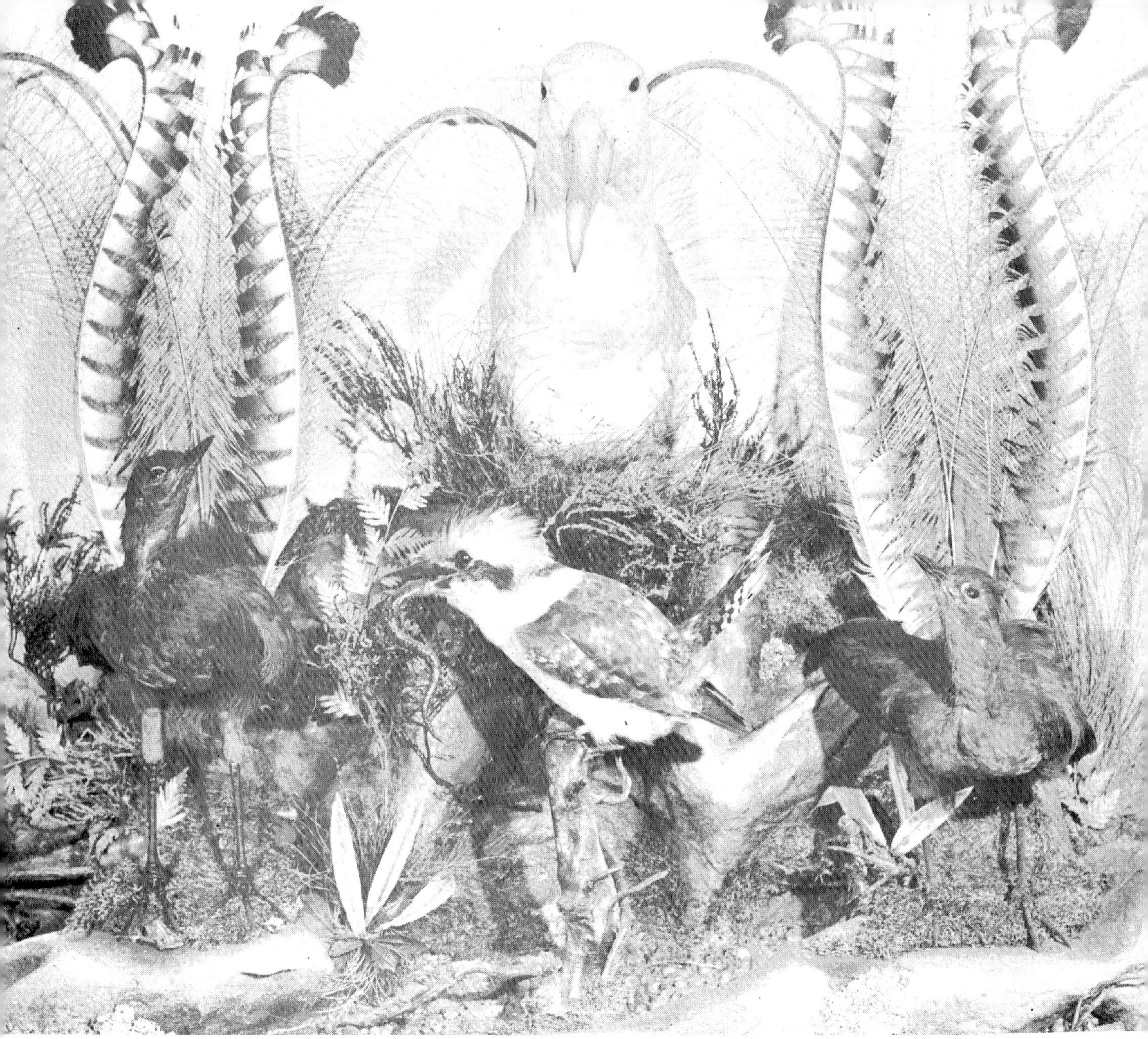

A case of stuffed birds, *c.* 1910. The kookaburra shares the case with lyrebirds and an albatross

OTHER DECORATIVE KOOKABURRAS

Decorative kookaburras are to be found in many other media. They were painted on silk and velvet, appliquéd onto teacosies, stuffed and put into cases – even, in one extraordinary example, semi-stuffed and made into a fan. Leatherwork was a popular craft and many leather collar boxes and bookmarks were decorated with kookas. Gesso-work kookaburras have also been found.

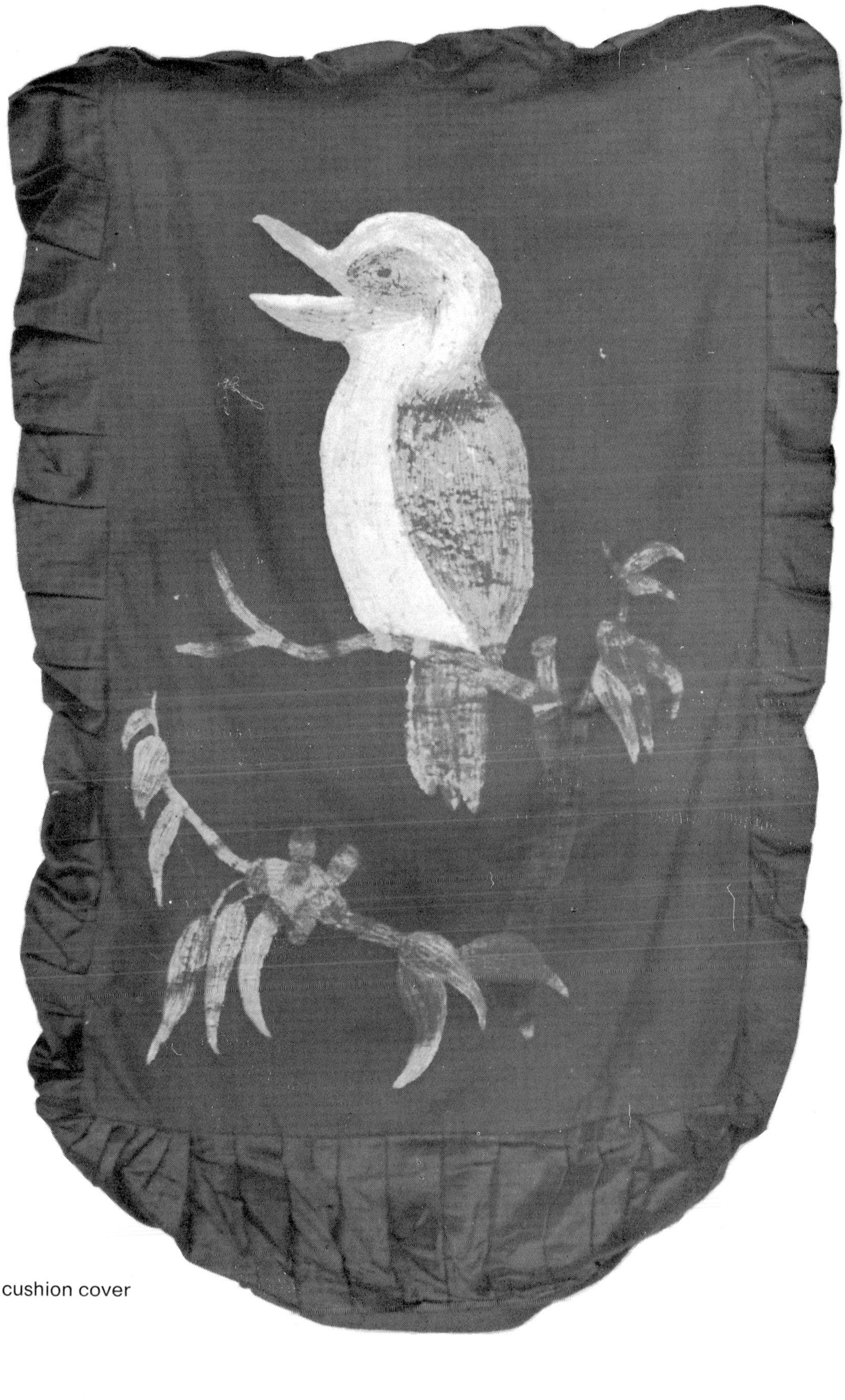

Painted silk cushion cover

Pressed leather collar box and two bookmarks

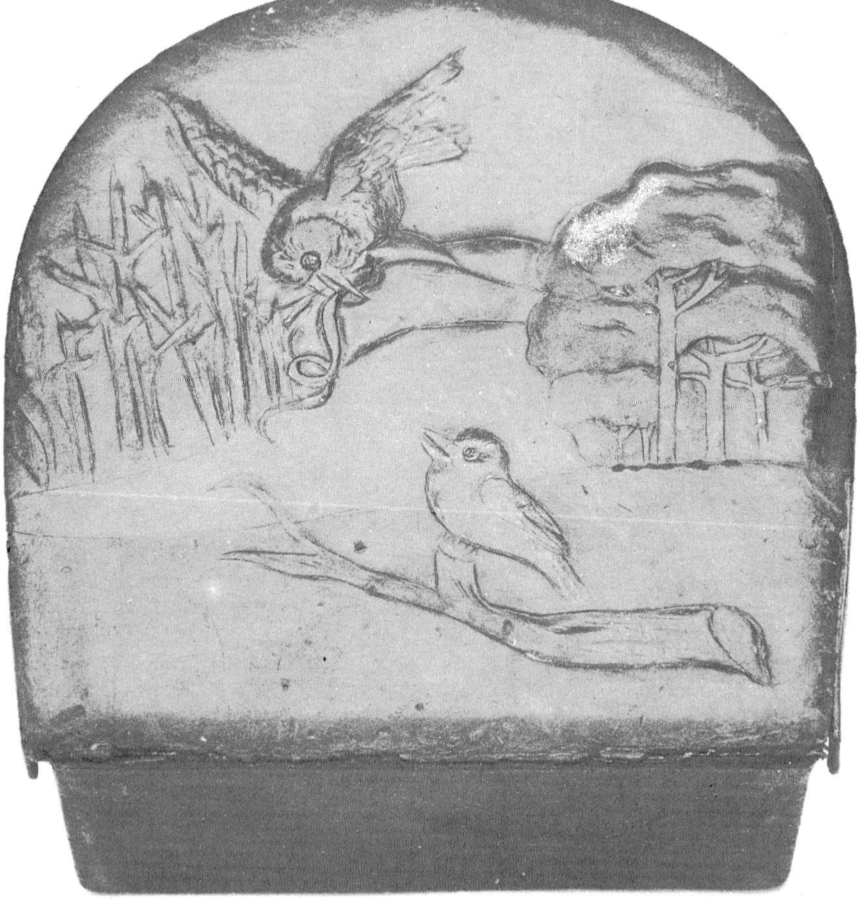

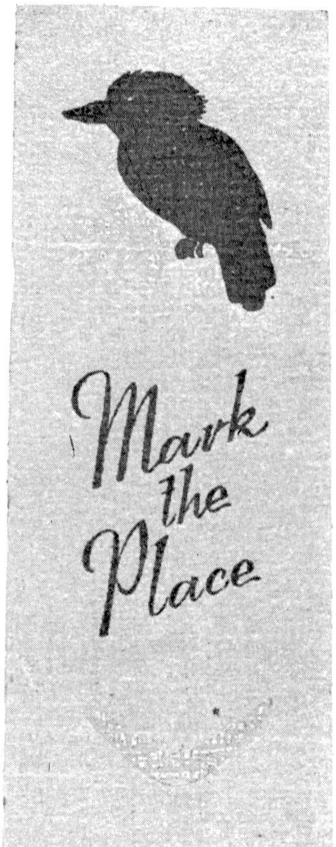

Painting on velvet

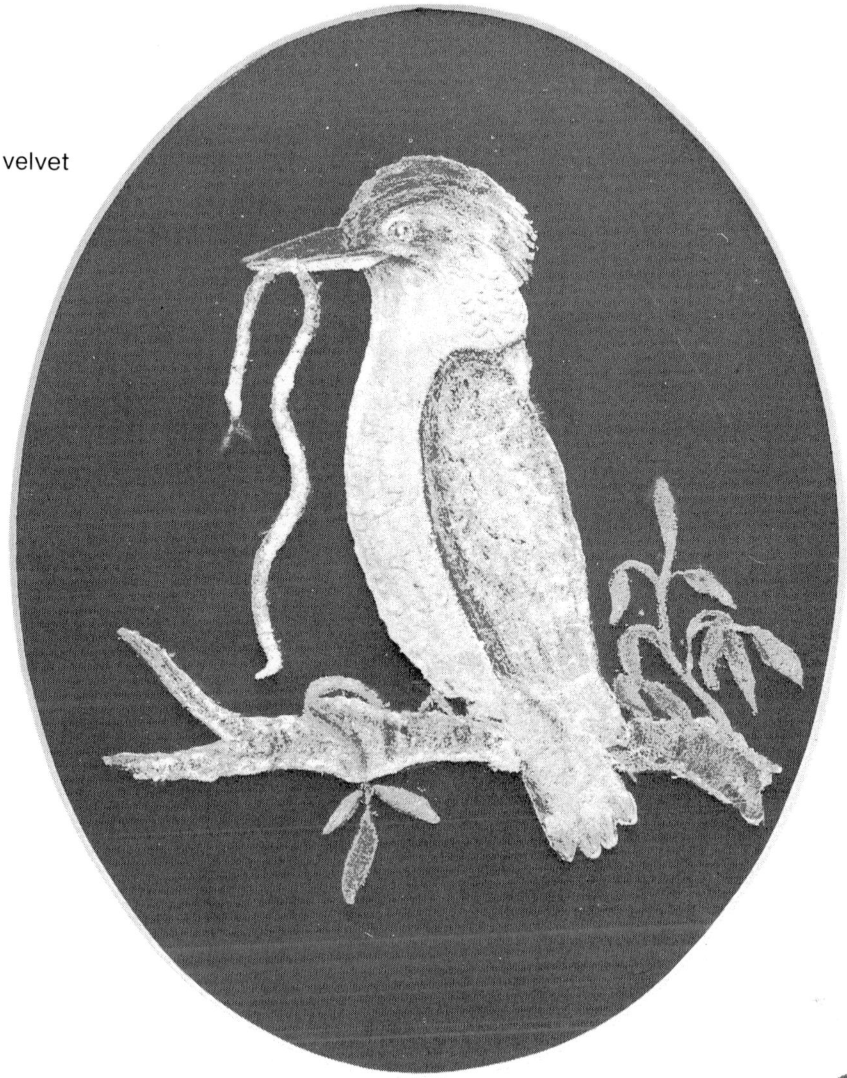

Plastic cigarette dispenser. When the kookaburra is pushed down, the tray opens and the kookaburra picks up the cigarette in his beak (below)

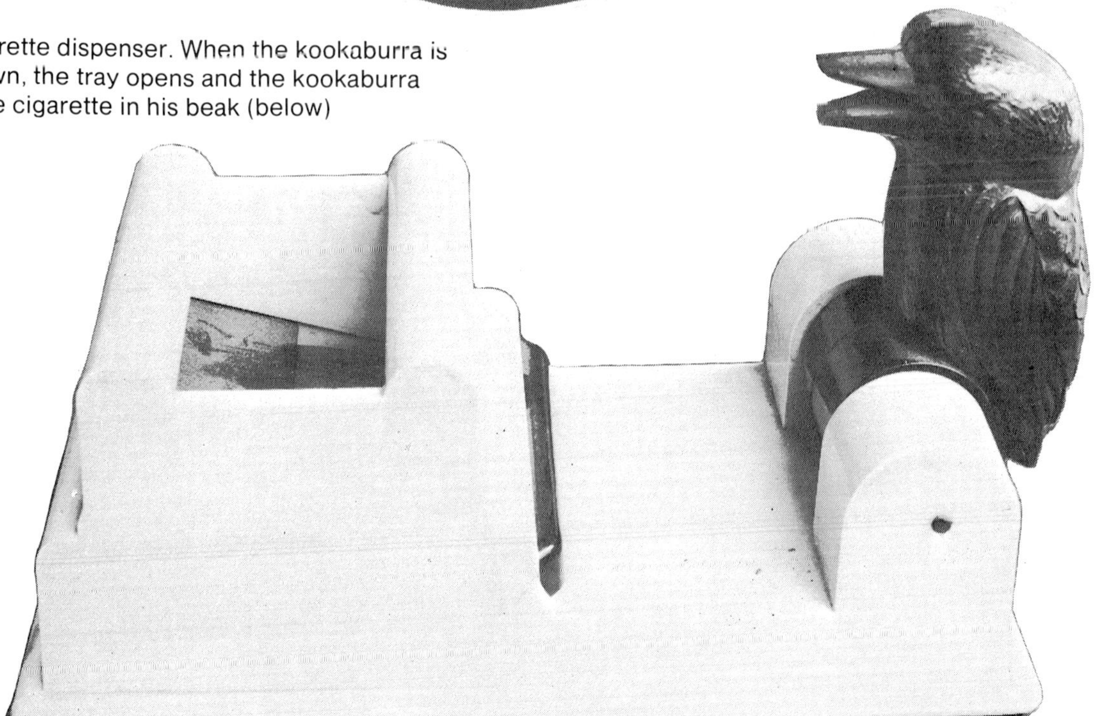

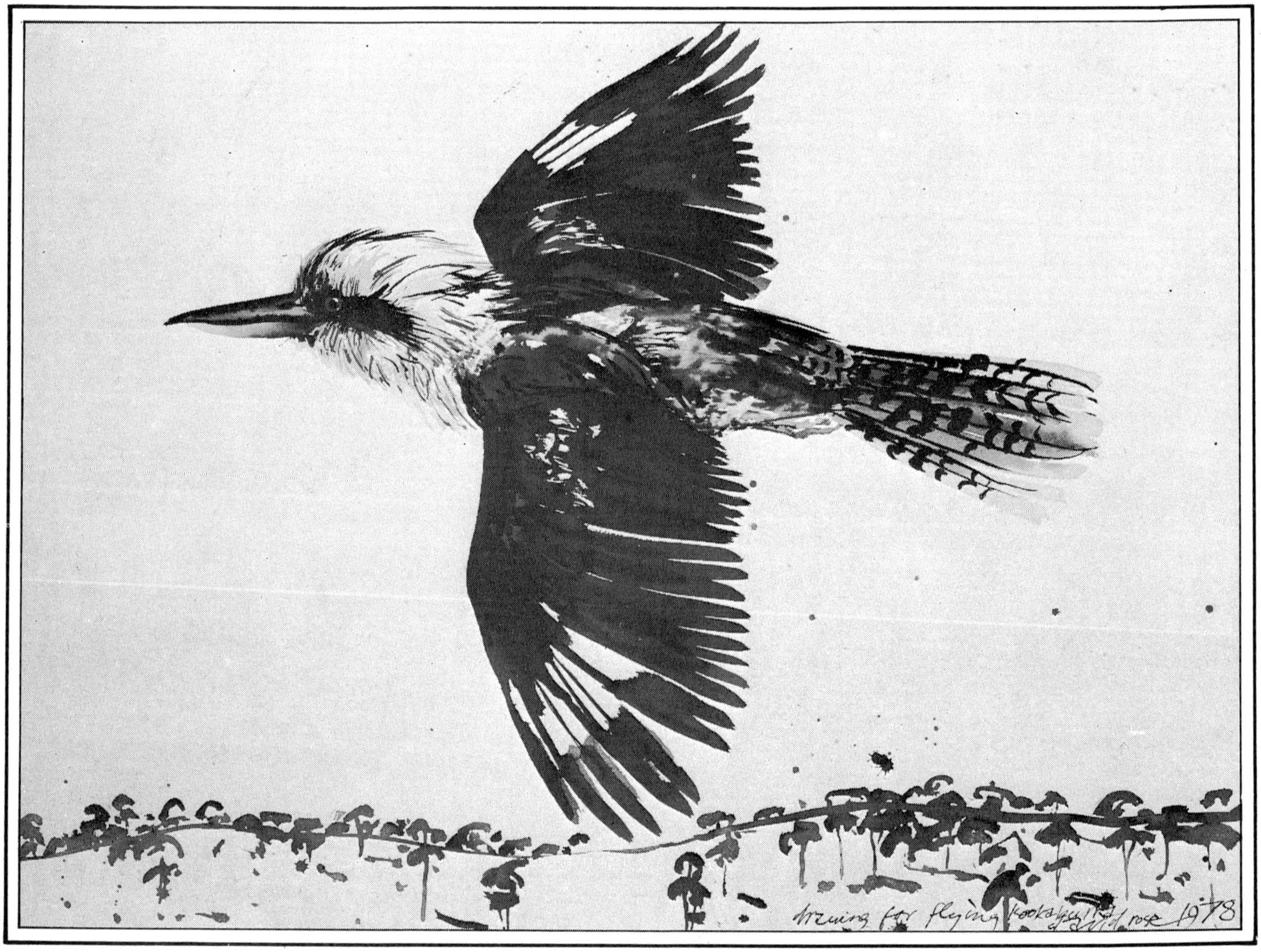

Drawing by David Rose, 1978

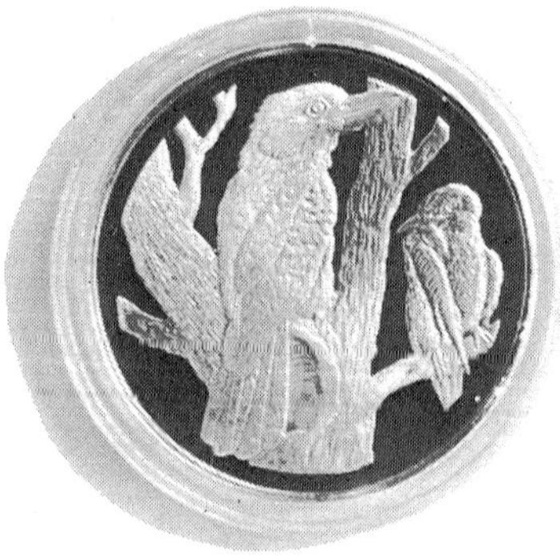

Stuart Devlin's silver kookaburra in the Birds of Australia series for the Franklin Mint

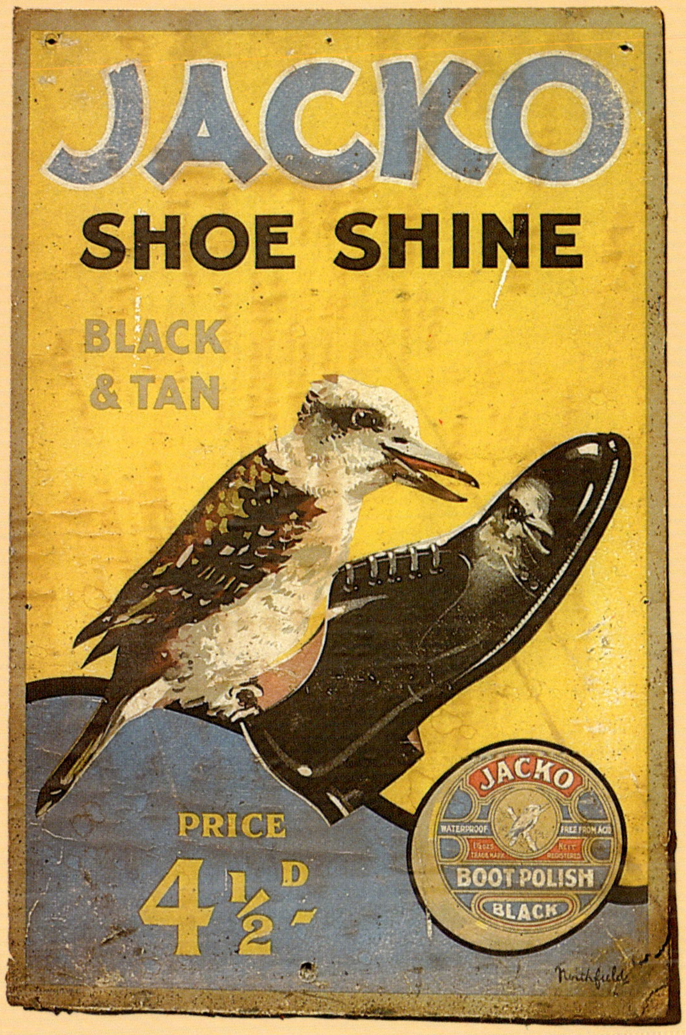

Jacko Shoe Shine advertising poster

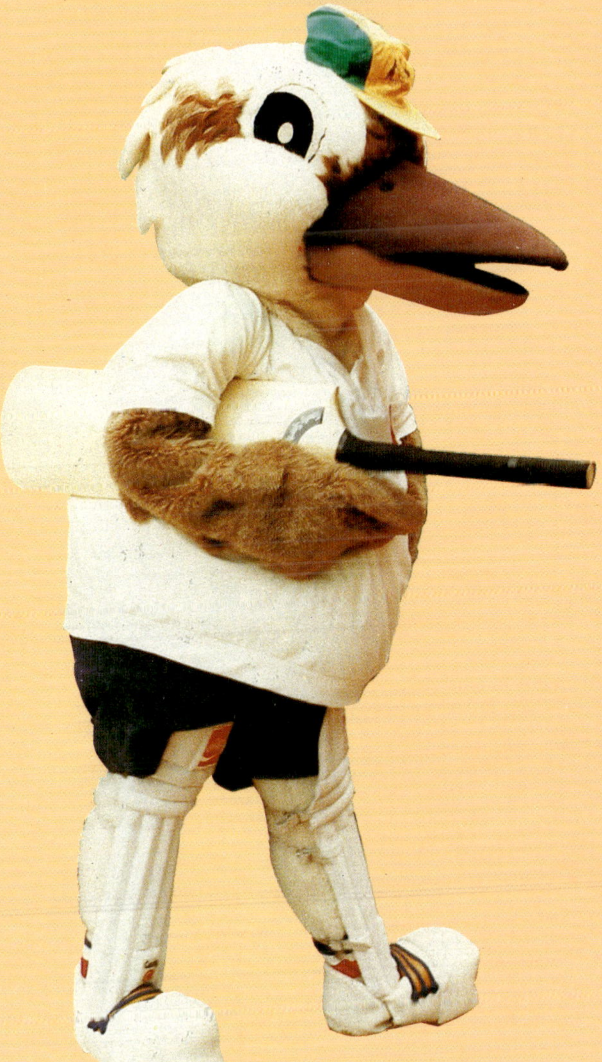

Kickaburra, the Coca-Cola Export Corporation's relative of the kookaburra, also plays cricket

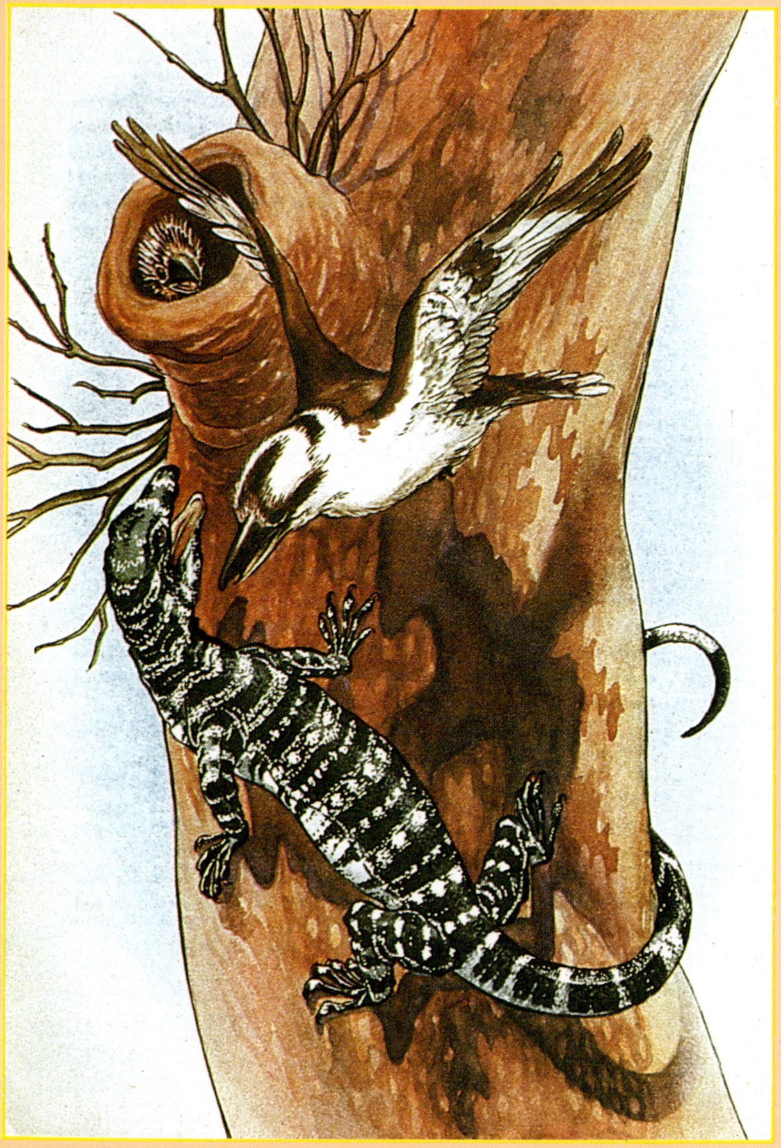

Protecting the fledglings from their chief predator, the lace goanna. Illustration from *The Story of Kurri Kurri the Kookaburra* by Leslie Rees, originally published in 1948 and still in print for children to enjoy today

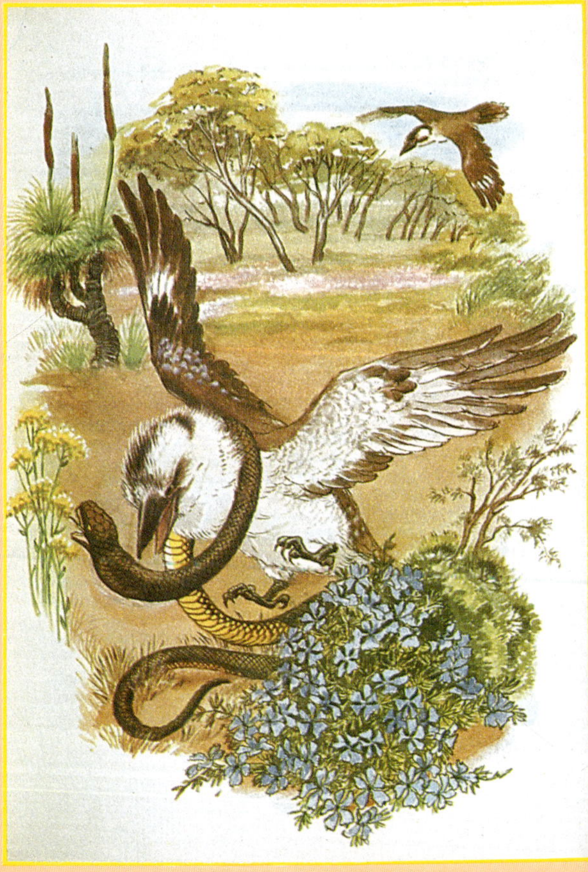

A savage battle. Another illustration from *The Story of Kurri Kurri the Kookaburra*

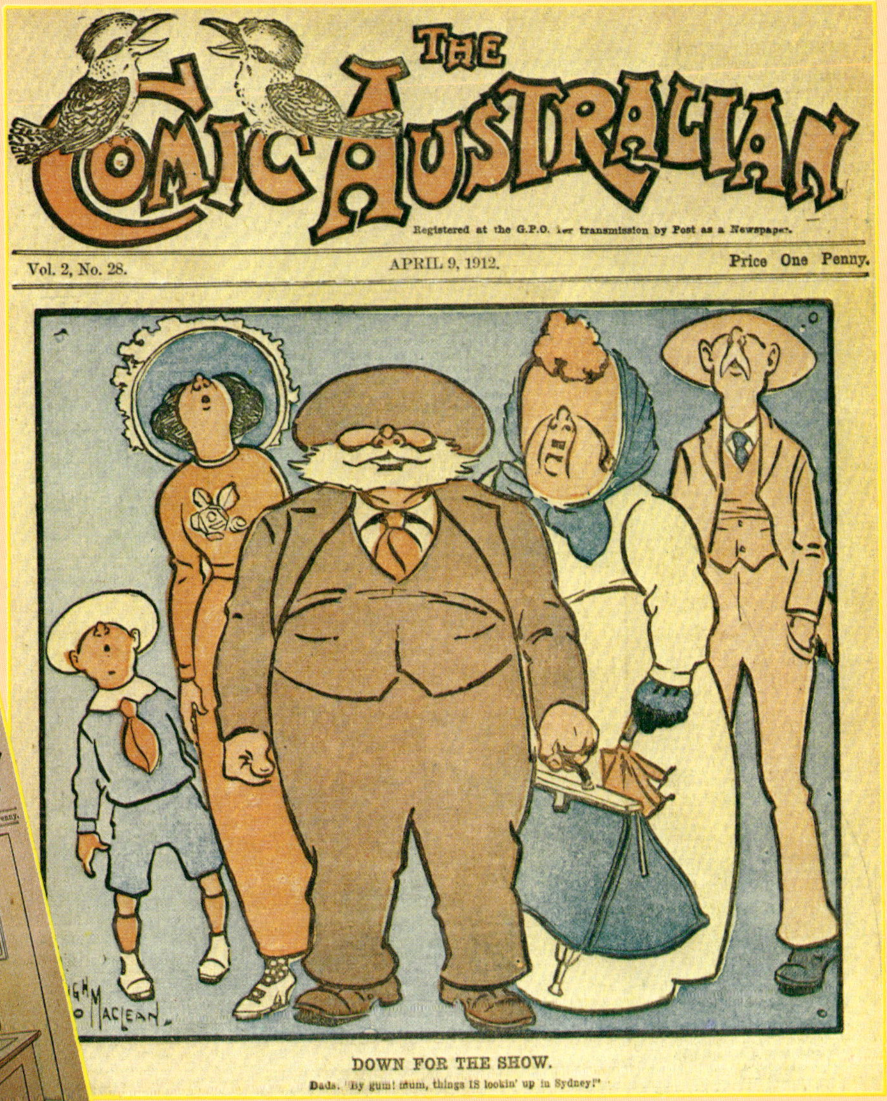

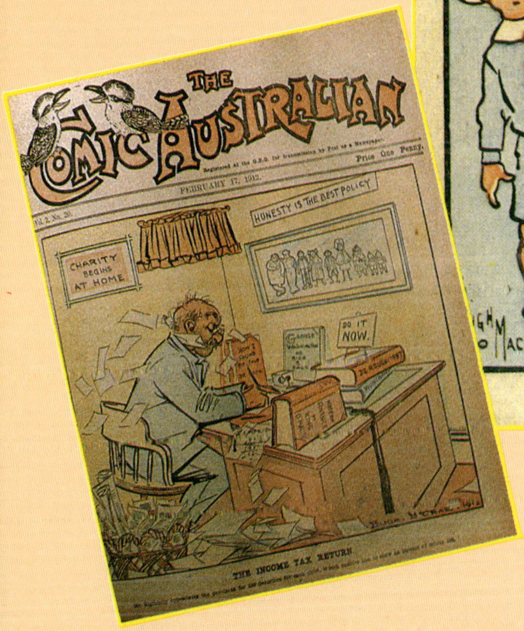

A suitable emblem for *The Comic Australian*

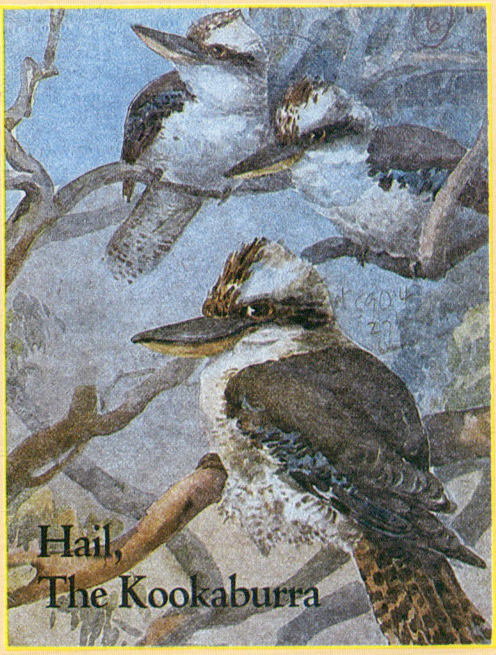

Hail the Kookaburra, by A. H. Chisholm and Dorothy Drewett, was published in Sydney in 1931

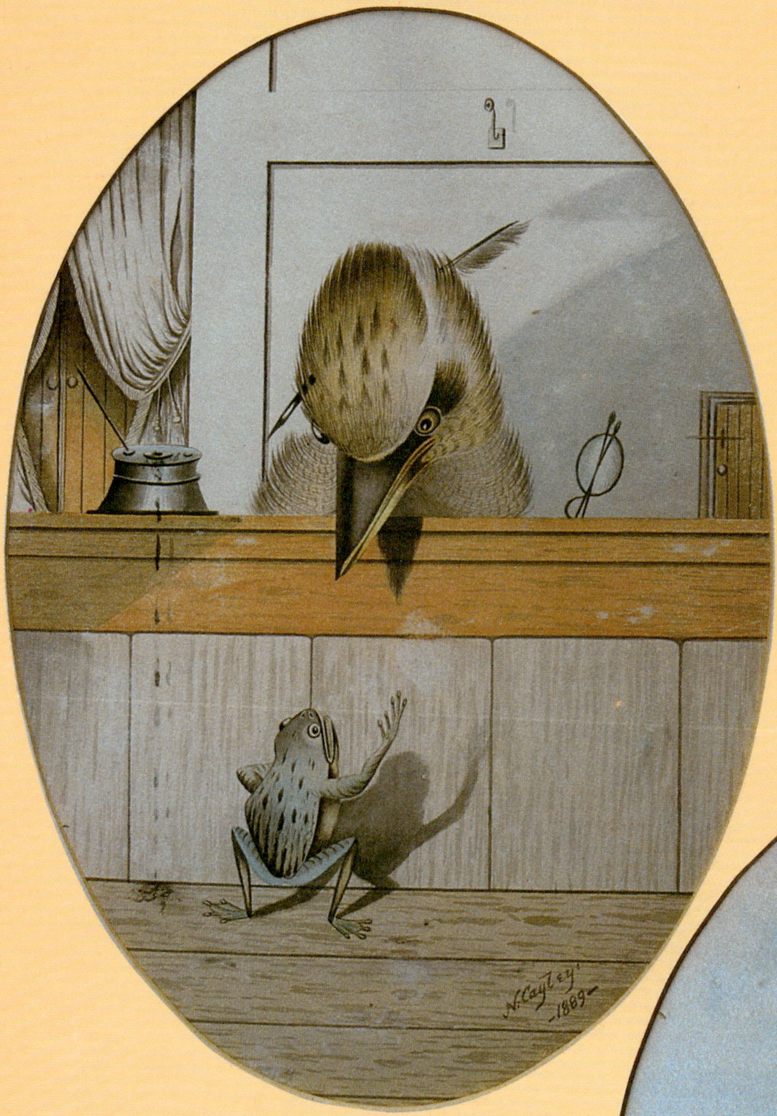

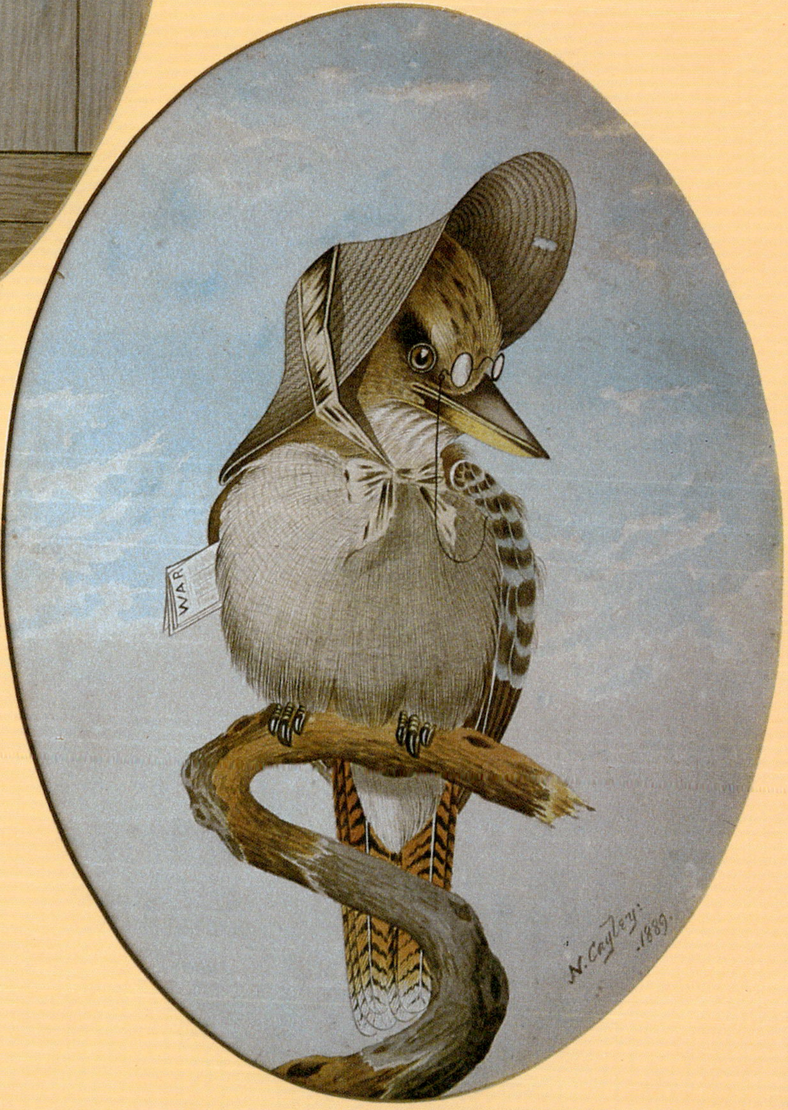

These two charming watercolours by Neville Cayley senior, dated 1889, are in a private collection

MODERN KOOKABURRAS

A question that arises is, why did all these kookaburra crafts taper off after World War II? Our own theory is that in the wake of World War II we became 'sophisticated' and 'international' and rather self-conscious about our Australian heritage. But the wheel has turned almost full circle, and there are new signs in the 1980s that many young craftspeople and artists – often first and second generation Australians – have discovered our own national nostalgias and heritage and are using them again. In recent years the kookaburra motif and other national symbols have once more become a part of the national consciousness. Australiana shops have sprung up selling Australian crafts of a much higher standard than most souvenir items.

In the early 1980s modern ceramic kookaburras began to appear. During the same period Peter Stripes in Melbourne produced some stunning kookaburra fabrics, while both Art Knitwear from Flamingo Park in Sydney and Rachelle King in Melbourne featured the kookaburra. Mark Arbuz in Sydney also celebrated the kookaburra in leather.

A new wave of young silversmiths and jewellers have featured Australian flora and fauna, including the kookaburra, in their works. Hendrich Forster, Geoffrey Ince and Mike Wilson in Melbourne and Ilaria Logi, Peter Tully and Elizabeth Olah in New South Wales have produced wonderful kookaburra objects.

The kookaburra has appeared in the drawings and original prints of David Rose and has been painted by artists like Brett Whiteley. Graphic designers have again used the kookaburra in their projects. Home crafts have begun to reflect the trend.

A silver kookaburra brooch by Hendrich Forster (right)

Can you find the kookaburra? The Australia Puzzle by Ilaria Logi (below)

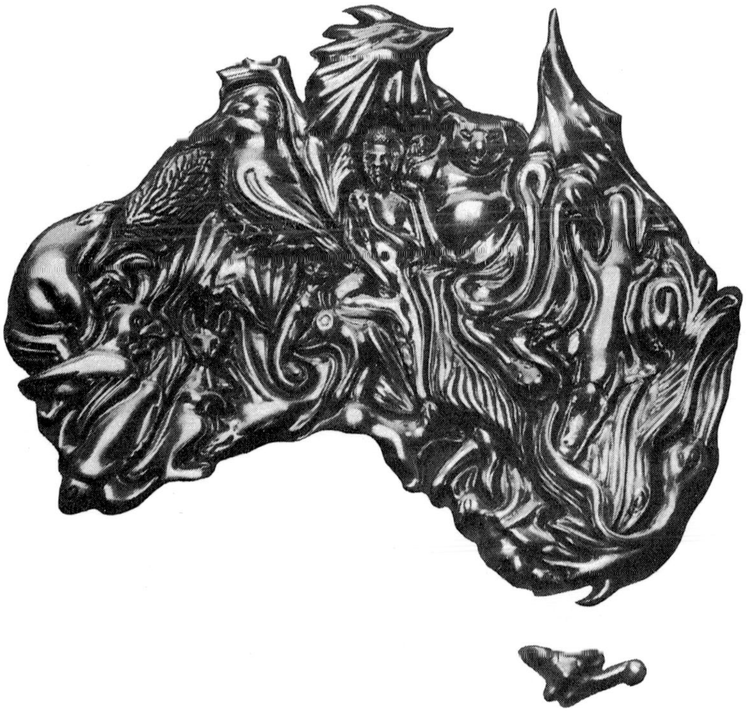

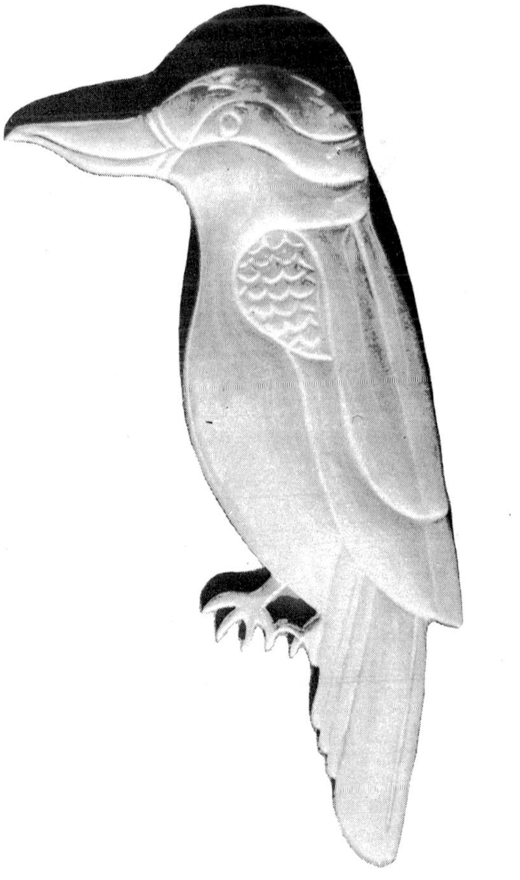

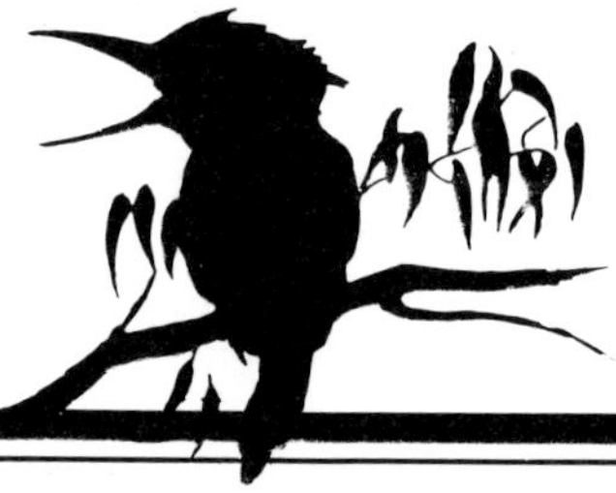

-8- KOOKABURRAS IN CHILDREN'S LITERATURE

The kookaburra features conspicuously in nineteenth-century Australian children's books, especially in his role as a snake catcher.

EARLY LITERARY KOOKAS

One of his earliest appearances was in *Who Killed Cockatoo?* by W. A. C. (William Alexander Cawthorne). This was written, printed and published in Adelaide in 1870. Here our greedy friend is gobbling a snail in the text but making a meal of a hapless frog in the illustration.

Another very early children's book was *The Young Australians' Alphabet*, which was 'printed and published at W. Calvert's Chromo-typographic Printing Office, 89 Little Collins Street East' around 1871: 'J is for JACKASS, A very strange bird, Whose laugh in the forest is very absurd'.

As an example of what was served up for children's amusement a hundred years ago, we reproduce Cyrus Mason's short story 'The Conceited Snake', which was published in 1871 by George Robertson of Melbourne in *The Australian Christmas Story Book*:

> There lived in the wild bush, where iguanas trailed over stumps, flying squirrels swung from bough to bough, and opossums scuttled up and down trees undisturbed, a comfortable snake family. She wore a sober bluish-brown dress, which, as decent bodies do, she changed occasionally, and passed a happy time to the terror of all frogs and lizards within fifty yards.

One morning, instead of one snake living in this way, there were twenty, for this sober lady-snake had a family of nineteen young snakes – and great was the joy of the maternal heart on witnessing her family taking a morning crawl out of the rock in which they were born.

But if mother snake was pleased, so was a bird which sat on a bough, with his great head on one side, for he saw his breakfast waiting for him.

When the whole nineteen had wriggled out and were fairly in the sun, Master Cockie Laughing Jackass pounced among the infant snakes and polished them off like a little boy eats shrimps. One little snake escaped by pushing his brothers and sisters aside and leaping down his mother's throat.

This was an undoubted family loss, and the maternal snake felt it keenly as the young snake tickled her inside, whilst chuckling over his own narrow escape – asking himself the question, if his brothers and sisters felt as comfortable inside the bird with the big head as he did – whilst his disconsolate parent carried him to their now cheerless home and the bird with the big head laughed so heartily it was a wonder his sides did not crack.

Louisa Anne Meredith was a notable early colonist whose writings and chromolithographs bring us an accurate picture of genteel life in nineteenth-century Australia. In 1878 she published in Tasmania *Grandmama's Verse Book for Young Australians*, which includes a poem 'Laughing Jackasses'. She had also lived on the mainland, which is where she must have encountered the Laughing Jack. They did not occur naturally in Tasmania and were introduced to that state in 1905.

Another charming sketch of the 'goburra' occurs in *Australian Fur and Feathers* by Mary Anne Fitzgerald. This was illustrated by W. T. Anderson and published by Edwards, Dunlop and Co. Ltd in 1889. Mary Anne Fitzgerald notes that 'its laughter is not always indicative of mirth, but is the natural sound of its voice'. Also 'it is most valuable as a destroyer of vermin and particularly for killing small snakes and lizards . . . So useful is this bird considered, that

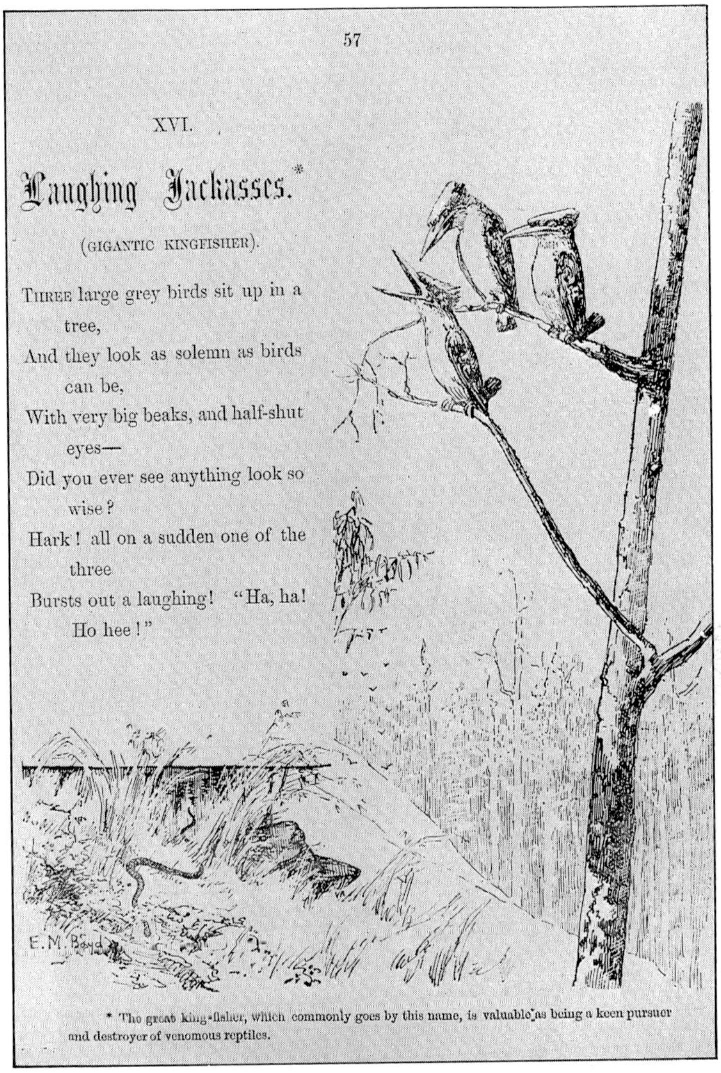
57

XVI.

Laughing Jackasses.*

(GIGANTIC KINGFISHER).

THREE large grey birds sit up in a tree,
And they look as solemn as birds can be,
With very big beaks, and half-shut eyes—
Did you ever see anything look so wise?
Hark! all on a sudden one of the three
Bursts out a laughing! "Ha, ha! Ho hee!"

E. M. Boyd

* The great king-fisher, which commonly goes by this name, is valuable as being a keen pursuer and destroyer of venomous reptiles.

'Laughing Jackasses', by Louisa Anne Meredith was first published in *Grandmama's Verse Book For Young Australians* in 1878

a law has been made to protect it from wilful injury'.

Mrs K. Langloh Parker published *Australian Legendary Tales* in 1896. In this and other subsequent volumes for children she recounted Aboriginal legends, including some concerning the kookaburra.

By the last decades of the nineteenth century, a now-accepted kookaburra was carving out his special niche in Australia's affections.

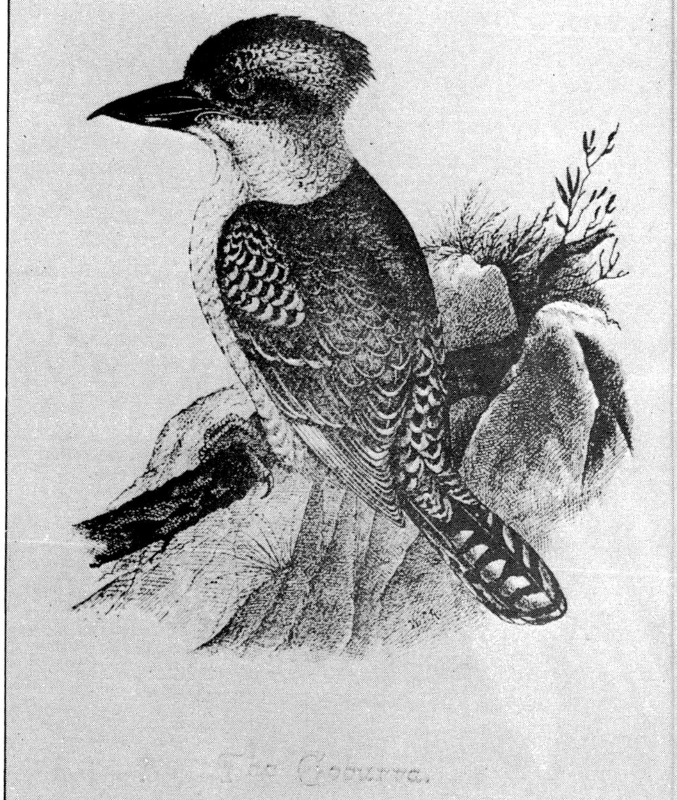

The Goburra. (*Dacelo Gigas.*)

THE Goburra is also called the Laughing Jackass, and Settler's Clock, the latter name because its loud strange laugh is heard at early morning and again at sun-set. The Aborigines of the various districts have different names for it, as *Kukuburra, Goburra,* and *Gogoburra,* all given in imitation of its curious note. It is also known as the "Giant Kingfisher," and "Great Brown Kingfisher," because it belongs to a tribe of birds called Kingfishers, but the Goburra does not live near water nor seek for fish. It frequents different localities, the rich brushes along the coast, also

'The Goburra', from *Australian Fur and Feathers* by Mary Anne Fitzgerald, 1889 (above). 'The Good Little Jackass', a nineteenth-century jingle (below)

The Good Little Jackass

A good little Jackass sat in a high tree,
He was laughing "Ha, ha!" and laughing "He, he!"
He saw a fat tiger snake crawl slowly by,
"Ha, ha," chuckled he, "to the ground I will fly
For that naughty snake very quickly must die."

So down he flew laughing "Ha, ha!" and "He, he!"
And carried that tiger snake up to the tree
Laughing "Ha, ha!" and laughing "He, he!"
And dropped him and killed him as quick as could be
Laughing "Ha, ha, ha, ha, he, he, he, he!"

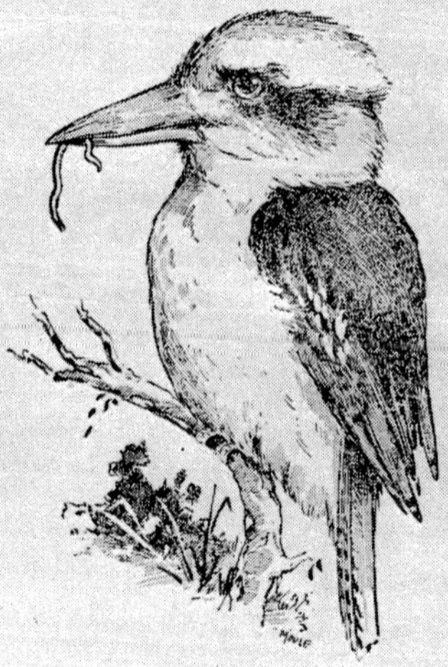

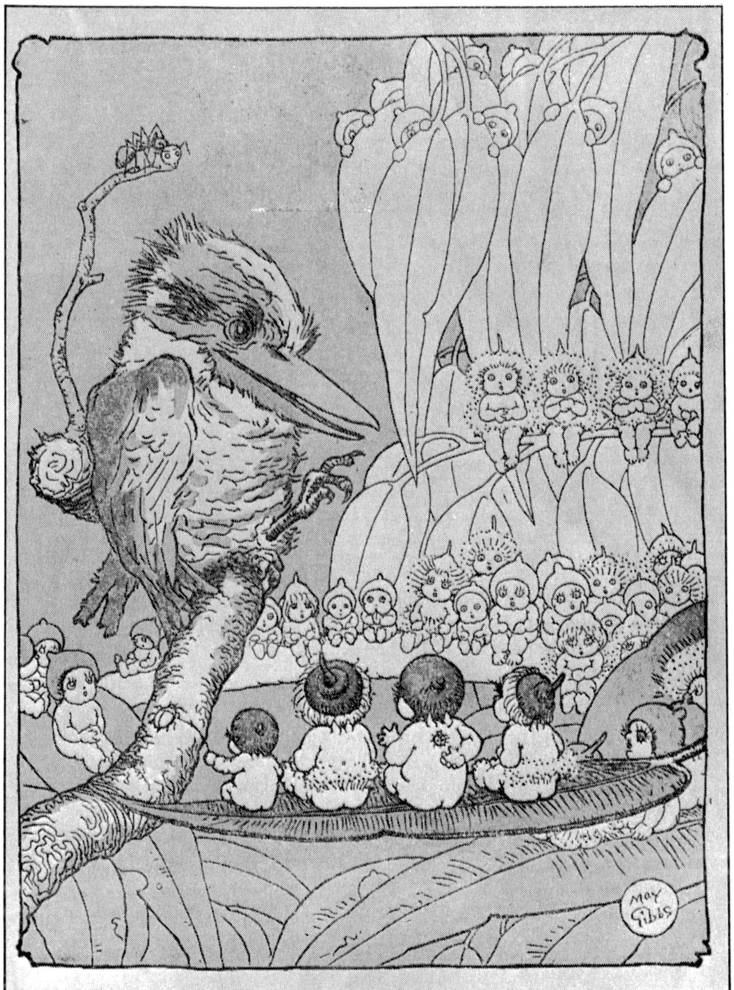

The Lecture

The Lecture from May Gibbs' *Tales of Snugglepot and Cuddlepie*

TWENTIETH-CENTURY CHILDREN'S LITERATURE

Kookaburras abound in twentieth-century children's literature. All the most famous authors used them, always humorously and usually endearingly. Among others, Norman Lindsay, C. J. Dennis, May Gibbs, Ida Rentoul Outhwaite, Banjo Paterson and Peg Maltby produced memorable tales.

Norman Lindsay's kookaburra is the ultimate larrikin in *The Magic Pudding*. There is such a strong larrikin element in the kookaburra's laugh that the association is an excellent one. Norman Lindsay also did a cheeky kookaburra illustration for Banjo Paterson's yarn about the kookaburra and the Boastful Crow.

May Gibbs used kookaburras as 'goodies' in the war against wicked Mrs Snake and the Banksia men in *Tales of Snugglepot and Cuddlepie*. She has given us two absolutely wonderful depictions of kookaburras. One is entitled *The Lecture* and shows a wise old kookaburra lecturing the gumnuts on those dreaded beasts 'the humans'! The other is *Mrs Kookaburra's Dinner Party* where Snugglepot and Cuddlepie have some difficulty matching Mrs Kookaburra's appetite for the huge snake smorgasbord.

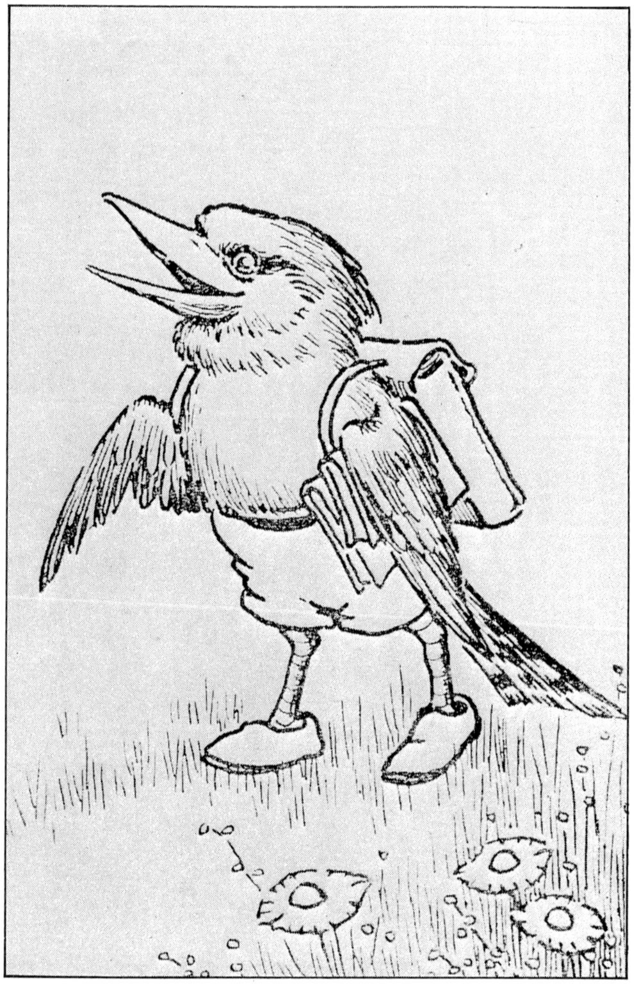

Ida Rentoul Outhwaite's Johnny Kookaburra: from *Sixpence to Spend*

From Ida Rentoul Outhwaite's *The Little Fairy Sister*: Fairy Bridget chatting to a kookaburra (opposite page)

Ida Rentoul Outhwaite was the creator of many charming kookas. One of our favourites is Johnny Kookaburra from *Sixpence to Spend*. Complete with shoes, schoolbag, shorts and books, he has a good laugh at the little koala children and calls them crybabies. The larrikin element creeping in again! Another of I. R. Outhwaite's kookaburras is a much more snuggly little chap who cuddles up very close to fairy Bridget in *The Little Fairy Sister*. This illustration was also used as a postcard, which we show in colour opposite page 88.

In the 1970s, when we started to look for Australian children's books for our eldest child we were horrified at how few books with Australian themes were in print. Admittedly some of the classic Australian stories have been reprinted, but there is little evidence in the bookshops of much that has been written this century. Many charming books have vanished completely. Nevertheless, when we began searching for Australian children's books featuring the kookaburra we discovered a real treasure trove in specialised collections. More recently the situation has changed with the publication of wonderful new Australian material.

At the end of this book there is a list of twentieth-century children's books featuring the kookaburra.

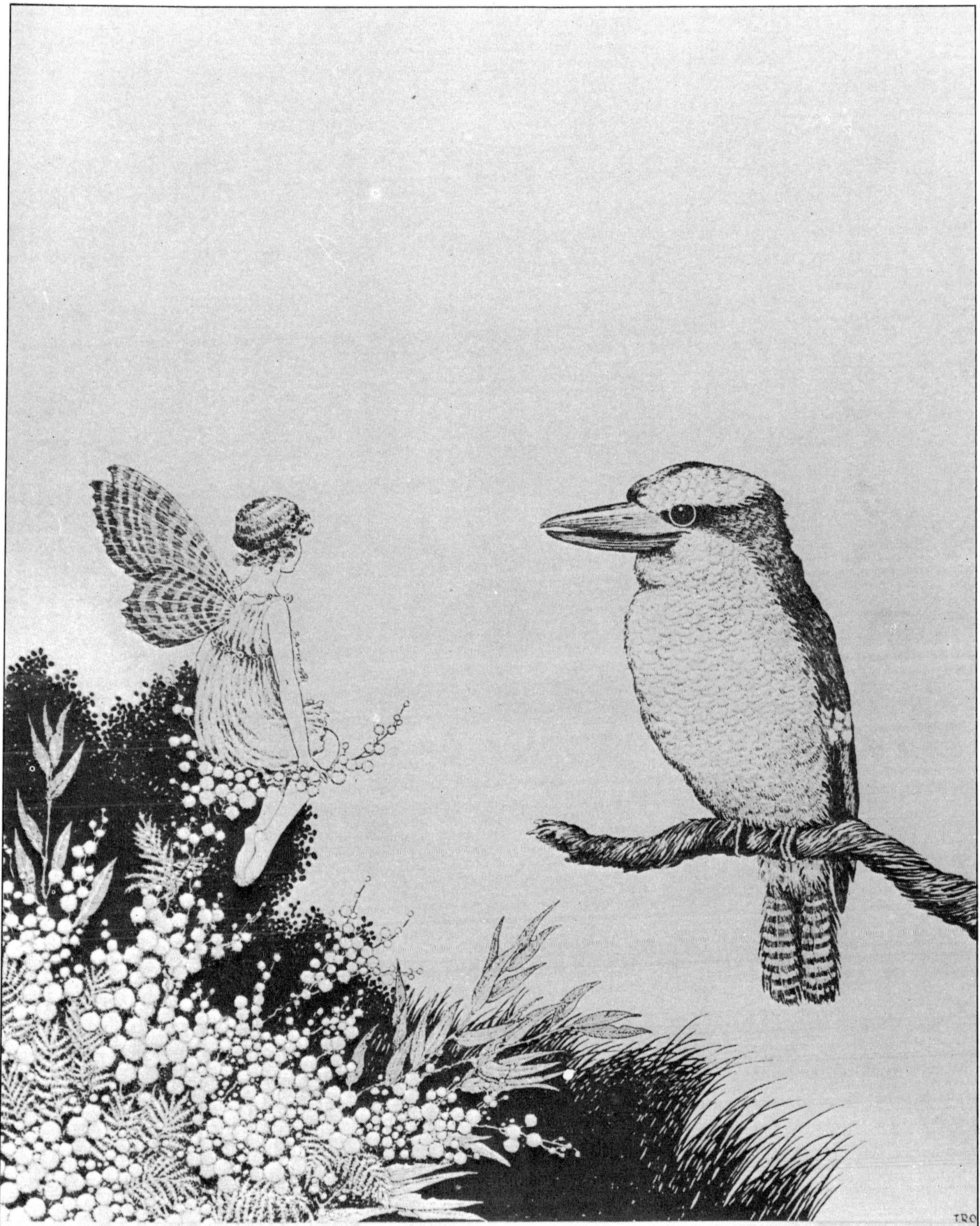

"While She Sat Chatting to a Kookaburra."

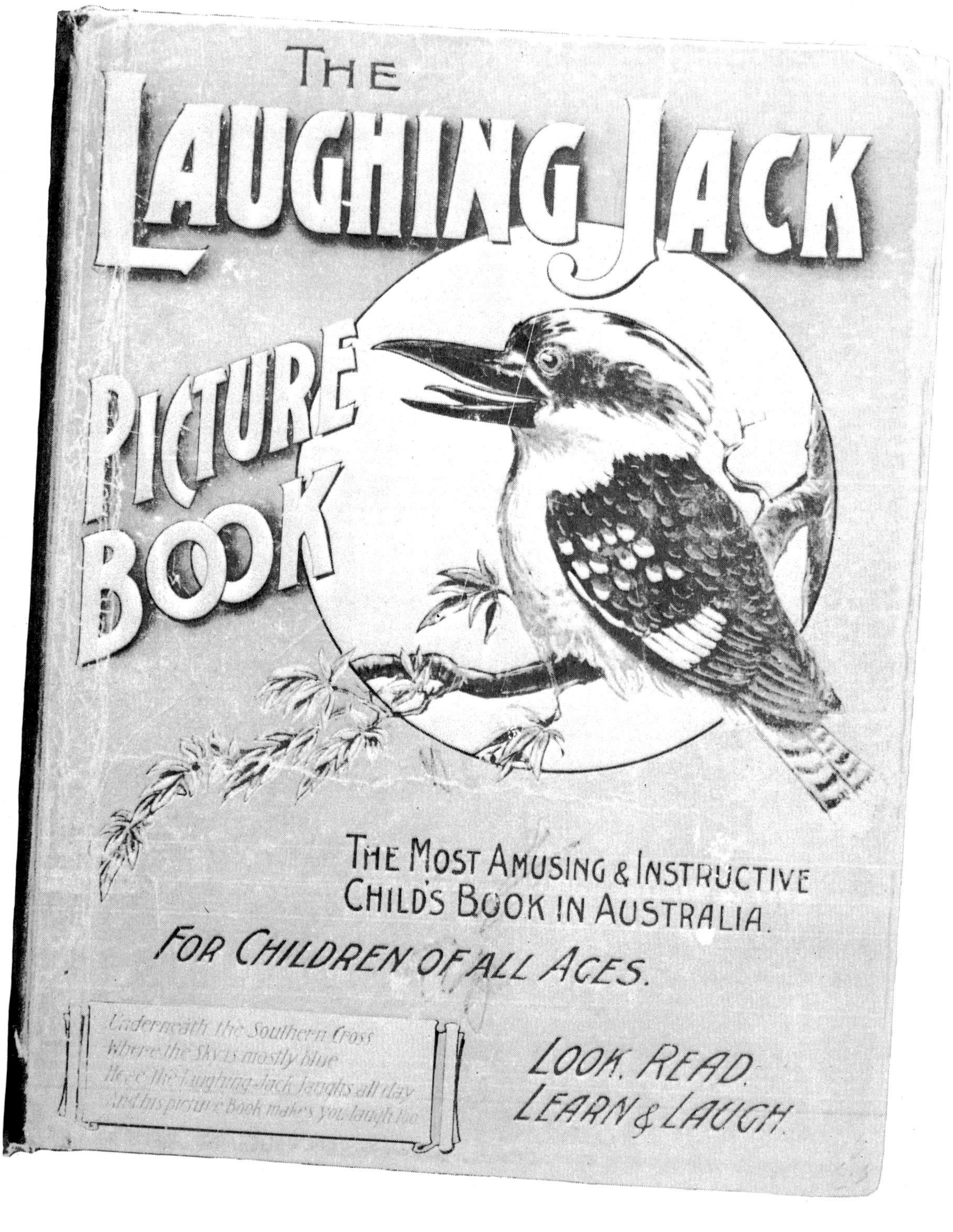

Cover of *The Laughing Jack Picture Book*, published *c.* 1910

Illustration from Harold Gaze's *The Simple Jagajay*, published by Whitcombe & Tombs in Melbourne, 1919 (right)

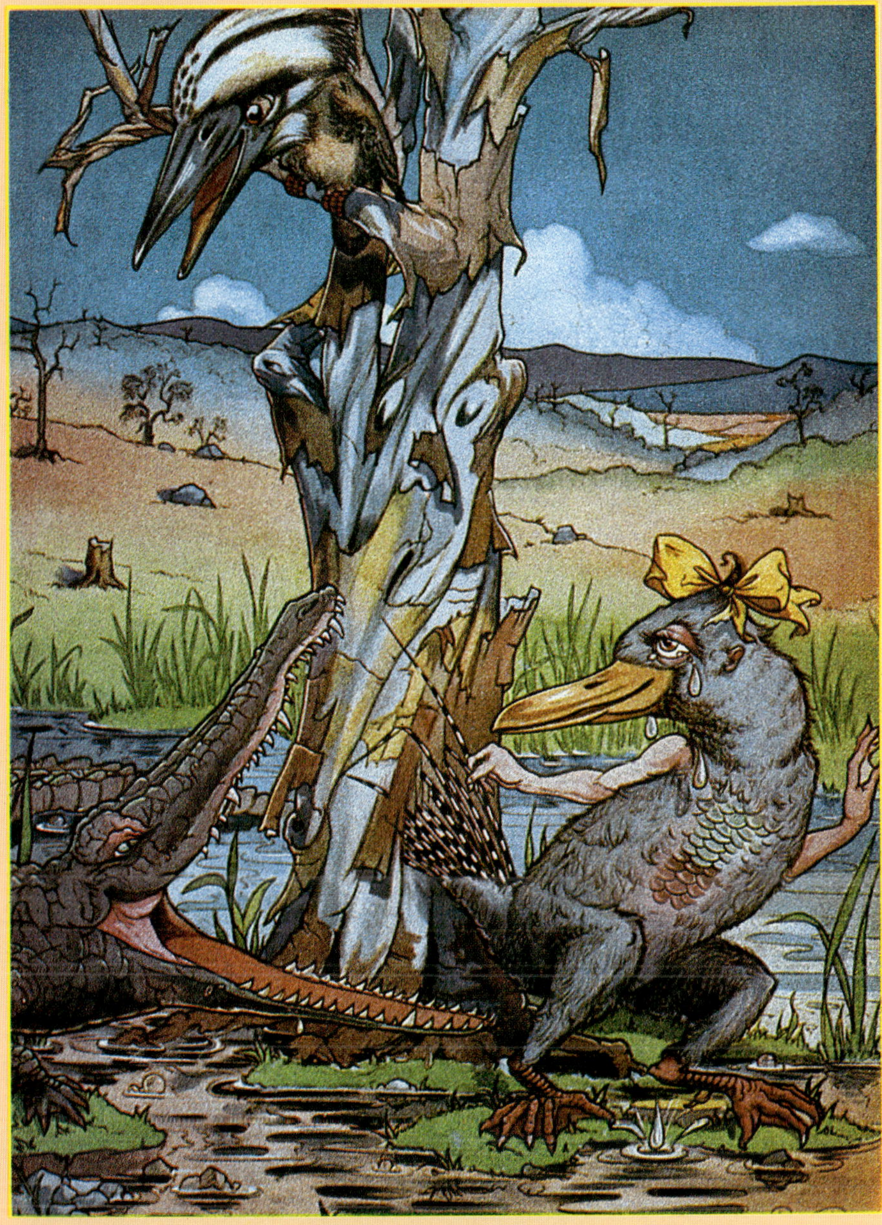

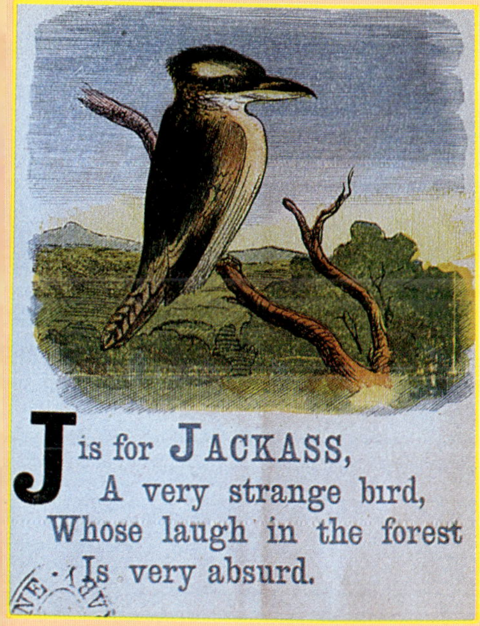

From *The Young Australians' Alphabet*, a children's book printed and published by W. Calvert c. 1871 (above)

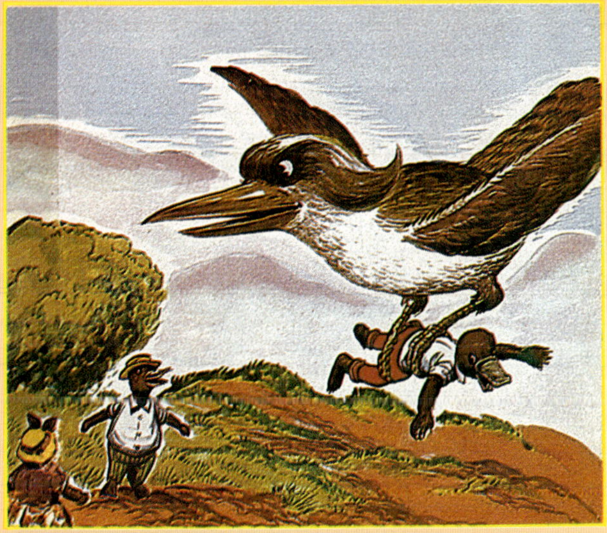

This illustration (right) is from a children's book probably published in the 1950s, Barbara Herbert's *A Camping Holiday in Australia*

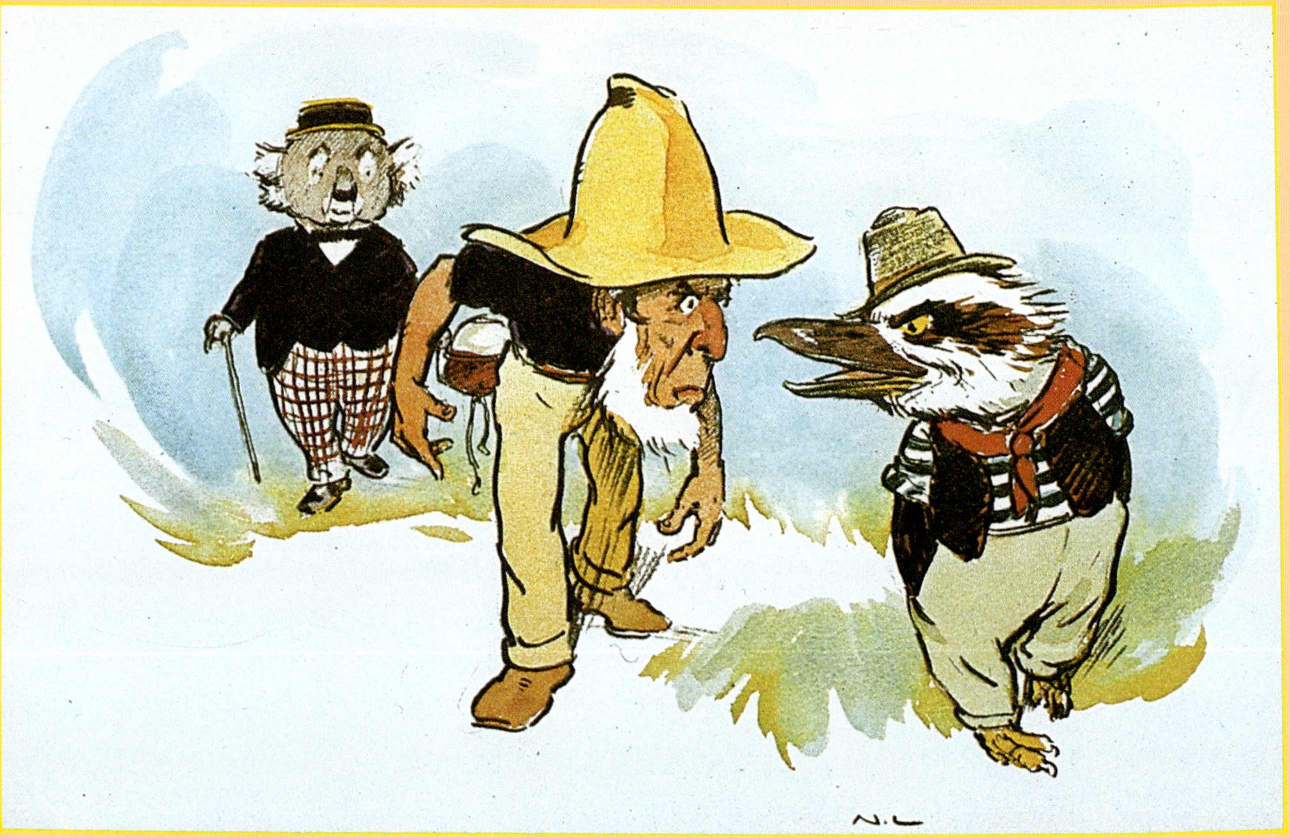

A low larrikin upsets Bill Barnacle in *The Magic Pudding*, Norman Lindsay's classic story for children, published by Angus & Robertson

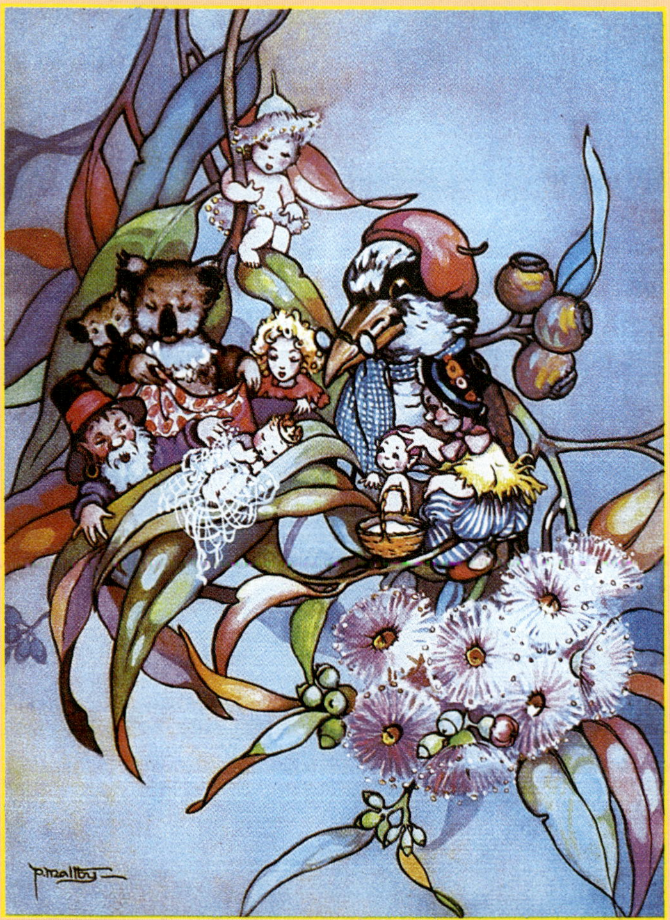

One of Peg Maltby's kookaburras from *Peg's Fairy Book*

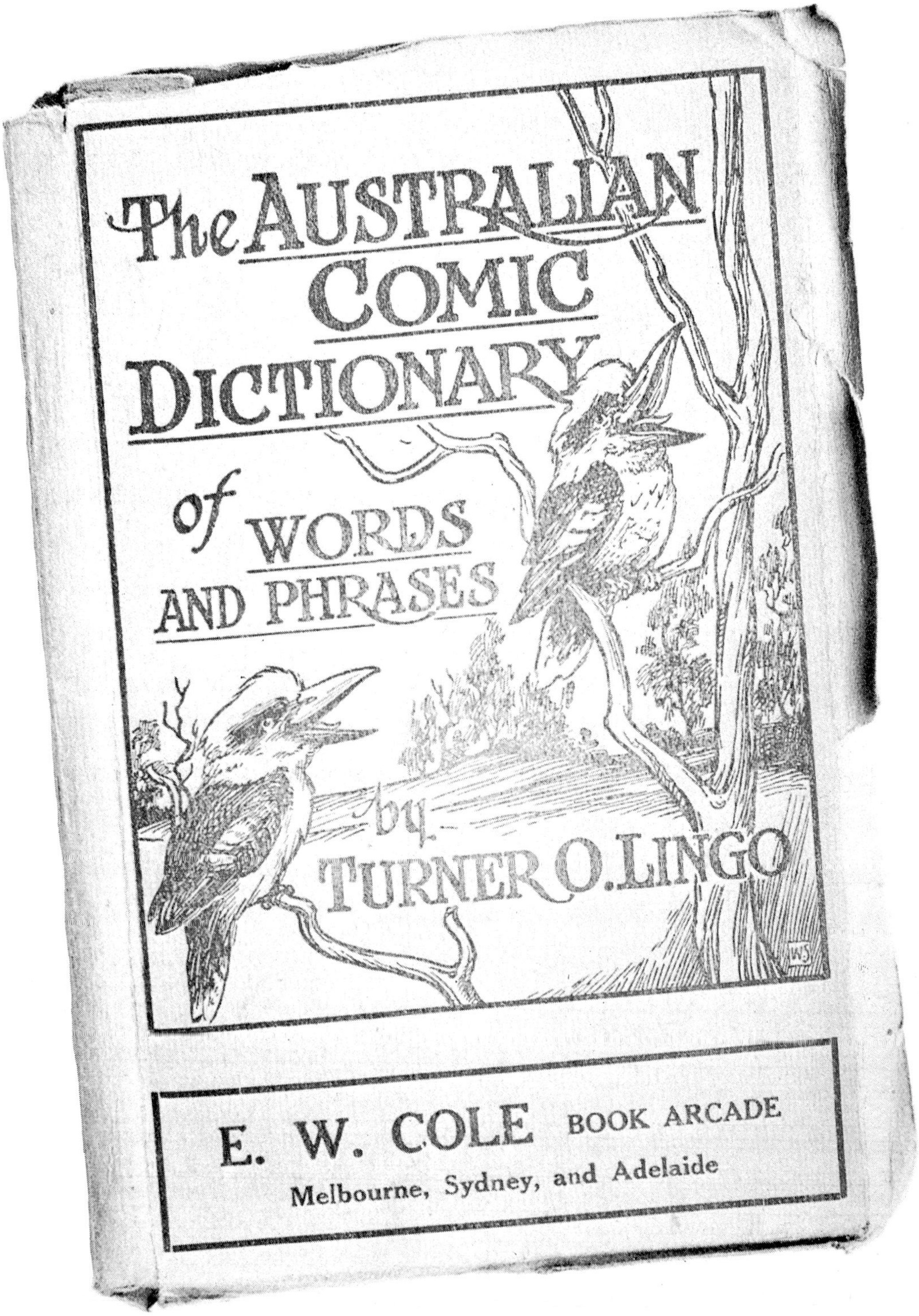

A book cover from E. W. Cole

Kookaburras and children in an idyllic setting: an Ida Rentoul Outhwaite illustration from *Bush Songs of Australia for Young and Old*

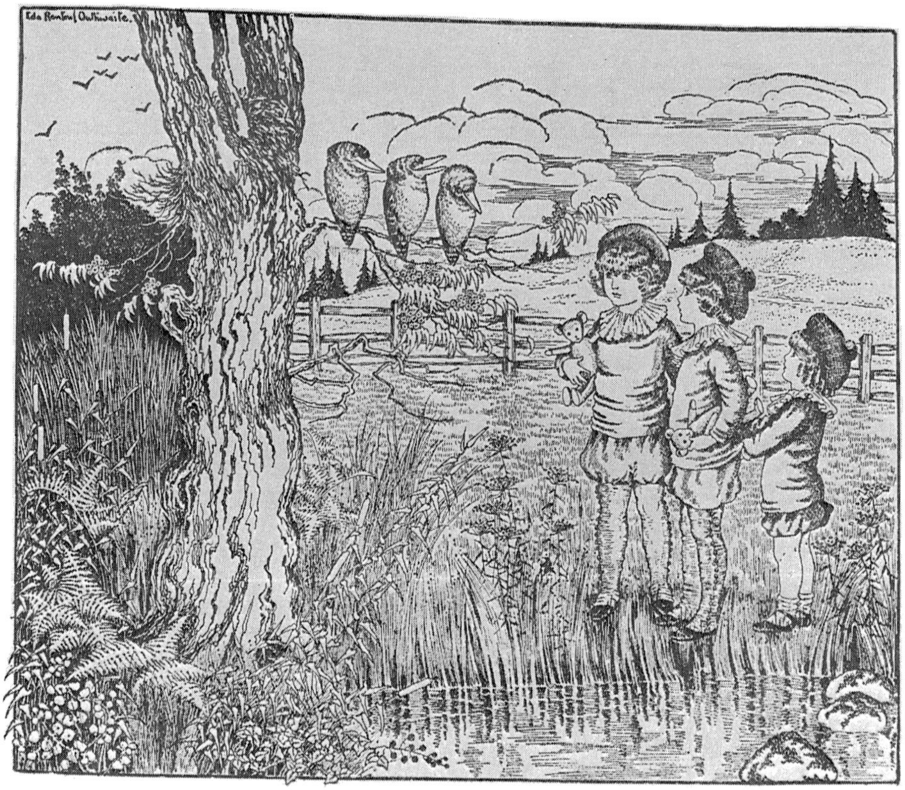
KOOKABURRA

Australian Songs for Young and Old must have whiled away some happy musical hours in the 1930s

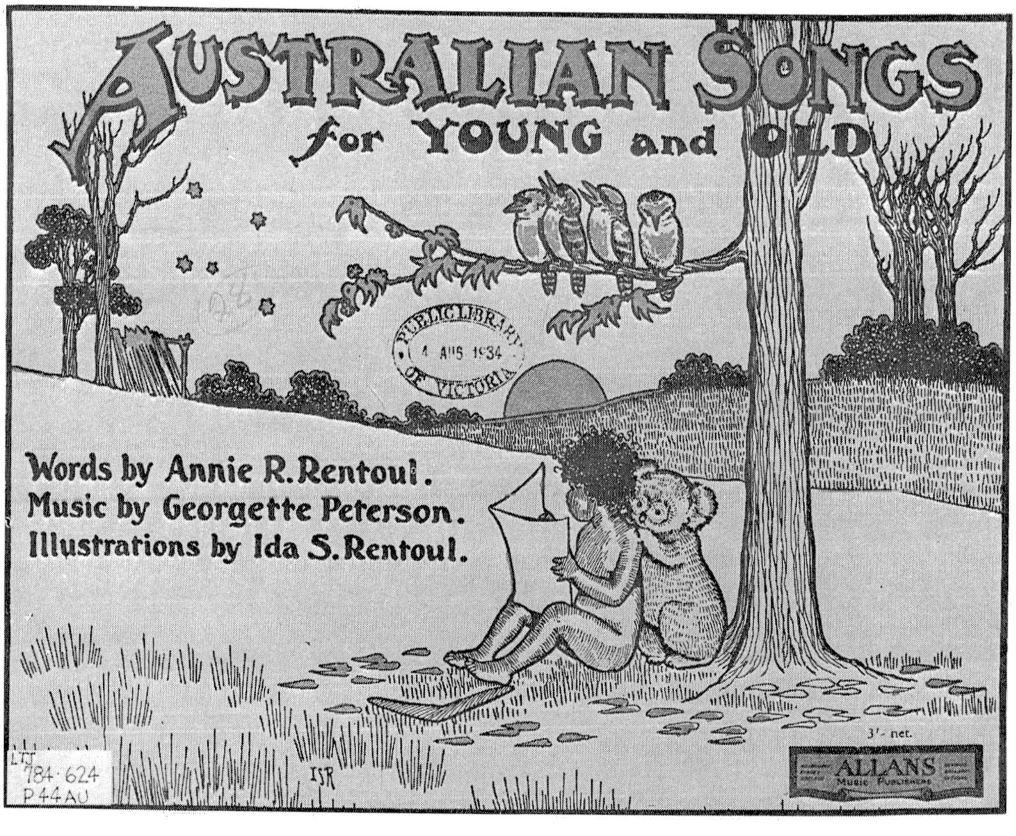

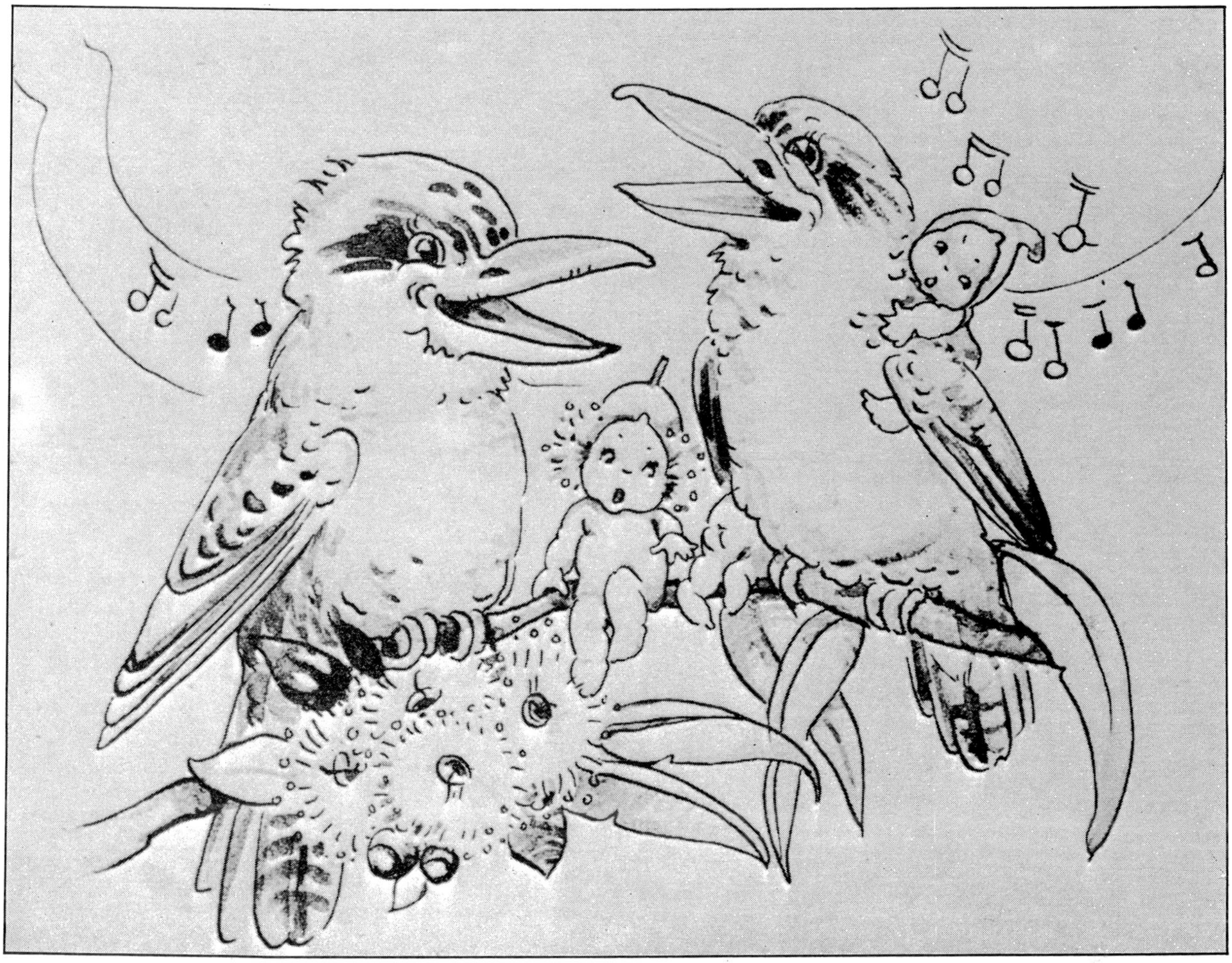

KOOKABURRA POEMS AND JINGLES

You're a bonzer joker, dear old,
Queer old Laughing Jack!

– *F. Hayward*

The kookaburra inspired an enormous number of poems and jingles. We include a selection for your enjoyment.

'Mr and Mrs Kookaburra high in the tree tops, laughed and laughed till the woods rang with their merry echoing song.' This is from Peg Maltby's *Ben and Bella in the Hills* (above)

Kookaburra

The King of Laughter.

Listen! . . How the clatter of the
Kookaburra's song
Echoes thro' the Wattles, Tree Ferns,
Gums, and Currajong.
Hear his shouts of dinkum laughter!
Wonder what's the joke!
Heard a funny story, Jack, from
Other Jackass folk?
Now the jolly Winds blows in, to
Tell the trees the fun.
See their heads bent close together,
Nodding in the sun.
Sapling Gums, all fuss and flutter,
Shake their leaves with glee,
Little gossips, full of mischief,
Whisp'ring tree to tree!
Till their leaves all flutter like a
Million little wings,
As they chuckle at the story
That the Bush Wind brings.
Kookaburra hears them laughing.
Laughs an answer back!
You're a bonzer joker, dear old,
Queer old Laughing Jack!

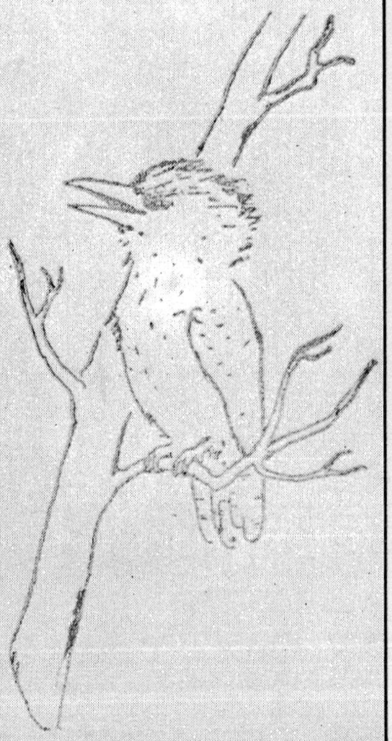

37

Marjorie D. Kay illustrated F. Hayward's *Tails and Tales of Tails and No Tails*, an Adelaide picture book of 1920

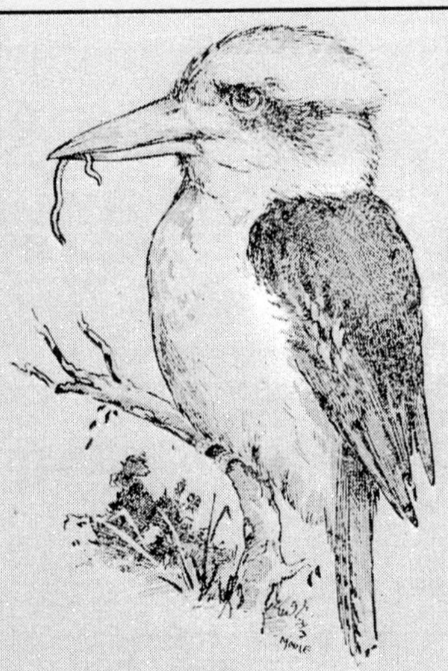

Laughing Jack.

From out the eucalyptus tree
Kookaburra laughs with glee,
He, he, ho, ho, ha, ha, he,
Such a merry bird is he,
How he laughs, ho, ha, ha, he.

He laughs when shines the morning light,
And looks about with glances bright
When finished is his daily flight,
He laughs again when comes the night.

Should another add his song,
Soon there'll be a laughing throng,
He, he, ha, ha, ho, ho, he,
What a merry bird is he.

Anon

From *The Laughing Jack Picture Book*

THE KOOKABURRA

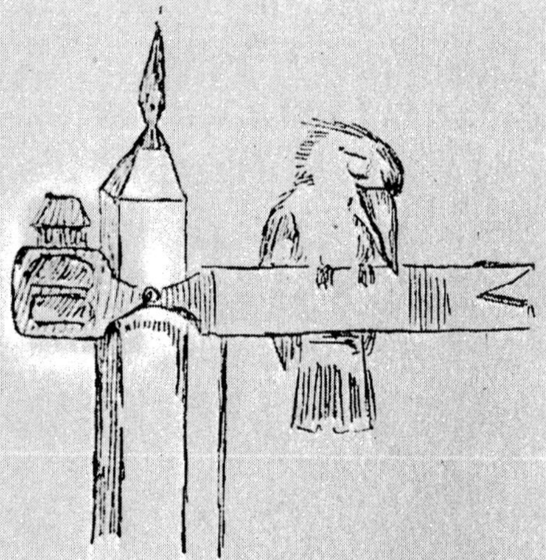

The Kookaburra sat
On the signal arm;
Along there came
A train;

The
arm
went
down,

And
so
did
Jack,

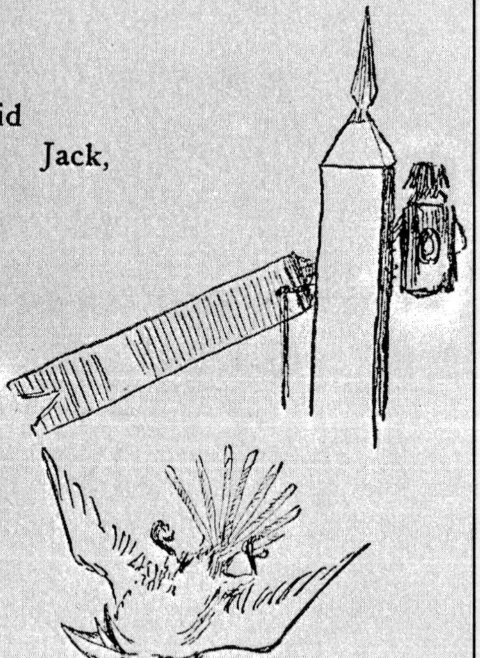

**And he'll not
Sit there
Again.**

Tails and Tarradiddles: an Australian Book of Birds and Beasts by The Perfesser and Alter Ego, Esquire (Launcelot Harrison), was published in 1925 by Cornstalk Publishing, Sydney

THE KOOKABURRA

OR LAUGHING JACKASS.

1

You laugh ! An echo-raising sound: a comic "He-he-Ha" !
A positively tonic sol, fah, te, doh, ra, me, fah.

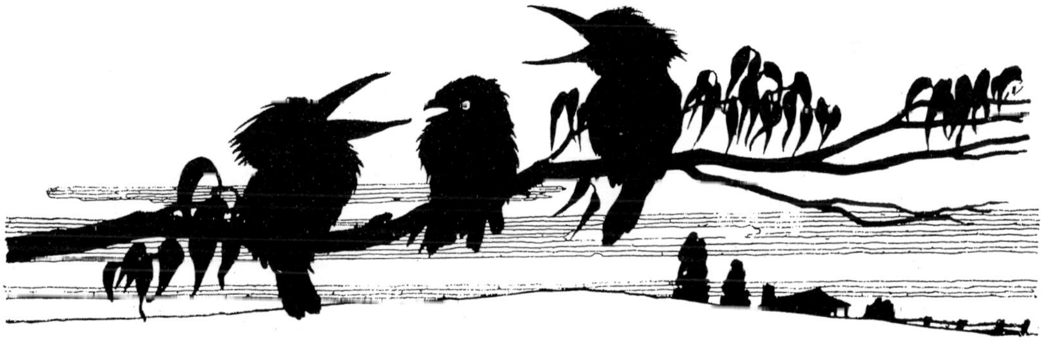

From *A Jackaroo's Jingles* by Alan Edmunds

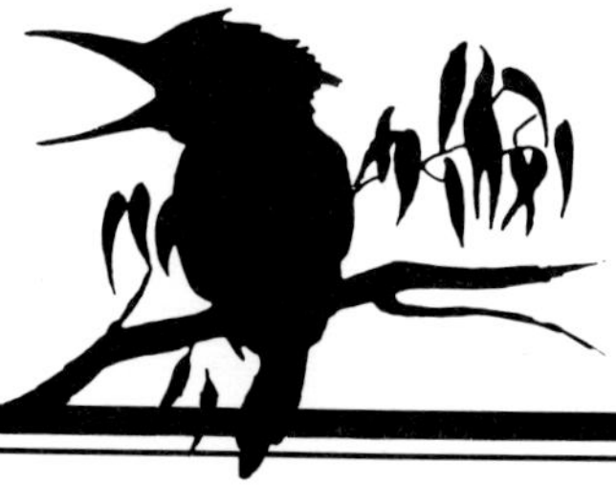

-9-
STAR OF STAGE AND SCREEN

With such a zany character as the kookaburra, it is no wonder that a few choice oddities occurred. For example, there was Jacko, the broadcasting kookaburra – a phenomenon of the 1930s. Jacko, who had been caught at Healesville, was taught to laugh on command. First he made a record, then a movie, then he went to a wireless station in Melbourne where fiction claims that he said 'As well as laughing when I was told, I laughed at everything and everybody. They couldn't stop me'.

Jacko made a highly successful concert tour of eastern Australia where people came from miles around to hear him. Children brought their worms and grubs to tempt the famous star. His laugh was recorded and his 'autobiography' created by Brooke Nicholls. There were wonderful illustrations by Dorothy Wall, the author of *Blinky Bill*, one of Australia's most famous koalas. Who should have been chosen as Blinky Bill's godfather but the famous Jacko himself. Jacko had many products named for him – even shoe polish.

Another curiosity of the 1930s was Little Miss Kookaburra of 3LO Melbourne. Little Miss Kookaburra told stories for the children and opened her programme with a kookaburra laugh. Her real name was Hazel Maude, and her imitation of the kookaburra's laugh was said to be 'remarkably faithful'. The real testimony of her skill came from Jacko himself. After Jacko had done his solo at the radio station, he and Little Miss Kookaburra did a duet. No doubt you'd prefer to hear Jacko's words:

> I started first, when she joined in I stopped short and looked at her. It was the first time I had heard

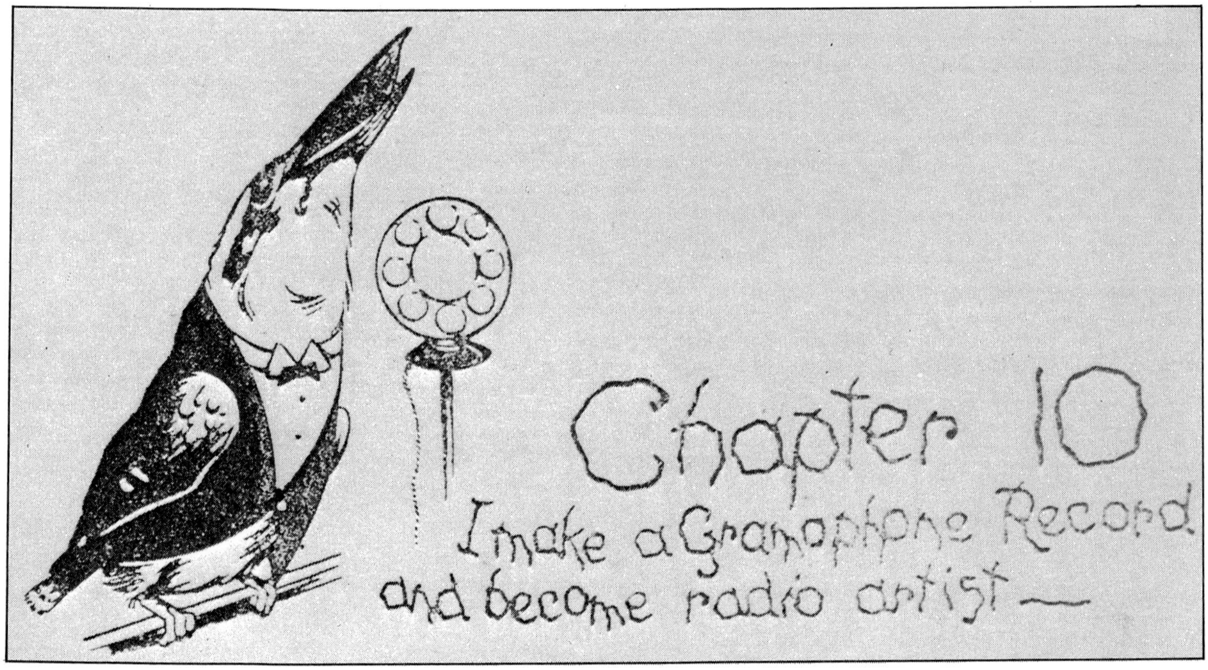

Jacko the broadcasting kookaburra (above and right)

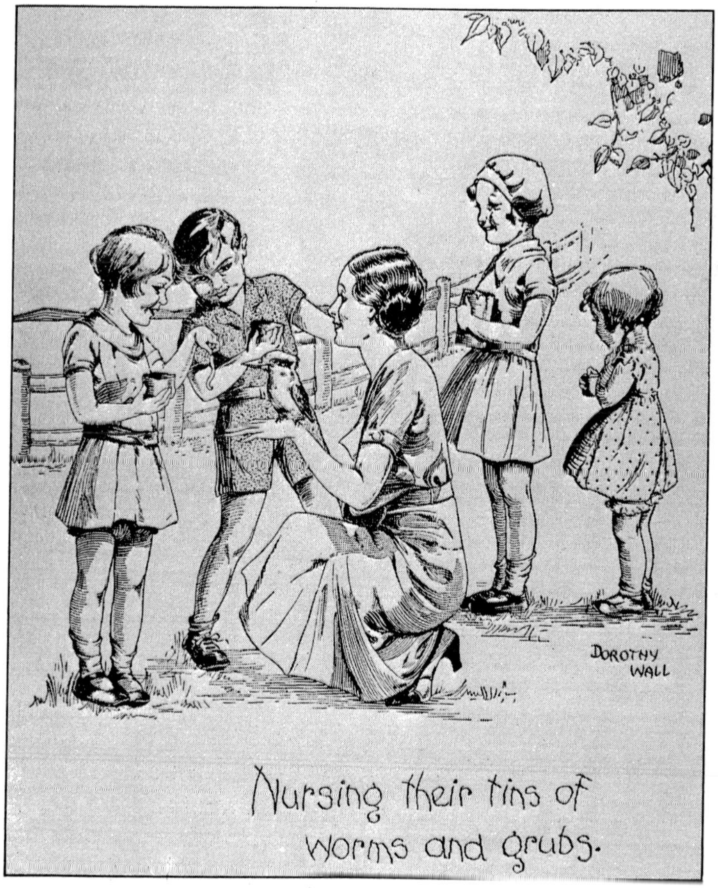

a human laugh really like a kookaburra. Then I joined in again and laughed my hardest. We cackled and gurgled and chuckled together. Our voices blended perfectly. If Miss Kookaburra had not been a really good mimic, I would not have joined in with her. I once heard a lyrebird broadcast his imitation of my laugh. I took no notice of it.

Jacko's voice was heard in a twenty-second burst of hilarity for twenty-five years on radio by millions of listeners in Asia, North America and Europe. It was the call sign for Keith Glover, on Radio Australia's longest running programme 'Mail Bag'. On Sunday, 28 January 1981, Keith's and Jacko's voices were heard for the last time when the programme was discontinued.

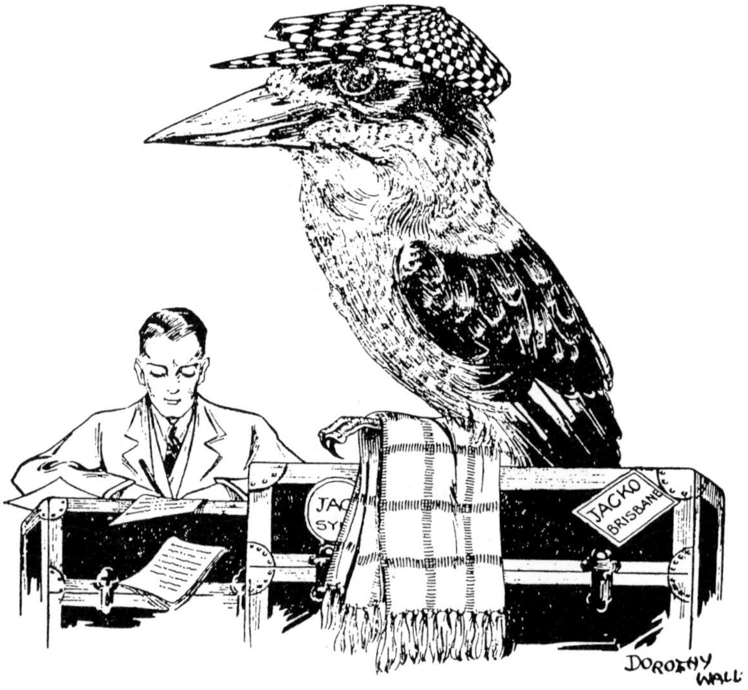

Jacko's travels & triumphs.

TOLD BY HIS FRIENDS

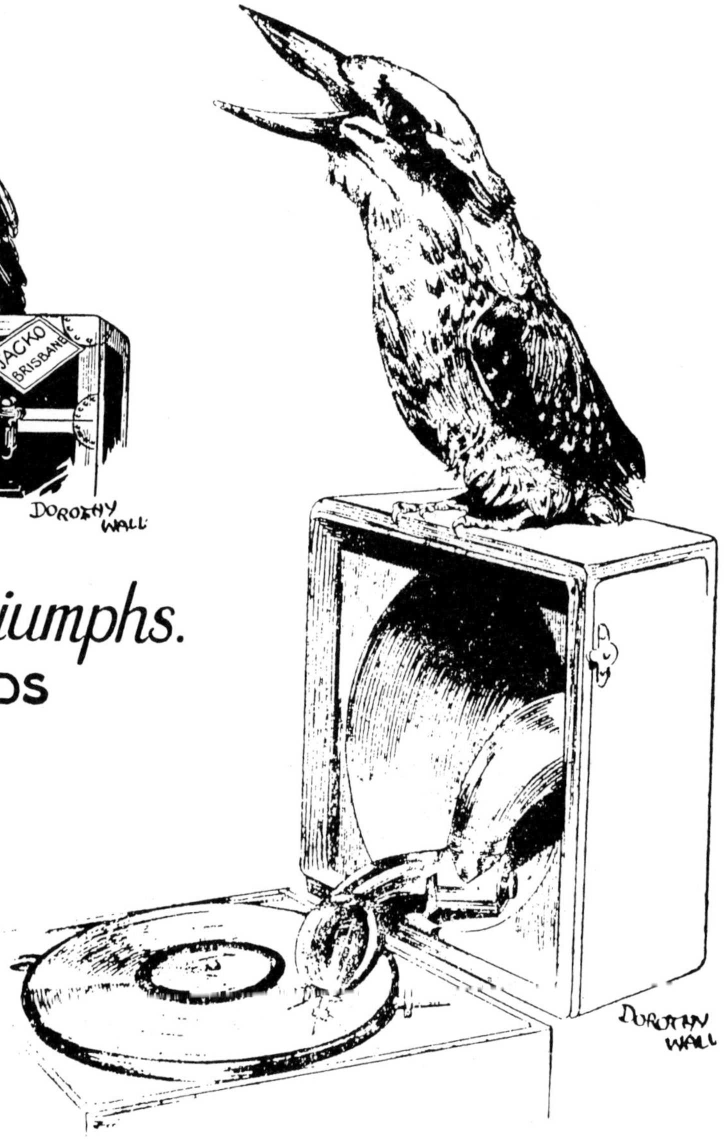

From Jacko's 'autobiography', illustrated by Dorothy Wall. Angus & Robertson published Jacko's life story, written by Brooke Nicholls

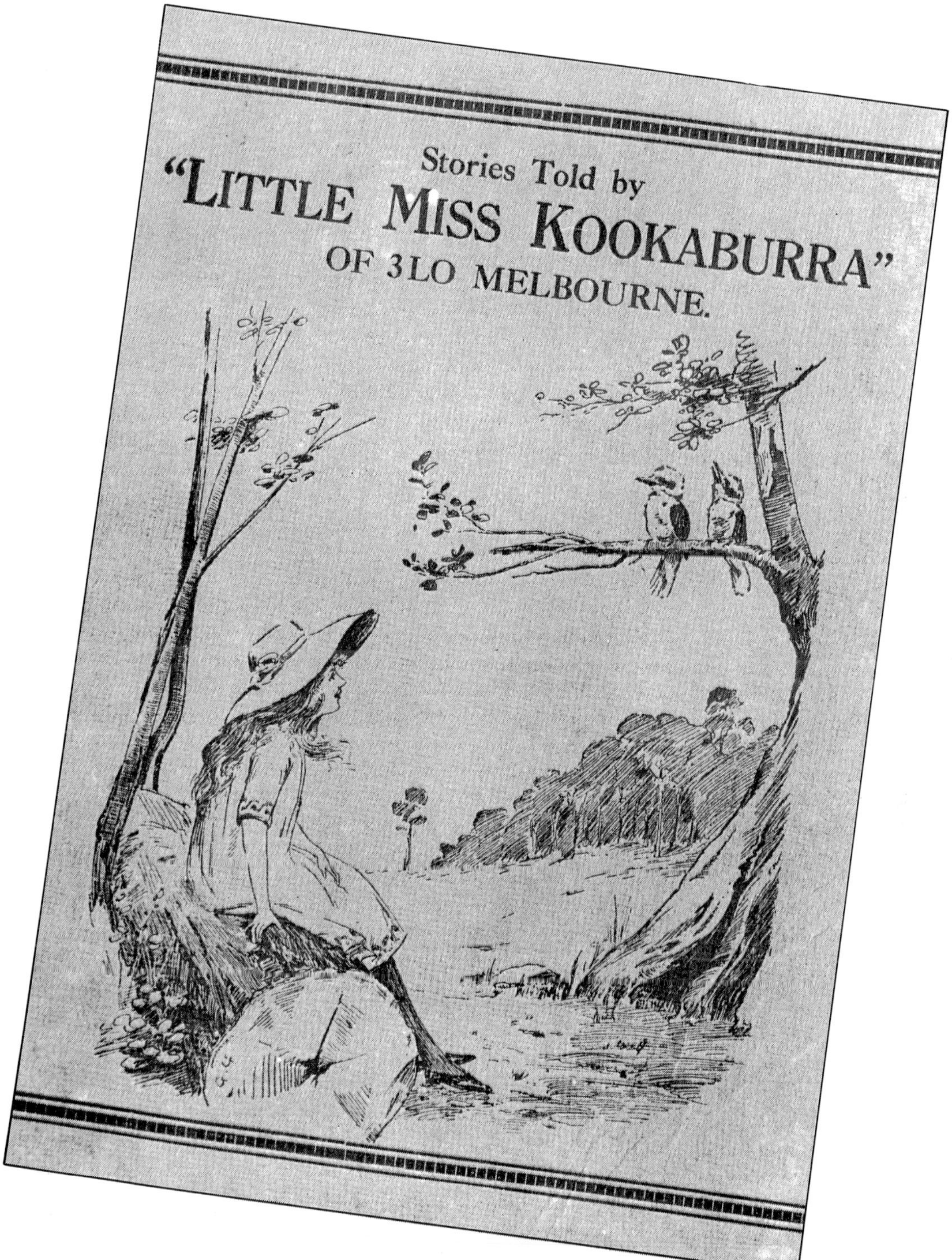

Little Miss Kookaburra of 3LO, Melbourne, opened her children's programme each day in the 1930s with a most realistic kookaburra laugh

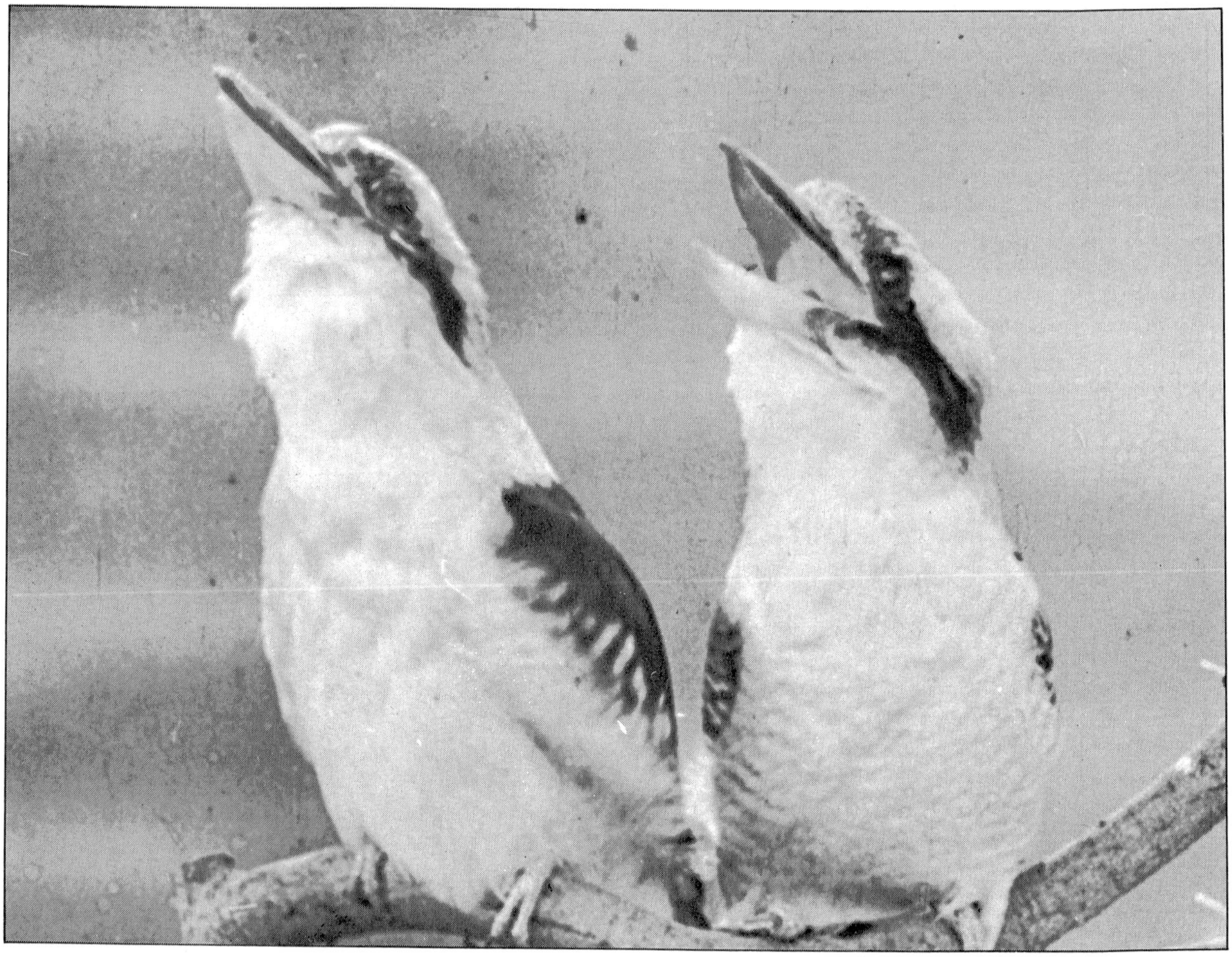

A concerted effort

Many Australian moviegoers were startled to hear the kookaburra's merry laugh being used as an eerie background sound effect in various everglades and jungles in Hollywood movies.

Another famous kookaburra film star was seen every week at the 'pictures', noisily heralding Movietone News. After seeing *Newsfront*, a film that recalled Movietone News, a number of people were overwhelmed by the nostalgic power of the sound of the introductory kookaburras' laugh. It conjured up a past era. As a nation, we had been in danger of forgetting our national identity. We must be thankful to find that Australian folklore is having a renaissance. As usual, Jacko is in the vanguard.

Long may Australian children sing the familiar round:

Kookaburra sits in the old gum tree,
Merry, merry, king of the bush is he,
Laugh kookaburra, laugh kookaburra,
Gay your life must be.

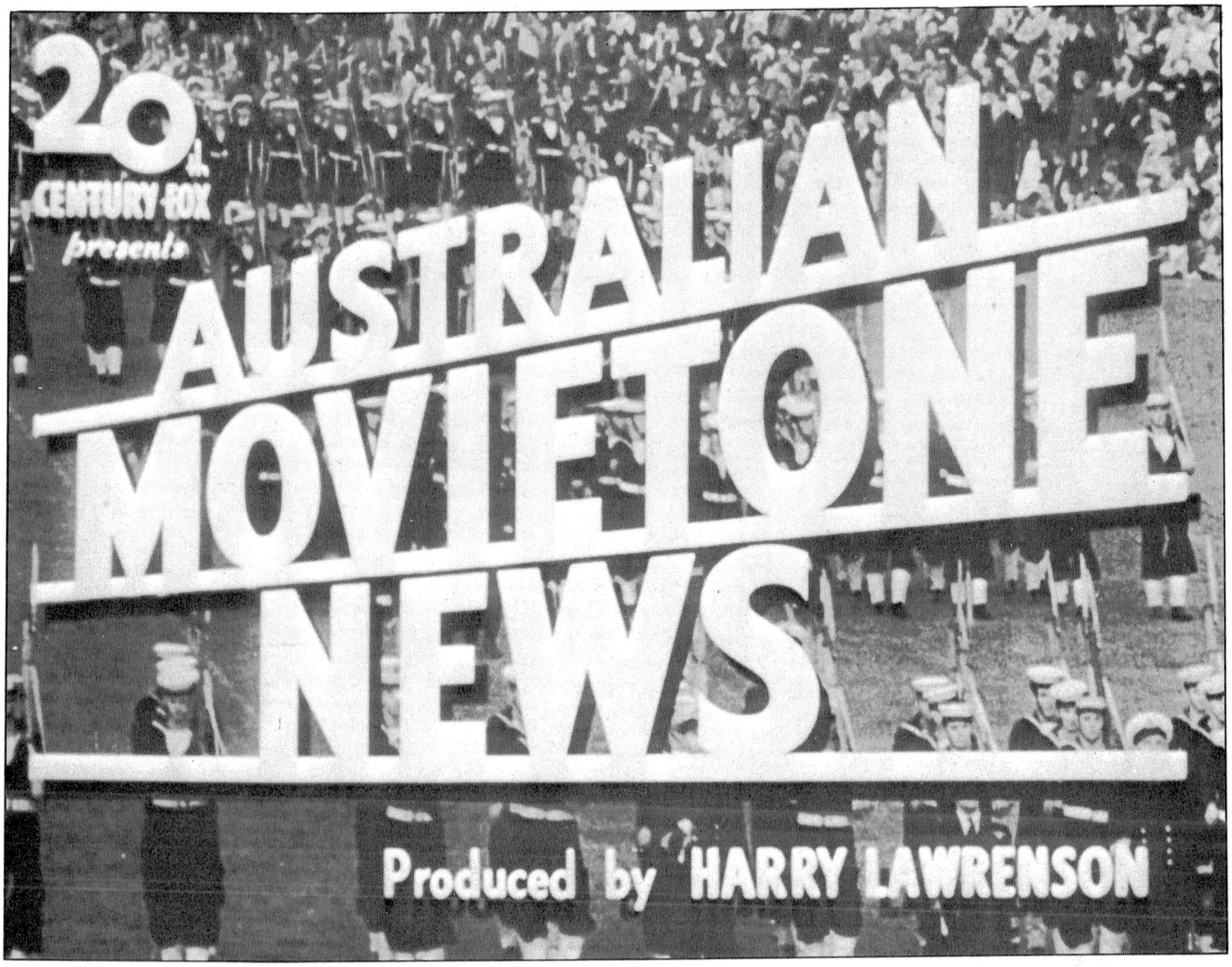

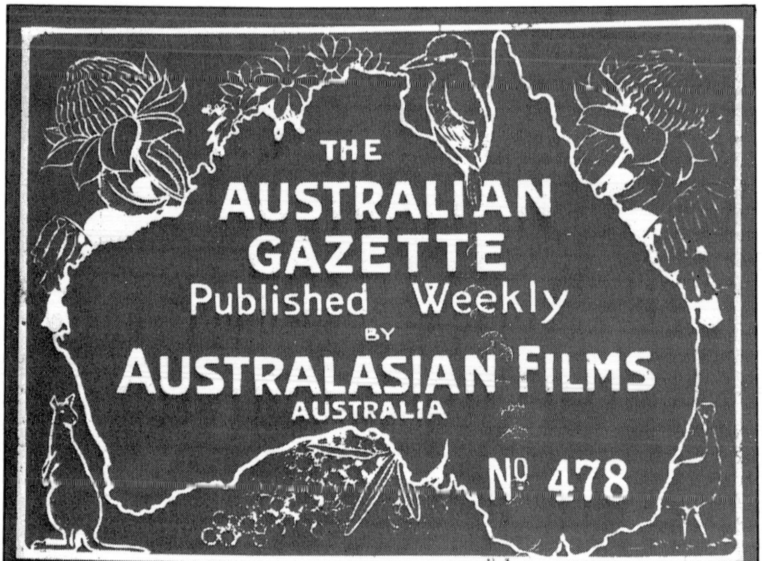

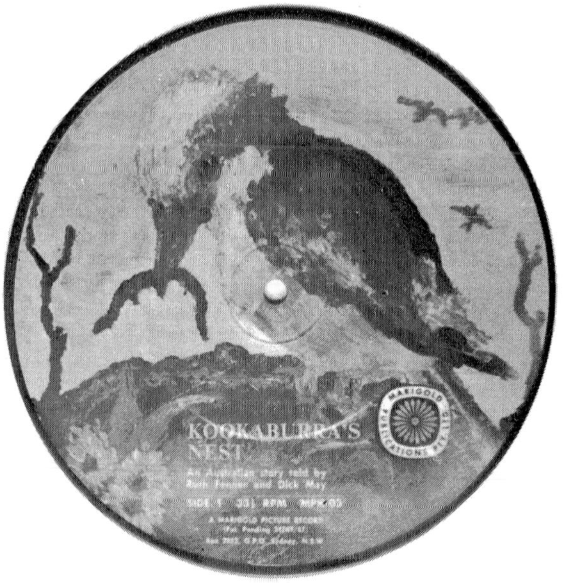

Kookaburra's Nest,
an Australian story on record

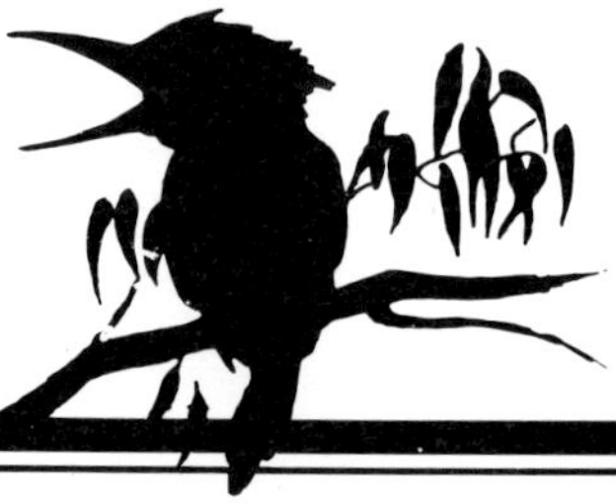

-10-
KOOKABURRAS IN THE 1980s

In 1885 English historian James Anthony Froude marvelled at the kookaburras living in the gardens of the Melbourne Club. One kookaburra, Jack, was almost regarded as a member. When he died his body was stuffed, and displayed at the club for years.

A hundred years later the kookaburra is regarded as fondly as ever. In an upsurge of national feeling, Australian motifs have made a triumphant comeback. Suddenly they have become an important part of our design, much sought after in fashion circles here and overseas. And among these motifs the kookaburra has been one of the most popular. Holeproof, for example, chose a kookaburra image for the T-shirts and windcheaters in their co-ordinated range of sportswear and knitwear, and for their labelling, a stylised kookaburra motif that emphasises the bird's primeval appearance.

The kookaburra's great attraction as a symbol is its appeal for Australians in all walks of life. One of the most memorable images of the kookaburra was associated with the defence of the America's Cup in Fremantle, Western Australia, in 1987. When Taskforce '87, with chairman Kevin Parry, built three Kookaburra 12-metre racers, the sponsors used a bold kookaburra logo and adopted a 'Captain Kooka' motif, in a number of different forms, for their packaging and promotion. In December 1986 the kookaburra was set opposite another Australian symbol, the boxing kangaroo, when Taskforce '87 challenged and beat the 12-metre yachts of the Bond Corporation. With

KOOKABURRA

TASKFORCE '87 AMERICA'S CUP DEFENCE

VOLUME 1 NUMBER 5 The [illegible] Publication of **TASKFORCE '87 LIMITED.** 1986

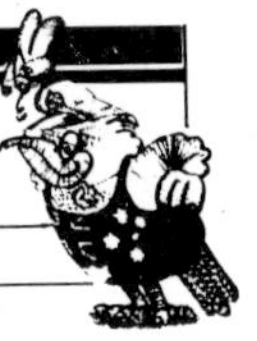

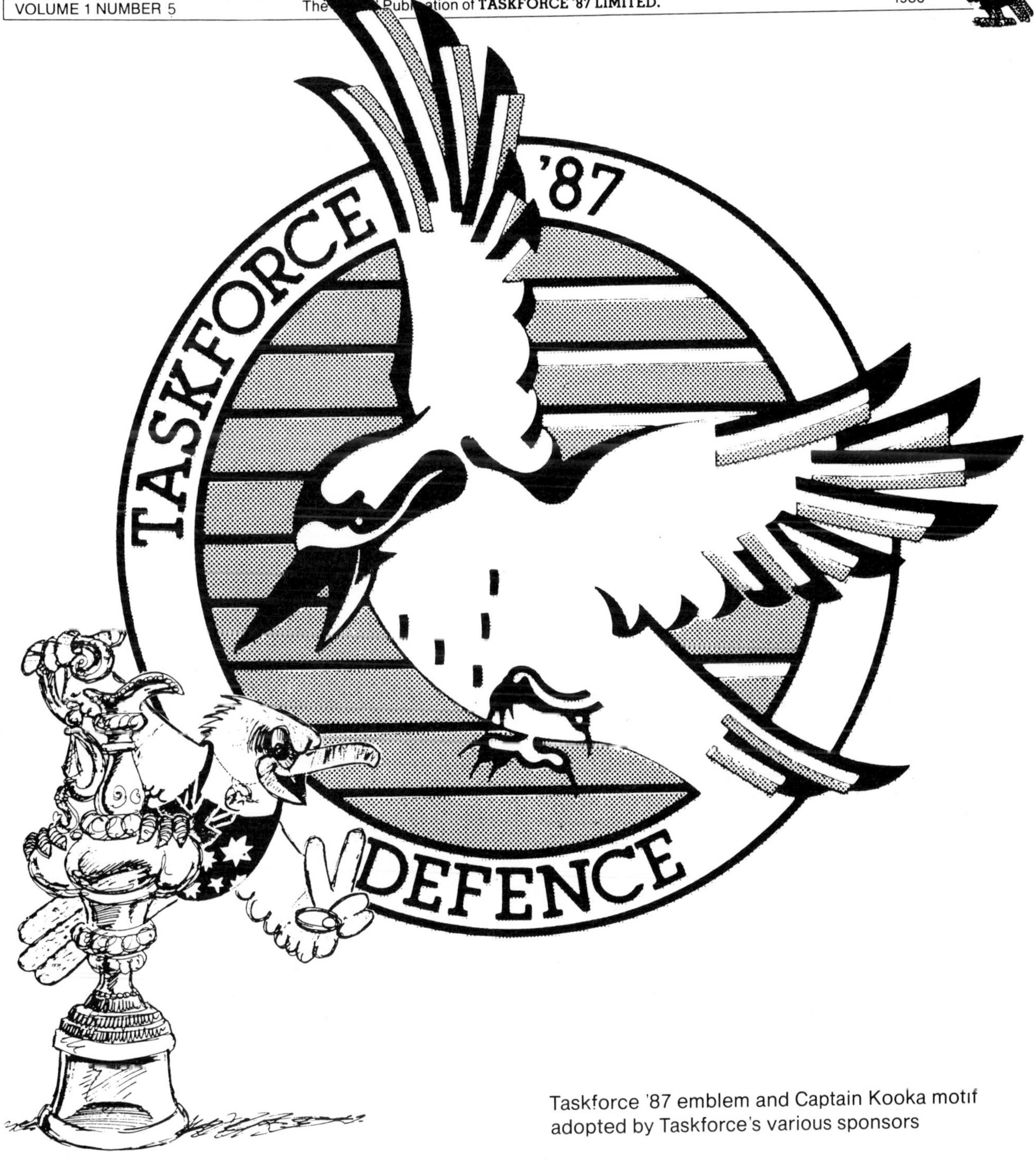

Taskforce '87 emblem and Captain Kooka motif adopted by Taskforce's various sponsors

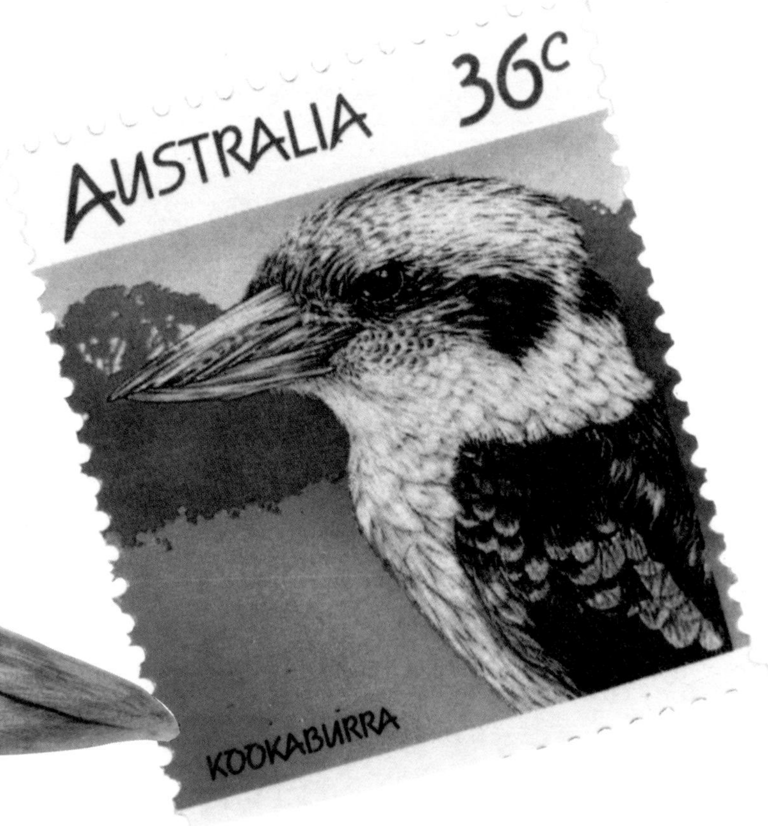

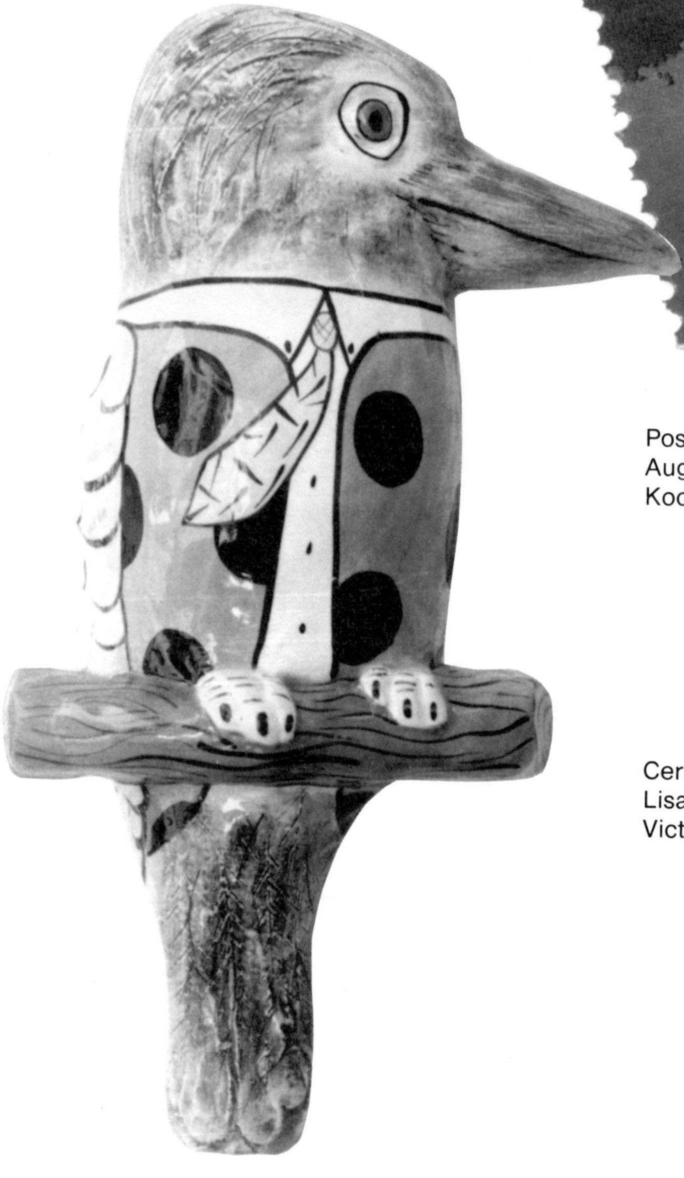

Postage stamp from the Wildlife series (issued August 1986) depicting the Laughing Brown Kookaburra (above)

Ceramic kookaburra (left) hand-made by John and Lisa Nye, 1986 (By courtesy of Distelfink Gallery, Victoria.)

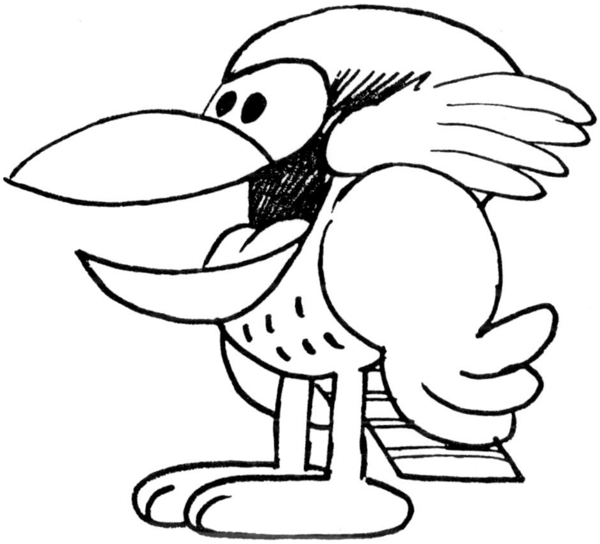

Alex Stitt's Bicentenary creation, Kev Kookaburra (above)

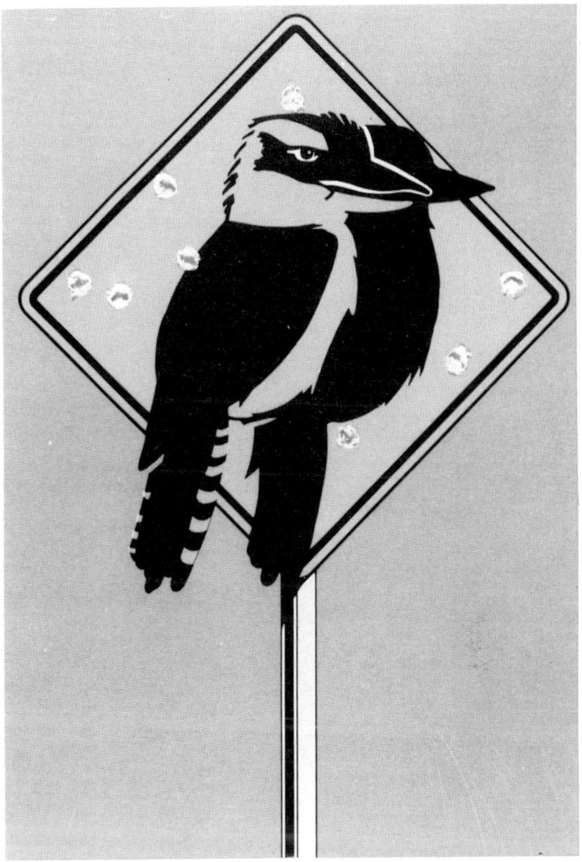

Bush images in a postcard design by Mimmo Cozzolino and David Hughes: the kookaburra country road sign complete with bullet holes (above)

Taskforce's victory, kookaburras of every conceivable kind appeared all over Fremantle, and racing news was on everybody's lips. Although destined not to triumph in the defence of the America's Cup itself, the kookaburra symbol rode high again on Australia Day 1989 when a challenge between *Kookaburra I* and *Kookaburra II* took place on Sydney Harbour with America's Cup skippers Dennis Conner and Iain Murray as helmsmen. On this occasion there were so many spectator craft on the Harbour that the race was inconclusive.

In the 1980s the kookaburra has made a fitting symbol for events so keenly expressive of our national consciousness.

The 1988 Bicentennial of European settlement in Australia encouraged a nationalistic focus for the decorative arts. The kookaburra became one of the most popular images for the creation of new forms by our artists, sculptors, potters, woodcarvers and jewellers. A novel example came from John and Lisa Nye, who used the trade name Mad in Australia for their kitsch objects. They believed that this engaging bird was just right for the kind of in-joke they convey through their pieces.

When David Johnston established Kookaburra Country in 1980 to promote his food products, he selected the kookaburra symbol because 'the Kookaburra is uniquely and identifiably Australian'. There is little doubt

KOOKABURRA
INDUSTRIES PTY LTD

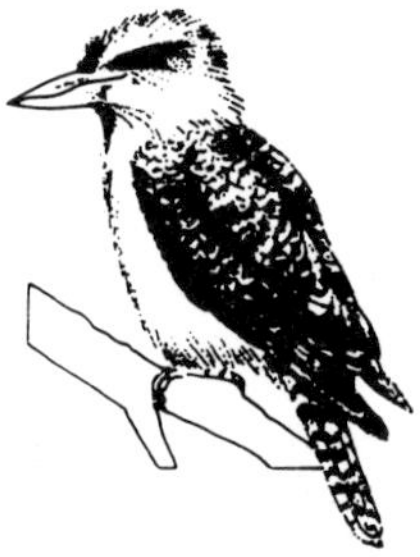

KOOKABURRA CHILD CARE CENTRE
256 Bedford Road, Andergrove. Qld. 4740.
PHONE (079) 55 2398

KOOKABURRA

Kookaburra
PROP. H.C. & E.M. HOUTEPEN
Antiques & Old Wares

Mildura Kookaburra Club
265 TENTH ST., MILDURA, 3500
Telephone: (050) 22 1933

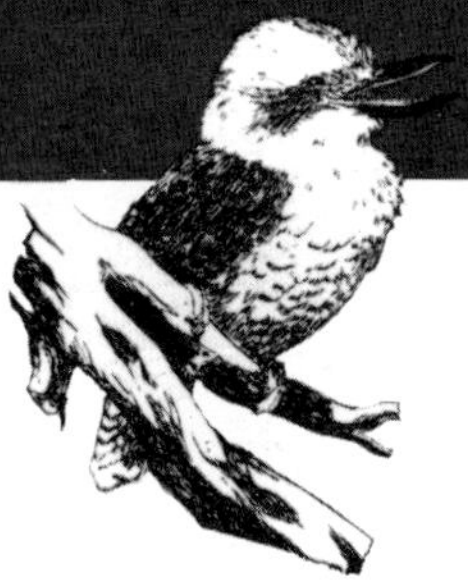

HOOPERS
TOBY & JULIANA HOOPER
545 High Street Prahran 3181 Phone 521 2278 51 3260 (H)
SPECIALIST DEALERS IN AUSTRALIANA
REGISTERED COMMONWEALTH VALUERS Est. 1969

FOUNTAIN ANTIQUES

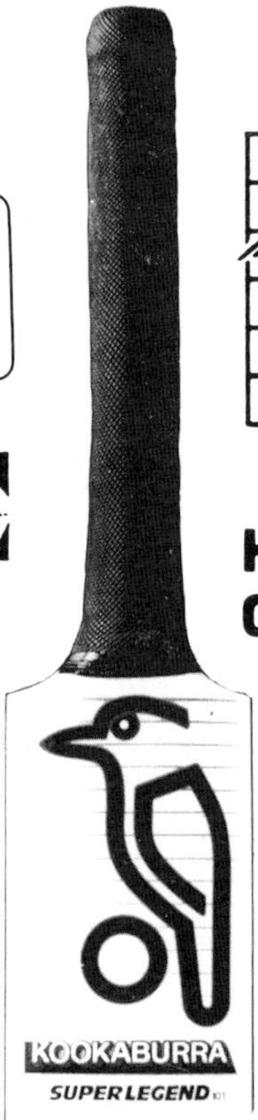

KOOKABURRA COMPUTERS

YUNGABURRA
Atherton Tablelands
KookaBurra Motel

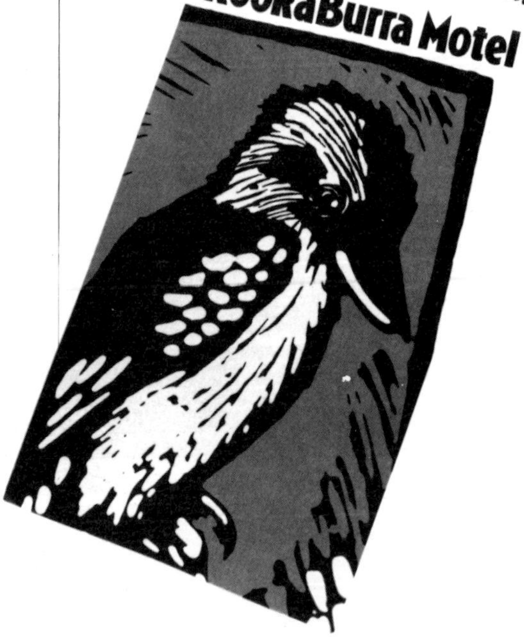

Examples of the kookaburra image in recent commercial design (above)

A Steve Graham cover design for the *Age* magazine *Good Weekend*: the kookaburra is linked with that other national symbol, the beer can (opposite page)

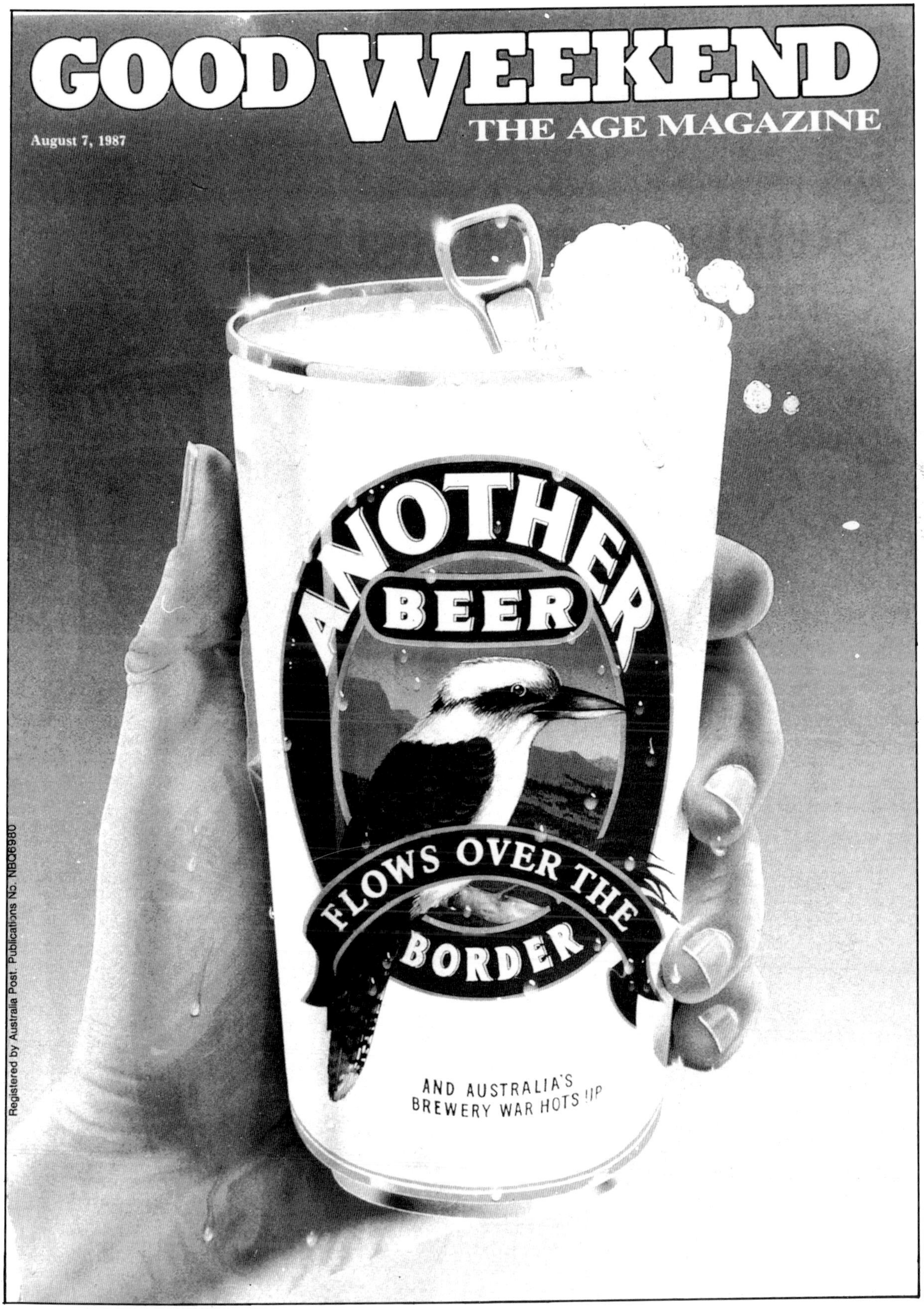
GOOD WEEKEND
THE AGE MAGAZINE
August 7, 1987
ANOTHER BEER
FLOWS OVER THE BORDER
AND AUSTRALIA'S BREWERY WAR HOTS UP
Registered by Australia Post. Publications No. NBQ6980

that for Australians that symbol suggests something traditional, tried and true; in addition, however, the kookaburra's vigour and apparent sense of fun appeals to creative talents. Barbara Grollmus, a painter of silk screens, who spent hours watching and sketching the kookaburra, observed, 'He seemed such a friendly bird with his mischievous laugh and tubby appearance, but when he made a kill he became a warrior'.

The most frequent use of the kookaburra image in the 1980s was commercially: it was used for restaurants and food, antique shops, clothing and sporting products, wine, accommodation, photography, jewellery, blinds, computers, shoelaces, paper, and river boats. In some cases perhaps it was the first edition of this book in 1982 that encouraged the use of the kookaburra image for commercial purposes.

Although we are now predominantly a nation of urban dwellers, the bush is part of our subconscious: it still beckons, and its sounds continue to fire our creative imagination. As we develop a secure pride in our Australian heritage, the symbol of the kookaburra is likely to live on in a variety of enterprises.

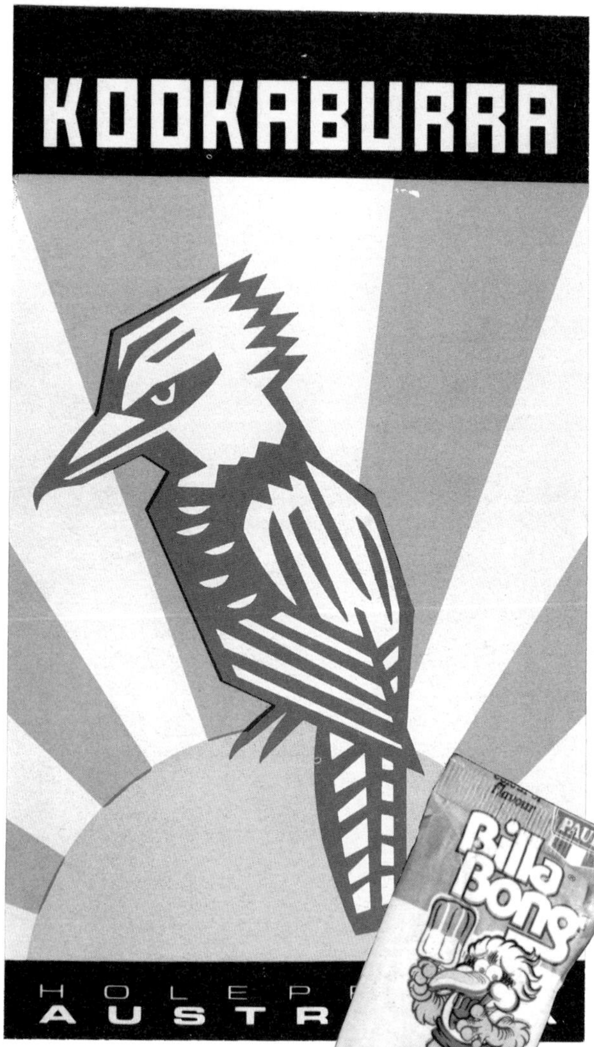

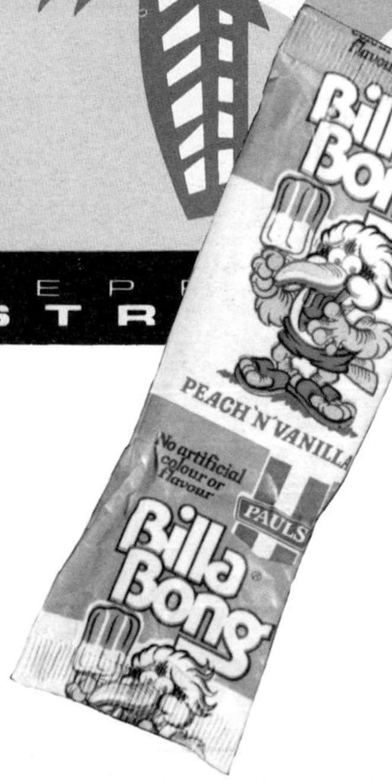

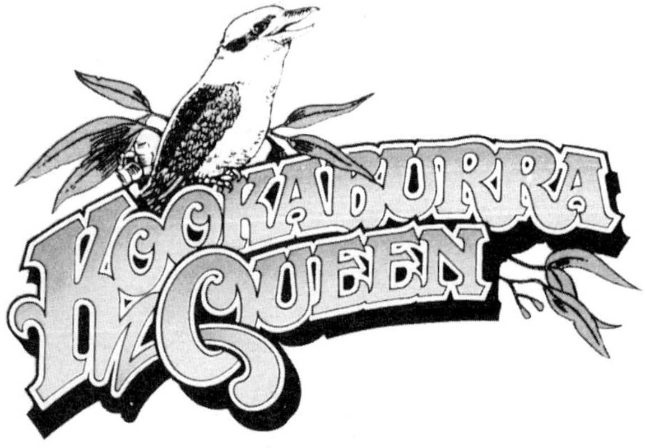

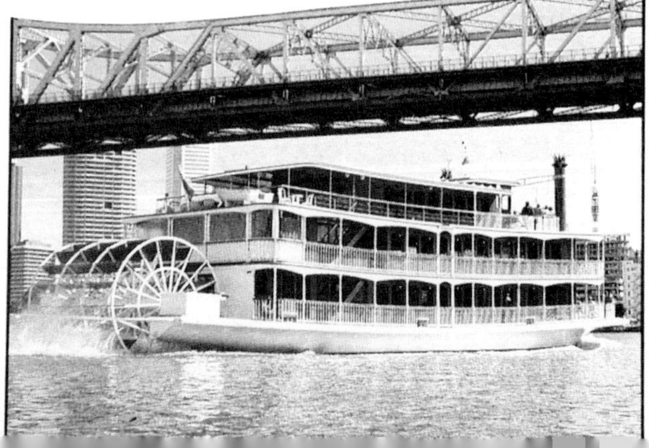

Stylised kookaburra image used for Holeproof's labels and packaging (top)

Paul's Billa Bong icy-pole, depicting the kookaburra in hot-weather gear (above)

Brisbane River's *Kookaburra Queen* carried thousands of visitors during the Bicentennial Expo in 1988 (right)